CITIZENSHIP 2.0

Princeton Studies in Global and Comparative Sociology
Andreas Wimmer, Series Editor

Citizenship 2.0: Dual Nationality as a Global Asset by Yossi Harpaz

Nation Building: Why Some Countries Come Together While Others Fall Apart by Andreas Wimmer

The Paradox of Vulnerability: States, Nationalism, and the Financial Crisis by John L. Campbell and John A. Hall

Citizenship 2.0
Dual Nationality as a Global Asset

Yossi Harpaz

PRINCETON UNIVERSITY PRESS
PRINCETON AND OXFORD

Copyright © 2019 by Princeton University Press

Published by Princeton University Press
41 William Street, Princeton, New Jersey 08540
6 Oxford Street, Woodstock, Oxfordshire OX20 1TR

press.princeton.edu

All Rights Reserved

LCCN: 2019942872
ISBN 978-0-691-19405-9
ISBN (pbk.) 978-0-691-19406-6

British Library Cataloging-in-Publication Data is available

Editorial: Meagan Levinson and Jackie Delaney
Production Editorial: Nathan Carr
Jacket/Cover Design: Layla Mac Rory
Production: Erin Suydam
Publicity: Nathalie Levine and Kathryn Stevens

This book has been composed in Adobe Text Pro and Gotham

Printed on acid-free paper. ∞

Printed in the United States of America

10 9 8 7 6 5 4 3 2 1

The passport is the noblest part of a person. It isn't generated in the plain and simple way people are. A person can be begotten anywhere in the world, in the most frivolous of ways—but not a passport. That's why a passport, so long as it's a good one, is recognized—whereas a person can be ever so good and yet be denied recognition.
—BERTOLT BRECHT, *CONVERSATIONS IN EXILE*

It becomes more and more clear that, when that religious adoration of the state, which makes it into a *mysterium* and a transcendent institution, is shaken, along with it goes the reverent and pious relationship. Henceforth, individuals see only the side of the state that can be helpful or harmful to them, and press forward by any means to gain influence over it.
—FRIEDRICH NIETZSCHE, *HUMAN, ALL TOO HUMAN*

CONTENTS

    Introduction 1

1 Dual Citizenship as a Strategy of Global Upward Mobility 15

2 Serbia: Becoming Hungarian, Returning to Europe 39

3 Mexico: Strategic Birth as Elite Investment 67

4 Israel: European Passports as Insurance and Restitution 97

    Conclusion: The Rise of the Sovereign Individual 126

    Acknowledgments 145
    Methodological Appendix 147
    Notes 153
    References 175
    Index 199

CITIZENSHIP 2.0

Introduction

For most of the twentieth century, citizenship was an exclusive bond between an individual and a state. Countries refused to share their citizens with other countries just like they do not share their territories. Since the 1990s, the principle of exclusive citizenship has been abandoned, and dozens of countries moved to permit dual citizenship. Today, toleration of multiple citizenship has become the norm, and tens of millions of persons around the world hold citizenship in two—sometimes even three or four—countries.[1]

The legitimation and proliferation of multiple citizenships is creating new realities on the ground, reshaping patterns of international migration, political participation, global security, and ethnic relations.[2] Scholars have analyzed the causes that are driving this global shift, especially the legal and political dynamics behind permissive policy changes. Its consequences, however, remain understudied and undertheorized. The key question that this book aims to answer is: What happens to the institution of citizenship when the basic rules governing it are changed? What does national membership look like in age of flexible, overlapping, and nonterritorial citizenship?

Previous studies mostly examined dual citizenship in the context of immigration to Western Europe and North America. In this book, I focus instead on the strategic acquisition of dual citizenship by nonimmigrants from outside the West.[3] Once we shift the empirical focus, a crucial but overlooked aspect comes into sharp relief: the disparity in the value of the "citizenship packages" that different countries offer, and the tremendous practical usefulness that a second citizenship from a more developed country may provide.

Analyzing the rise of dual citizenship through the prism of global inequality highlights a mostly overlooked consequence of this shift: the creation of new opportunities for people around the world to obtain premium citizenship from

EU countries, the US or Canada. Millions of people from Latin America, Eastern Europe, the Middle East, and Asia strategically draw on resources like European ancestry, ethnic origin, migration history, or economic capital in order to obtain a second nationality. The second citizenship operates as *compensatory citizenship*. It does not necessarily lead them to emigrate and does not replace their original nationality. Instead, it makes up for its deficits by providing additional opportunities, an insurance policy, a high-mobility passport, and even elevated social status. Dual citizenship constitutes a new kind of global asset.

This book analyzes the emergence and proliferation of compensatory citizenship through in-depth analyses of three case studies: Hungarian-speaking Serbians who obtain Hungarian citizenship (and an EU passport) thanks to a policy of ethnic preference; upper-class Mexicans who strategically give birth in the United States to secure citizenship for their children, and immediately return to Mexico; and Israelis who acquire EU citizenship from their European countries of origin, over five decades after their families have left those countries as refugees.

In each case, I combine interviews and statistics to analyze applicants' motivations and explore the dynamics of citizenship acquisition on the ground. There is substantial variation in the motivations to obtain dual citizenship: for example, Israelis mainly seek EU citizenship as an insurance policy and status symbol, whereas Serbians acquire it to facilitate emigration and secure travel freedom. Nevertheless, a common logic operates across all those cases. Dual citizenship allows for the conversion of resources between local and global systems of stratification. It leads to a revaluation of characteristics such as ancestry or ethnicity, which gain newfound practical value and are reinforced as axes of within-nation inequality. The rise of compensatory citizenship is associated with the diffusion of a new view of state membership: perceived as a piece of private property, citizenship is increasingly a domain for strategizing and maximizing utility. This new attitude can be described as "the sovereign individual."

To get a sense of this new approach to citizenship, consider the two following cases. Ya'akov, a Jewish Israeli engineer in his fifties, was born in Romania and came to Israel as a child.[4] I interviewed him at the Romanian embassy in Tel-Aviv, where he applied to reacquire his citizenship and register his daughter as a Romanian citizen. Ya'akov felt entirely Israeli and had no nostalgia for Romania, he said. In fact, he was only interested in securing a "European passport." "This [citizenship]," he added, "is like a luxury article that you buy, a fine watch or a laptop computer. You will probably not use all of its features . . . but you are willing to pay extra for the potential." His wife, Sarah, said: "It's good to have another passport. We live in a very volatile country. Who knows what will happen here in ten years?"

Ricardo, a Mexican businessman in his late thirties, lives with his wife in Monterrey, Mexico, but their four children were born across the border in the United States. In three of these births, Ricardo's wife crossed the border especially to give birth, in order to make sure that their children will have US nationality in addition to their Mexican nationality. These births took place at a private clinic, at a cost of $20,000 per birth. Discussing his and his wife's decision to give birth in the United States, Ricardo explained, "We wanted to give [our daughters] the option to choose where to live, study and work . . . Also, we had a big security crisis here before, and many people went to live abroad. So we wanted to give them flexibility to move between the territories."

The attitudes that are reflected in these short vignettes starkly diverge from traditional conceptions of citizenship. They include strategically acquiring citizenship; experiencing the acquisition as an economic transaction; imagining citizenship as a luxury product; mentally detaching the "European passport" from the country that granted it; conceiving of nationality as a source of security, flexibility, and freedom; and believing that good parents should obtain this asset for their children. This book will explore these emergent understandings of citizenship in three case studies, and thereby shed light on the new forms that this key institution assumes in our times.

Why Citizenship Matters

In a world that is dominated by nation-states, citizenship is the master status.[5] Citizenship defines the scope of rights that an individual may claim and specifies which state is expected to answer those claims. Until the 1990s, formal citizenship (or nationality) was mostly neglected as an object of study by social scientists.[6] In recent decades, however, academic interest in citizenship has boomed. This interest was initially driven by the dilemmas of immigrant integration in Western Europe and the dynamics of nationalist resurgence in the new countries of Central and Eastern Europe.[7] More recently, citizenship also emerged as a key perspective for studying inclusion and exclusion within nations (including in the context of diaspora politics) as well as analyzing the structure and dynamics of global inequality.[8]

Below, I briefly outline four key dimensions of citizenship. The first three dimensions—status, identity, and rights—draw on a classic formulation by Christian Joppke.[9] The fourth dimension, citizenship as global sorting mechanism, captures an emergent perspective that has grown in importance in recent years, and which will be central to this book.

Citizenship as status. Citizenship signifies the formal status of state membership. It is, as the sociologist Rogers Brubaker noted, an instrument of closure that serves to exclude those who are not members of the national community.[10] Citizenship-based closure comes in multiple forms: territorial closure (exclusion of unauthorized noncitizens from the national territory), political closure (exclusion of noncitizens from political decision-making), economic closure (exclusion from the labor market and welfare rights) and social closure (exclusion from the national community). States use bureaucratic mechanisms to ensure citizenship-based closure: proof of nationality is often required in order to vote and receive some services, and border control officials routinely verify the nationality of persons who wish to enter a territory.

Citizenship, Brubaker points out, is not just an instrument of closure; it is also a contested object of closure. In other words, the boundaries of citizenship reflect the distribution of power in society, and determine the present and future contours of the national collective. Citizenship laws, Brubaker famously argued, are shaped by national legacies.[11] According to this logic, countries of immigration would have citizenship regimes that facilitate the integration of immigrants by providing automatic citizenship to anyone born in the territory, including the children of noncitizen immigrants. This is called the principle of *jus soli*, or the right of soil. Automatic, unconditional *jus soli* citizenship is found in most countries in the Americas, including the United States and Canada; a qualified version of it exists in France, which employs "double jus soli" (the children of French-born persons are automatically French).

Meanwhile, countries that are defined by a connection to a particular ethnocultural group will use descent rather than place of birth as the main criterion for citizenship (the principle of descent is called *jus sanguinis*, right of blood). Such policies make it easy for emigrants who leave the country to retain citizenship and pass it on to their descendants, while restricting the access of immigrants and their children.[12] This principle is dominant in European and Asian countries, where the nation is often imagined as synonymous with a particular ethnic group. Another mechanism of ethnic nationalism consists of citizenship laws that offer facilitated access to members of a defined ethnic, religious, or cultural group: variants of such laws exist in Germany, Spain, Poland, Greece, Romania, Hungary, Israel, Japan, and other countries.[13]

Arguing against the "traditions of nationhood" approach, Patrick Weil has demonstrated that citizenship laws are actually highly responsive to changing historical circumstances.[14] When political conditions call for it, countries with ethnonational traditions may liberalize their citizenship laws to include and accommodate immigrants.[15] The most salient example is Germany. Previously a paradigmatic case of ethnic citizenship, Germany enacted a series of policy changes after 1999. These included a limited toleration of dual citizenship, a qualified form of *jus soli*, and the phasing out of ethnic preference.[16] Marc Howard has shown that the presence of anti-immigrant populist parties may block such liberalizing moves.[17] These works are part of a large body of literature that has demonstrated the dynamic and instrumental nature of citizenship policies: far from blindly enacting national legacies, policymakers are strategic in their use of citizenship to include or exclude individuals and populations based on changing criteria (ethnic, economic, or others).[18]

Citizenship as rights. Citizenship is a set of rights that an individual may claim vis-à-vis a specific state. In a classic essay, Thomas H. Marshall has identified three categories of citizenship rights. These include civil rights (equality before the law and individual freedoms), political rights (political voice and, above all, the right to vote) and social rights (welfare, education, and health).[19] Note that these rights—and, more generally, the public goods produced by a state's institutions, such as infrastructure, public safety, the job market, a clean environment—can usually only be enjoyed by persons who are present in the state's territory. Given that control over movement into and within national territory is a key prerogative of the modern state, the right to be admitted to and reside in the national territory should be considered a crucial component of citizenship.[20] We should therefore add territorial rights as a component that complements Marshall's model. Today, many scholars understand citizenship as a package of civil, political, social, and territorial rights that is supposed to provide the conditions for human flourishing.[21]

Reality is more complicated and more dynamic than this idealized picture. Most countries do not offer the full package of rights described by Marshall. For example, since the 1970s many Western countries have cut down on social rights (e.g., welfare benefits) while introducing new kinds of civil rights (above all, rights to nondiscrimination).[22] Outside the West, few countries even come close to providing the full package of citizenship rights. About half of the world's countries are not democratic and their citizens' political and civil rights are severely curtailed.[23] Many countries simply lack the resources to offer their citizens substantial rights of any kind, due to ineffective and underfunded institutions. Any examination of citizenship rights must go beyond the abstract ideal of citizenship and take into account the huge variation in states' ability to realize the ideal.

Citizenship as identity. Historically, citizenship has evolved as a master status that ensures national unity and supersedes all subnational distinctions based on social class, ethnicity, religion, or race.[24] The growth of citizenship is a story of expansion, from an exclusive status that was restricted to a small percentage of the population to a status that unifies an entire nation.[25] The bureaucratic leveling of a state's population through the imposition of a uniform status was associated with the creation of a unified national identity. Citizenship, therefore, is a key manifestation of national identity.

The identity aspect of citizenship has been studied in the context of the literature on immigration. Scholars traditionally treated an immigrant's decision to take up citizenship in her country of residence (a procedure called naturalization) as an indicator of successful integration and the adoption of a new national identity.[26] Empirical research has shown that immigrants who naturalized in European countries were more likely to identify with their new nations. In a parallel finding from the United States, it was found that immigrants who naturalized tended to speak better English than those who did not become citizens.[27]

This effect extends to the second generation. Second-generation immigrants in the United States, who enjoy automatic *jus soli* citizenship, seem to be better integrated and are more likely to identify with the nation, compared to second-generation immigrants in Europe, many of whom do not have citizenship in their country of residence.[28] Citizens do not just have a greater sense of belonging; they are also more likely to be perceived by others as full members who are worthy of solidarity and trust. For example, courts in the United States apply harsher sentences to noncitizens (including legal immigrants) relative to Americans who committed the same crime; employers in Germany are much more likely to call back applicants with foreign-sounding names if their job applications indicate that they hold German citizenship.[29]

The association of citizenship with national identity stands at the root of the citizenship allocation policies that were described above, under "citizenship as status." Israel's Law of Return, which offers automatic citizenship to any Jew who moves to Israel, or the United States' Fourteenth Amendment (which establishes automatic *jus soli* citizenship) are not just technical definitions of who may claim rights. They also serve a performative function as statements of national identity. In the Israeli case, the law embodies the principle that Israel "belongs" to the Jewish people; US policy is founded on the idea of a nation that belongs first of all to native-born Americans (the same conception informs the restriction that bars an immigrant from becoming President).[30] Citizenship policies are used to tie a particular population to a state in both institutional and symbolic terms.

Citizenship, as traditionally understood, is not just one aspect of an individual's identity. Rather, it is constructed as a sacred form of membership.[31] Citizens are expected to make sacrifices for their nation and to avoid calculations of individual utility. The clichéd quotation from John F. Kennedy's 1961 inaugural address—"Ask not what your country can do for you, ask what you can do for your country"—captures this spirit. For most of the twentieth century, the sacred character of citizenship entailed the stigmatization of individuals who gave up their country's citizenship or became citizens in another country. In many countries, persons who emigrated or took up another nationality were condemned as "traitors," "sellouts," or "weaklings."[32] The prevalence of such epithets reflects the traditional assumption that when individuals behave instrumentally in the domain of citizenship, this defiles the sanctity of citizenship and casts shame on the national collective.

In recent years, a growing literature has argued that instrumental attitudes toward citizenship are becoming more common. Christian Joppke coined the term "citizenship light" to describe this instrumental turn. He points out three examples of instrumentalism: citizenship-for-sale schemes, ancestry-based dual citizenship, and EU citizenship. Joppke argues that EU citizenship is the avant-garde of citizenship light because "[it is] exclusively about rights with no complementary duties whatsoever, decoupled from even the thinnest of identities."[33] Other authors who have studied the rise of instrumental attitudes toward citizenship described them as "flexible citizenship," "citizenship á la carte," "passport citizenship," or "strategic citizenship."[34] The instrumentalization of citizenship—a conspicuous symbol of a change in values—has encountered fierce political resistance. Claims that citizenship is being cheapened, diluted, or desecrated, along with calls to reinforce national identity, regain control of borders and make the nation "great again," figure prominently on the agendas of populist movements in the West and beyond it.[35]

Citizenship as global sorter. The three dimensions of citizenship discussed above pertain to a dyadic relationship between an individual and a specific state (when an individual holds dual citizenship, this is actually a triad).[36] A fourth dimension focuses on the way that the possession of a particular citizenship defines an individual's relation to the entire global system. Viewed from a global perspective, Brubaker argues, citizenship is "an international filing system, a mechanism for allocating persons to states."[37] The underlying legal doctrine has been described by Rainer Bauböck as the "Westphalian conception of citizenship": every human being must belong to a sovereign nation-state.[38]

After World War II, Hannah Arendt famously wrote that citizenship was "the right to have rights." A person without citizenship did not have recourse to any law that would protect her. Thankfully, this principle is not applied today with the same ruthlessness. A series of international conventions provide some (limited) protections for stateless persons.[39] Nevertheless, statelessness remains highly problematic from the point of view of states, constituting a disruption to the entire international system—"matter out of place" in the words of anthropologist Liisa Malkki.[40] Dual nationality, potentially, may be equally problematic. Concerns about the neat sorting of persons into states have led most states to resist dual citizenship for a long time. Today, however, a growing number of countries no longer view overlapping memberships as ipso facto problematic.[41]

In theory, global sorting by citizenship places persons into equivalent categories. The "Westphalian" legal imagination at the root of international law treats the world's countries as sovereign and equal units. In reality, there are vast disparities in value and prestige between the citizenships of different countries. The sorting function of citizenship places people into hierarchically ordered categories. It is therefore a mechanism of stratification.[42] Audrey Macklin suggested that we can rank countries by the heft of citizenship that they offer.[43] One of the most eloquent formulations of the connection between citizenship and global inequality is Ayelet Shachar's concept of the "birthright lottery": a critique of the fact that the status that has the largest impact on individuals' life chances is ascribed at birth, according to particularistic principles.[44]

The key institution that enacts this hierarchical sorting by citizenship is the international system of passports and visa restrictions. This system accords extensive travel freedom to the citizens of rich countries while imposing strict limits on citizens of less developed countries: a "global mobility divide," in the words of Steffen Mau and his collaborators.[45] In this book, I focus on the sorting function of citizenship, which—as I will show—is indispensable for understanding how dual citizenship is perceived and used by individuals on the ground.

The Global Shift Toward Dual Citizenship

For most of the nineteenth and twentieth centuries, most countries prohibited dual citizenship and made significant efforts to suppress it. This ban was enforced through a combination of bilateral treaties, international conventions, and attempts by individual states to monitor their citizens. The view of dual citizenship as an unwelcome anomaly is captured in the words of the nineteenth-century American statesman George Bancroft, who compared it to bigamy.[46] Since the 1990s, however, a new permissive approach to citizenship has been gaining dominance.

Figure I.1 presents the dual citizenship policies of eighty-eight countries in the Americas, Europe, Oceania, and Asia (comprehensive data for the Middle East and Africa were not available). The graph shows the percentage of countries in each region that permitted dual nationality at naturalization in 1990 and in 2016.[47]

Figure I.1 demonstrates the shift in states' acceptance of dual nationality: in 1990, only 28 percent of countries in the sample tolerated it; by 2016, it was accepted by 75 percent of those countries. This represents a dramatic change in the relation to a status that until recently was considered highly problematic, even scandalous. Over the past three decades, toleration of dual nationality has grown in all the examined regions, albeit at different paces. The two Western regions included many "early adopters" of multiple citizenship. By 1990, the United States, Canada and New Zealand already permitted dual citizenship; Australia joined them in 2002. In Western Europe, about 30 percent of countries permitted dual citizenship in 1990 (including France, Britain, Ireland, and Portugal); between 1990 and 2016, half the countries in Western Europe changed their laws to permit dual citizenship.

In Latin America and Central and Eastern Europe, pre-1990 acceptance levels were very low—under 20 percent of countries. In those regions, the permissive shift was rapid and dramatic. Today, dual citizenship policies increasingly converge across Europe and the Americas: the acceptance of dual nationality is becoming a new norm in those regions, where over four-fifths of countries permit dual citizenship.[48] Asia also shows a trend toward the greater acceptance of dual citizenship, but at a much slower pace. While the majority of Asian countries do not permit dual citizenship, the number of accepters has tripled since 1990.

Citizenship in Europe and the Americas has undergone a *post-exclusive turn*. Countries no longer require exclusive allegiance from their citizens. This change is inseparable from another transformation: a *post-territorial turn*, whereby many

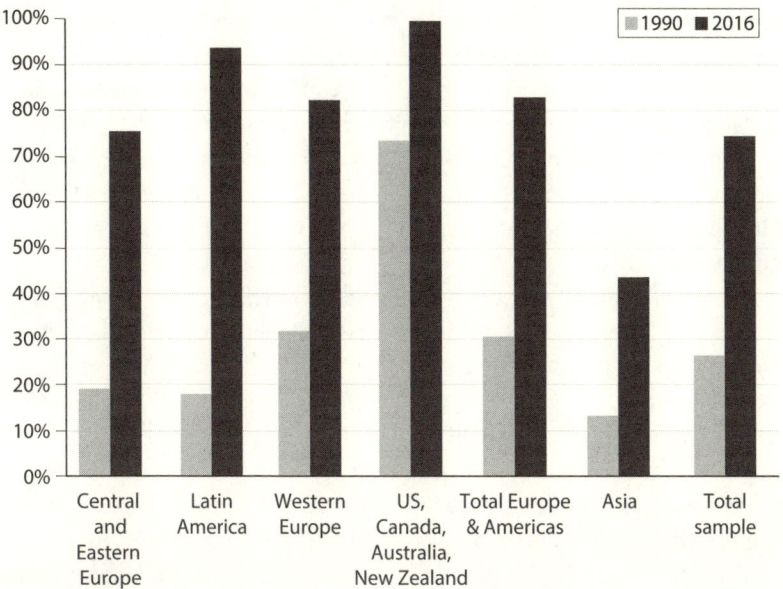

FIGURE I.1. World regions by percentage of countries that permitted dual citizenship at naturalization in 1990, 2016
Note: The bars show the percentage of countries in each world region that permitted dual citizenship at naturalization in 1990 (lighter bar) and 2016 (darker bar). The sample includes 72 countries in 1990 and 88 in 2016. Countries were coded as permitting dual citizenship if they formally allowed foreigners to naturalize while retaining their original citizenship ("immigrant dual citizenship") *or* allowed their citizens to naturalize elsewhere without expatriating them ("emigrant dual citizenship").
Sources: Author's calculation based on GLOBALCIT citizenship reports retrieved from www.globalcit.eu, and Liebich 2000; Bloemraad 2004; Escobar 2007; Blatter et al. 2009; and Pogonyi et al. 2010. See also Harpaz and Mateos 2019.

countries expand the scope of rights that they offer to their citizens abroad, including absentee voting and consular protection.[49] These two shifts are connected: the vast majority of dual citizens reside in just one country and their second citizenship comes from a country in which they do not reside. The proliferation of dual citizenship is also the spread of nonresident citizenship. Here, I will refer to a dual citizen's residence-country citizenship as their primary citizenship and to their nonresident citizenship as their secondary citizenship.

Pathways to Dual Citizenship

What explains the new permissive attitude toward dual citizenship? Analysts have pointed out changes in the global legal and normative context that have made multiple citizenship increasingly acceptable. They include the end of the Cold War, the abolition of conscription, processes of democratization and liberalization, new norms of gender equality, intensified international migration, and more.[50] While these contextual factors are important, we should remember that governments do not change citizenship laws in response to a general ambience of tolerance. Instead, governments and lawmakers move to permit dual citizenship because they believe that it will further the well-being, power, or prestige of the nation, as defined by their political ideology and interests.

Different countries have made the move toward the permission of dual citizenship for different reasons. Studies of legal and policy dynamics highlight this diversity.[51] In the United States, the toleration of dual citizenship was pushed by the Supreme Court, which, in a series of rulings since the 1950s, limited the government's authority to expatriate US citizens against their will.[52] In most other cases, dual citizenship became accepted in the context of migration or ethnic politics. Immigrant-receiving countries such as Sweden and Finland permitted dual citizenship in order to facilitate the integration of immigrants and their children.[53] Emigrant-sending countries such as Mexico or Turkey permitted dual citizenship to encourage emigrants to naturalize abroad while holding on to their original citizenship and identity.[54] Countries that had lost territories in the twentieth century—including Hungary, Romania, Bulgaria, Croatia, and Serbia—offer dual citizenship to cross-border ethnic kin to bring them back into the national fold.[55]

In all of these cases, the actual scope and impact of dual citizenship go beyond the initial motivations that have inspired its acceptance. Once states offer individuals the possibility to become dual citizens, bottom-up dynamics inevitably lead to a host of unintended consequences. In contrast to the extensive literature that adopted a state-centered approach, fewer studies have explored the implications of dual citizenship for the individuals who acquire and use it. The existing case studies on dual citizenship outside the West (which will be discussed in detail in chapter 1) reveal some common patterns that this book will explore in a more systematic comparative manner.

While researchers have analyzed data on dual citizenship from the European Social Survey, selected censuses and surveys and official statistics from citizenship-granting countries, the statistical picture is far from complete.[56] There is still a need for statistics that would shed light on the global demographics of dual citizenship, including comparative data on prevalence and demand.[57] In chapter 1, I will present such a dataset, that I constructed from original data.

In order to formulate a new analytical approach to citizenship, we also need to expand our theoretical toolbox. Social scientists' understanding of citizenship has traditionally been framed by concepts and theories that were developed to analyze immigrant integration, minority politics, and transnationalism.[58] The approach I propose in this book builds upon this literature, but also expands the theoretical lens by integrating the global, population-sorting function of citizenship, and highlighting its role as a marker of differential status within a global hierarchy. This reframing broadens the analysis beyond questions of national identity and loyalty, bringing to the fore the practical value of dual citizenship as a source of additional opportunities, security, rights and travel freedom.

A New Approach: Investigating Compensatory Citizenship

This book focuses on a mostly overlooked type of dual citizenship that I call *compensatory citizenship*: dual citizenship from a Western or EU country that is acquired by individuals living outside Western Europe and North America. At least three million people in Latin America, Eastern Europe, and Israel have acquired dual citizenship from EU countries. Hundreds of thousands worldwide have acquired compensatory citizenship through other means, such as strategic birth or residence. The rise of compensatory dual citizenship is a direct consequence of the post-exclusive turn in citizenship.

There are six main pathways that citizens of countries outside the West use to secure a second, Western citizenship. Chapters 2, 3, and 4 of this book will analyze three study cases that represent the three pathways that involve the largest number of persons.

> 1. *Ancestry-based citizenship acquisition.* Descendants of European emigrants living outside Western Europe and North America obtain EU dual citizenship from their origin countries. Major citizenship-granting countries include Italy, Spain, Poland, and Germany. Applicants mostly hail from Latin American countries (including Argentina, Brazil, Mexico, and Venezuela) as well as Israel.[59]
>
> I study this pathway by focusing on the case of Israelis who apply for EU citizenship.[60] Between the 1920s and the 1960s, about a million Jews from Poland, Germany, Romania, and other countries settled in Israel (before 1948, the Palestine Mandate). They mostly came as refugees who fled persecution, and typically severed all links to their origin countries. Since 2000, over 85,000 Israelis with roots in Central and Eastern Europe have applied to reacquire citizenship in their countries of origin. Their declared aim is to secure a "European passport," and they show minimal interest in their countries of origin.
>
> 2. *Coethnic citizenship acquisition.* Individuals obtain dual citizenship from kin-states on the basis of ethnic origin. Numerous countries in Central and Eastern Europe offer coethnic citizenship, including Hungary, Romania, Bulgaria, and Greece, among others. Applicants

mostly come from neighboring countries in the region, especially those that are not EU members, such as Serbia, Ukraine, Macedonia, and Moldova.[61]

I study the coethnic pathway through the case of Hungarian dual citizenship in Serbia. The multiethnic region of Vojvodina, now in northern Serbia, is home to a sizable Hungarian minority. In 2011, Hungary enacted a new policy that made Vojvodina's ethnic Hungarians eligible for dual citizenship. By 2018, over 180,000 citizens of Serbia had obtained a second citizenship from Hungary. This demand is driven in part by an authentic identification with Hungary among cross-border Hungarians—but it also reflects the strong desire of Serbians to become citizens of the EU and earn the right to work and study in Western Europe. Not all applicants are ethnically Hungarian: many ethnic Serbs have begun to study the Hungarian language with the express aim of securing EU citizenship.

3. *Strategic cross-border birth.* Middle- or upper-class individuals from many countries in Asia, Latin America, and the Middle East travel to the United States or Canada in order to give birth there. After they secure citizenship for their children thanks to automatic *jus soli* laws, they return to their home country. There is evidence that this strategy—colloquially called birth tourism—is employed by citizens of Mexico, China, Turkey, Taiwan, among others.[62]

I study this pathway through the case of Mexican strategic birth in the United States.[63] In 1998, Mexico permitted dual nationality. This move was primarily intended to encourage Mexican immigrants to naturalize in the United States while retaining their nationality. An unintended consequence has been a growth in the number of dual nationals in Mexico. While most of this growth is the result of deportation and return migration, there has also been a rapid growth in the number of elite Mexican parents who travel across the border to the United States, give birth, and immediately return to Mexico. An estimated figure of 140,000 Mexicans have secured US citizenship for their children in this manner since 1990.

The book will focus on these three pathways to compensatory citizenship. There are at least three additional pathways to compensatory citizenship. While they form part of the same global phenomenon, they will not be analyzed in this book. These include (4) *residence strategies,* which involve individuals who naturalize in Western countries and then immediately return to their origin countries or migrate onward;[64] (5) *matrimonial strategies,* whereby individuals obtain dual citizenship through marriage;[65] and (6) *citizenship by investment,* which involves high-net-worth individuals who obtain a second citizenship by purchasing expensive real estate or making a monetary investment.[66]

The three study cases included in this book were selected to represent the three main pathways to compensatory citizenship: ancestry, ethnicity, and strategic birth. I collected extensive data on those cases through fieldwork and interviews (see methodological appendix). The diversity of cases also permits two additional axes of internal comparison. First, the Serbian and Israeli cases represent the dynamics of dual citizenship in the EU, where blood ties—ancestry and ethnicity—are central to citizenship allocation; the Mexican case illustrates the dynamics of dual citizenship from the United States, which is premised on the deliberate creation of citizenship ties (through strategic birth) where no prior connection exists.

The three-case design also makes it possible to compare countries with different positions in the global hierarchy. Serbia and Mexico are middle-income economies and massive senders of emigration; these countries' patterns of trade and migration show tight dependence on their respective adjacent Western blocs (the EU for Serbia, the United States for Mexico). In contrast, Israel is a high-income, low-emigration country that is not dependent to such a degree on trade with a single Western bloc.[67] This makes it possible to compare cases where the practical usefulness of dual citizenship is self-explanatory (Serbia and Mexico) alongside a case where the use of citizenship is less obvious (Israel).

Roadmap for the Book

This book aims to reposition the phenomenon of dual citizenship within the context of global inequality and analyze it as a strategy of resource accumulation. Chapter 1 lays out the theoretical framework for the book. It describes a model of the global citizenship hierarchy. Within this hierarchy, citizenship from Western or EU countries provides the highest level of rights, opportunities, and travel freedom. Once dual citizenship became available, millions of individuals from middle-tier nations in Latin America and Eastern Europe drew on their ancestry or ethnicity to obtain EU citizenship. For those individuals, compensatory citizenship is a deliberate strategy of upward mobility in the global hierarchy.

The following chapters explore three cases that illustrate the dynamics of compensatory citizenship on the ground. Chapter 2 explores the case of Hungarian dual citizenship in Serbia. Since 2011, Hungary has offered dual citizenship to cross-border Hungarians living in neighboring countries. Coethnic dual citizenship has complicated and contradictory effects on Serbia's Hungarian minority. On the one hand, they enjoy access to Europe, as well as elevated social status in Serbia. On the other hand, the proliferation of EU passports makes it easier for young Hungarians to emigrate, shrinking this beleaguered population even further. Meanwhile, thousands of ethnic Serbs have also begun to study the Hungarian language. They hope to take advantage of Hungary's generosity toward Hungarian speakers in order to thereby gain access to the EU.

In chapter 3, I study the growth in US dual nationality in Mexico, and specifically the phenomenon of strategic cross-borders births. This involves middle- and upper-class Mexican parents who travel to the United States to give birth, aiming to secure US citizenship for their children. The families who engage in this practice typically have little interest in emigrating. Instead, they mainly view the United States as a site of high-prestige consumption and wish to provide their children with easy access to tourism, shopping and education across the border. The American passport is also an insurance policy that allows easy exit at times of insecurity in Mexico. This strategic acquisition of US dual nationality by upper-class Mexicans can be juxtaposed with another recent trend: the deportation of hundreds of thousands of Mexican undocumented immigrants, who take their US-born children with them to Mexico.[68] For the former group, dual nationality is voluntary and practical; for the latter, it is an imposed disadvantage.

In chapter 4, I analyze EU citizenship in Israel. EU-Israeli dual citizens rarely refer to themselves as dual citizens, but instead see themselves as "Israelis with a European passport." The findings show that citizenship applicants are mainly driven by two motivations that were conditioned by Jewish history: the wish to hold an insurance policy against the possibility of Israel being destroyed, and the desire for a status symbol that signifies their elitist position in Israel as European-origin Jews. Ironically, the grandchildren of Jews who had left Europe for Israel now look to German or Hungarian passports for security.

In the conclusion, I discuss the theoretical implications of the book's findings. The proliferation of compensatory citizenship contributes to the commodification of nationality through multiple pathways: the emergence of citizenship industries, the exchange of citizenship for cash, and the instrumentalization of national belonging. Respondents exhibit an attitude that I call "the sovereign individual"; they understand citizenship status as a domain for individual free choice and maximization of utility, free from traditional collective dictates. In other words, citizenship is changing from an ascribed to an achieved status. The legal acceptance of multiple nationality has made Western citizenship into a valuable practical resource for elites in other parts of the world, allowing them to convert local advantages into a new kind of capital that elevates their position within the global system of stratification.

1

Dual Citizenship as a Strategy of Global Upward Mobility

Since the 1990s, states have become increasingly tolerant of dual citizenship. Who benefited from this new state of affairs? What are the forces that drive demand for dual citizenship? Social scientists have studied how immigrants in the West acquire and use dual citizenship, focusing on questions of ethnic and national identity, integration, and transnationalism. At the same time, they have tended to overlook a crucial element that plays a key role in the acquisition and use of dual citizenship: disparities in the practical value of different countries' citizenship. In this chapter, I introduce a new approach that posits that global inequality in citizenship value is the main factor that shapes the acquisition and use of dual citizenship.

The world's citizenships are not equal. Some citizenships–say, Canadian or Swedish—provide access to a secure and prosperous territory, guarantee extensive social and political rights, and come with a prestigious, high-mobility passport. On the other end of the spectrum, some citizenships are practically worthless in terms of economic access, social welfare, and political rights—and, moreover, mark their bearer as an automatic suspect when trying to cross international borders. This is the situation for citizens of most African and many Middle Eastern countries. Other citizenships occupy an intermediate position between those two poles, providing some degree of opportunities and entitlements but falling short of the ideal set by the rich West.

In this chapter, I take this global hierarchy as the point of departure and use it to explain variation in the way dual citizenship is understood and used. I introduce an index of citizenship value and analyze extensive data on the prevalence of dual citizenship and its acquisition. The analysis demonstrates three points. First, individuals' responses to the possibility to obtain dual citizenship are shaped by their position in the global hierarchy of citizenship value. Second, individuals are motivated to acquire a second citizenship if it is ranked higher in the global hierarchy than their primary, residence-country citizenship. Third, acquisition of dual citizenship is particularly high in countries that are in the middle of the global distribution (mostly in Eastern Europe and Latin America), where many citizens have both the practical incentive and the opportunity to obtain citizenship from a North American or an EU country.

The data show that millions of persons in middle-tier countries have acquired dual citizenship without immigrating; these persons draw on their ancestry, ethnicity, or economic capital to secure a second, Western citizenship. This second citizenship—which I call *compensatory citizenship*—is used as an enhancer of opportunities, an insurance policy, a premium passport, even a status symbol. In other words, compensatory citizenship operates as an instrumental strategy of global upward mobility.

Dual Citizenship: An Actor's Point of View

Most authors who have studied dual citizenship have focused on the legal and policy dynamics that led to its acceptance or prohibition by countries. Fewer works have studied it at the level of individuals: the motives and interests behind the acquisition of dual citizenship and its meaning and use once acquired. The existing individual-level, bottom-up literature mostly examined a particular set of cases: immigrants to North America and Western Europe who naturalized while retaining their origin-country citizenship. This literature explored the factors that lead some immigrants in the West to become dual citizens as well as the impact of dual citizenship on their social and political integration.[1] The analytical focus has been on the decision to acquire resident (i.e., primary) dual citizenship in the country where the immigrant lives.

In the context of immigration, nonresident dual citizenship (i.e., secondary citizenship) is created passively through the retention of origin-country citizenship or by transmission *jure sanguinis* from immigrant parents, without requiring any special action on the part of the dual citizen. Furthermore, for immigrants in the West, a secondary citizenship from their origin country (say, from Mexico or Morocco) typically carries relatively limited practical value. Nonresident secondary citizenship has been characterized by David FitzGerald as "citizenship à la carte," in reference to the autonomy that dual citizens enjoy in deciding when and how to use its benefits. However, it appears that, for dual citizens in the West, such uses typically remain only a potential.[2]

No more than a small minority of immigrants use dual citizenship to engage in transnational entrepreneurship—5 percent, according to an analysis by Portes, Guarnizo, and Haller—while other economic uses, such as inheriting property or relocating for work or lifestyle, are very specific and remain irrelevant for most immigrants.[3] Absentee voting in immigrants' country of origin is more common, but carries limited practical benefits for the voters. Many first- and second-generation immigrants (e.g., Algerian-French) retain dual citizenship to secure visa-free access to their countries of origin as well as safeguard their right to own and inherit real estate.

Nonetheless, for individuals who hold primary (i.e., resident) citizenship in a Western country, a secondary citizenship carries practical uses that are *specific* and *personal*. It makes it easier to capitalize on preexisting economic, political, or social ties, but does not usually act as an independent resource. Any additional citizenship beyond the primary Western one does not provide access to enhanced rights or opportunities on a global scale. Instead, it provides rights in an additional specific territory, one that is usually less prosperous and attractive than the country of residence (which is why those persons or their parents emigrated in the first place).[4] Therefore, dual citizens in Western countries do not typically treat their secondary, origin-country citizenship in an instrumental manner, but rather see it as a mark of identity and sentimental attachment.[5]

This explains why demand for dual citizenship among immigrants and their descendants in the West is relatively low, as evidenced by the relatively low percentage of dual citizens among first- and second-generation immigrants in countries like the United States, Germany, and Canada, compared to the potential number of those who could take up a second citizenship.[6] Moreover, the predominately sentimental value of dual citizenship in the West explains why the sociological literature has not developed a theory about the practical uses and meanings of dual citizenship and focused on its meaning as an indicator of assimilation and identity.

Beyond the Sentimental Approach

The noninstrumental approach to dual citizenship, that analyzes it through the prism of identity and sentiments, is theoretically valid within the empirical scope of the West. When applying this approach beyond the West, however, its limitations become apparent. Dual citizenship follows a different pattern in countries that occupy a lower position in the global hierarchy of citizenship value.

A number of recent monographs explore the meaning and uses of dual citizenship outside Western Europe and North America. Numerous researchers, including David Cook-Martin, Guido Tintori, Szabolcs Pogonyi, Pablo Mateos,

Eleanor Knott, and others (including the author) have examined specific case studies of dual citizenship. These included Bulgarian, Romanian, and Hungarian EU dual citizenship in neighboring non-EU countries (such as Macedonia or Moldova), Spanish and Italian citizenship in Argentina or Mexico, and EU citizenship in Israel. Typically, individuals in those countries do not acquire their second citizenship by way of naturalization, but rather on the basis of their ancestry or ethnic identity. Some studies—including works by Aihwa Ong, Evren Balta, and Özlem Altan-Olcay—analyze the practices of strategic residence and birth by Chinese, Turks, and others who seek US or Canadian citizenship for themselves or their children.[7]

Those case studies represent highly diverse contexts and pathways. Nevertheless, they have two key features in common: eligible individuals exhibited high demand for Western or EU dual citizenship, and the relation to such citizenship was strongly instrumental. While a small number of applicants were inspired by sentimental motives, most of them sought citizenship in countries to which they had no real connection and whose languages they often could not speak. This stands in marked contrast to dual citizens in the West, who are first- or second-generation immigrants and often have real experience of the "homeland." Many dual citizens outside the West denied feeling any identification or affinity with their countries of secondary citizenship (Israelis with German citizenship are a case in point). Moreover, most of them did not have concrete plans to immigrate to their new countries of citizenship.

Viewed from a traditional perspective that treats citizenship as a binding, socially significant tie to a specific nation-state, such attitudes appear puzzling. What could be the value of citizenship when detached from both residence and national identity? To answer this question, I propose an alternative way of looking at citizenship. This approach focuses on the function of citizenship as "marker in the international system of population management" (in the words of Barry Hindess) or, to put it differently, as position within a stratified global order.[8] Viewed from this angle, it should come as no surprise that individuals from outside Western Europe and North America are eager to acquire citizenship from any Western or EU country.

When individuals outside the West make decisions about whether to acquire a second citizenship, sentiments and identity do not seem to be the main criteria. They often evaluate citizenship on the basis of its potential to provide better opportunities, more extensive rights, improved security, and greater freedom of movement. The secondary citizenship operates as *compensatory citizenship* because it makes up for limitations in one's primary, residence-country citizenship. Given the practical usefulness of compensatory citizenship, we expect to find strong demand for it. This understudied type of dual citizenship is distinct from sentimental dual citizenship, which, thanks to its ubiquity in the

West, has been the focus of the sociological literature. In the remainder of this chapter, I present a model of the structure of global stratification and explore how it produces different formations of dual citizenship in different contexts.

The Global Hierarchy of Citizenship Value

Nation-state citizenship is the key principle of stratification in today's world.[9] Therefore, the quality of the citizenship that an individual already has will affect the likelihood that he or she will acquire a second citizenship and the way that they will use it. Below, I introduce an index that ranks the world's countries by the value of their citizenship and, moreover, groups them into three tiers (or classes) of citizenship that will differ in their relation to dual citizenship.

CITIZENSHIP: THE KEY TO GLOBAL STRATIFICATION

Citizenship is the most important factor that affects one's life chances—more than class, gender, or race.[10] In terms of income distribution, we are living today in what the economist Branko Milanovic has called a "non-Marxian" world. In 1848, Marx and Engels concluded the *Communist Manifesto* with the rallying cry, "Workers of the World, Unite!" At the time, the living standards of workers and peasants in England, Russia, and India were comparable, hovering around the level of subsistence. Under those conditions, it was plausible to envision the "workers of the world" as having a shared fate and common interests that might lead them to unite against a supposed common enemy. Over the past century and a half, however, the global distribution of wealth has changed dramatically. Today, between-country inequality (location, or citizenship) plays a bigger role than within-country inequality (class) in explaining economic gaps between individuals around the world—hence, a restructuring along "non-Marxian" lines.[11]

The fact that humanity is stratified by citizenship more than by class is evident in the vast income gaps that exist between rich and poor countries. To take an extreme example, the GDP per capita in Norway ($61,472) is over a hundred times higher than in the Central African Republic ($592), even after adjusting for different price levels (PPP). Even the poorest citizens of rich countries are well off relative to the world as a whole. Milanovic shows that the 5 percent of Americans with the lowest incomes are in the 60th percentile of the global income distribution (i.e., their income is higher than 60 percent of mankind); the lowest-income 5 percent of Danes are in the global 90th percentile. Note that, since the 1980s, within-country (class) inequality in the West has been growing while between-country inequality has diminished somewhat;

nevertheless, the gap in living standards between the West and (most of) the rest of the world remains very large.[12]

Global inequality in citizenship value is not limited to income; in fact, it extends to almost any conceivable domain of human flourishing, including security, political rights, access to health and social services and even clean air and water. Differences in access to education mean that over a third of young women in Pakistan cannot read, compared with practically zero female youth illiteracy in Europe. Gaps in access to healthcare make a child in Sierra Leone sixty times more likely to die before the age of five than a child in Norway. And differences in crime rates make a resident of Honduras fifty-six times more likely to be a victim of homicide than a resident of Canada.[13]

Furthermore, citizenship also stratifies individuals in terms of access to other national territories beside one's own country. The world's passports are not equal. Whereas citizens of rich Western countries may travel freely throughout most of the world, travelers from many other countries must expend substantial amounts of time and money on obtaining visas before they may venture abroad.[14]

The ranking of passports can be seen as a kind of "peer review" that states make of one another. The freedom to travel offered by a passport reflects the perception of the issuing country as a potential sender of unwanted immigrants, refugees, criminals, or terrorists. The citizens of rich, free and secure countries are welcome as tourists and business travelers and are admitted to many territories without a visa. Citizens of lower-ranked countries, in contrast, are seen as "automatic suspects," and their movement is controlled and restricted. This global system of citizenship-based mobility restrictions helps explain why, in spite of extremely high global income inequality, no more than 3 percent of mankind are immigrants.[15]

Legal scholar Ayelet Shachar describes this state of affairs as the "birthright lottery," arguing that citizenship transmission at birth operates as a kind of (untaxed and unregulated) intergenerational transfer of wealth.[16] Audrey Macklin has proposed the concept "heft of citizenship" to capture the different "packages" of rights and opportunities available to different individuals.[17] One can envision a graded spectrum of global citizenship value, extending from the stateless refugee to the citizen of a rich and secure country. Within the starkly stratified political-economic system that encompasses all of humankind, citizenship from a Western country acts as an entry ticket to the global elite.[18]

The model that is presented below uses a composite score that was calculated on the basis of four international indices to determine countries' relative positions within the hierarchy of citizenship value.[19] Each country's rank was determined by combining the value of its resident citizenship—represented by a Citizenship Quality Index (CQI) that will be introduced below—alongside an index that measures the international freedom of movement that its passport provides. The CQI represents the quality of a country's citizenship for residents in its territory, the passport ranking reflects the degree of recognition it receives abroad.

QUANTIFYING RESIDENT CITIZENSHIP: SECURITY, OPPORTUNITY, RIGHTS

The world's countries can be ranked according to their relative success in realizing an ideal of citizenship, meaning the rights and benefits that citizens expect to receive from the state. The institution of citizenship—and the nation-state more broadly—developed in Western Europe and North America and then diffused to other parts of the world, where it was emulated with varying degrees of success.[20] Therefore, I treat the ideal of citizenship not as an abstract vision derived from a priori reasoning about human nature but as a concrete model that corresponds to the standard set by rich and democratic Western nations.

The quality of resident citizenship is defined here as the full range of potential benefits that derive from the fundamental right to be present in the territory of one's state of citizenship (right of abode). There are three main components to resident citizenship: *security, economic opportunity, and civil and political rights*. Together, these elements constitute the ideal that modern individuals expect from their state when they are in its territory.

Security: this component of citizenship reflects states' relative success in minimizing the risk of violence—particularly political violence—and instability in their territory. I measure it using the State Fragility Index (SFI) published by the Center for Systemic Peace, which combines various measures that affect a country's security and stability, including external conflict, internal repression, regime stability, and social wellbeing.

Opportunity: this component captures states' relative ability to assure the prosperity of the population living in their territory. It is dependent on a range of factors, including labor markets, possibilities for education, and consumption and level of public services. I measure it using the Human Development Index (HDI) formulated by the United Nations Development Program, which combines measures of income, life expectancy, and educational attainment.

Rights: this component captures the relative degree of political rights enjoyed by citizens, including the basic democratic right to elect one's government, as well as civil rights like the freedom of expression and assembly. I measure it using the Democracy Index calculated by the *Economist* Intelligence Unit, which ranks countries using a composite democracy score that includes electoral process, government functioning, political participation, political culture, and civil liberties.[21]

These three measures were combined to construct the Citizenship Quality Index (CQI), a composite measure of the benefits that accrue from resident citizenship in a country.[22]

PASSPORT WORTH: STRATIFICATION THROUGH MOBILITY RIGHTS

The second index represents the degree of mobility freedom provided by each country's passport. I use the visa restrictions index published by the citizenship consulting company, Henley & Partners, which ranks passports by the number of countries to which they allow visa-free access. At the top of the list are the passports of Western European countries, the United States, Japan, and New Zealand, which in 2016 offered visa-free access to over 170 territories. Other countries with relatively strong passports were Hong Kong, Israel, Mexico, Poland, or Romania, whose citizens had free access to between 140 and 161 countries. Countries near the bottom of the list included China (visa-free access to 53 countries), India (49), Iran (40), and Afghanistan (24).[23]

Mapping Citizenship Value: A Three-Tiered Hierarchy

Figure 1.1 plots the CQI, which measures the quality of resident citizenship, on the horizontal axis, and the Passport Index, which measures global freedom of movement, on the vertical axis. It thus shows the ranking of the world's citizenships by their internal and external value.

Figure 1.1 illustrates the global stratification of citizenship value and shows the strong association between a country's CQI rank and its Passport Index rank. There was a rank order correlation (Spearman's rho) of 0.89 between the two indices at a significance level of $p<.0001$. This is consistent with the expectation that high-value resident citizenship would go together with extensive travel freedom. This correlation is visible in the graph.

I divide the world's countries into three tiers of citizenship value. These tiers roughly correspond to the top 10 percent of citizenship and passport value (first tier); the citizenships ranked between the fiftieth and ninetieth percentiles (middle tier); and those below the global median (third tier). The division of the world into three categories is consistent with preexisting conceptualizations, including the Cold War division into first, second, and third worlds, as well as Immanuel Wallerstein's world systems theory, which divides countries into global core, semiperiphery, and periphery.[24]

As can be seen in figure 1.1, there is a strong correlation between citizenship tier position and geographical region. The first tier is made up of Western European and North American nations, Australia, and New Zealand, as well as Japan and South Korea.[25] The middle tier is dominated by Central and Eastern European (CEE) countries (represented by triangles) and Latin American countries (shown as Xs). It also includes Israel, Taiwan, Singapore, Malaysia, Turkey, United Arab Emirates, Kuwait, Mauritius, and South Africa. The third tier mostly consists of Asian, African, and Middle Eastern

GLOBAL UPWARD MOBILITY 23

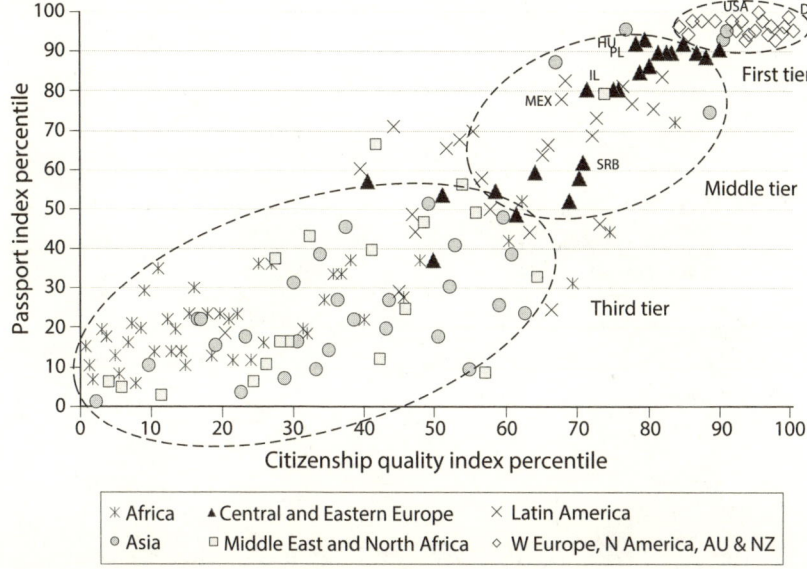

FIGURE 1.1. World's countries ranked by Passport Index and Citizenship Quality Index
Note: The x-axis represents the country's percentile rank in the Citizenship Quality Index. The y-axis represents its percentile rank in Henley's Passport Index (the number of countries its citizens may enter without visa). The small circle in the upper-right corner represents the first-tier citizenship category. The larger circle below and to the left represents the middle-tier citizenship category, and the bottom circle includes third-tier citizenship countries. The countries that will be discussed in this book are marked with labels on the graph: Germany (DE), USA, Hungary (HU), Poland (PL), Israel (IL), Mexico (MEX) and Serbia (SRB).
Sources: Author's calculation based on Henley & Partners Visa Restrictions Index 2016; State Fragility Index 2015; Human Development Index 2015; the *Economist* Democracy Index 2016.

nations. Figure 1.2 presents the citizenship tier breakdown on a map of the world.

The basic contours of this ranking are not surprising: it is well known that Norway is richer than Nicaragua, and Canada safer than Cameroon. The integrated model of citizenship value, however, is useful in highlighting the regional and path-dependent nature of citizenship value.

As figure 1.1 shows, the top rankings in citizenship value are dominated by a tight cluster of mostly Western European and North American countries. These countries have emerged as the world's first nation-states and have enjoyed hegemonic global positions for most of the past two centuries. The global middle tier is mostly composed of countries in Latin America and Eastern Europe that have gained independence during the nineteenth century or in the early twentieth century. These countries had strong historical ties with Central and Western Europe. The third tier is mostly composed of Asian and African countries that have gained independence relatively recently—usually after World War II.

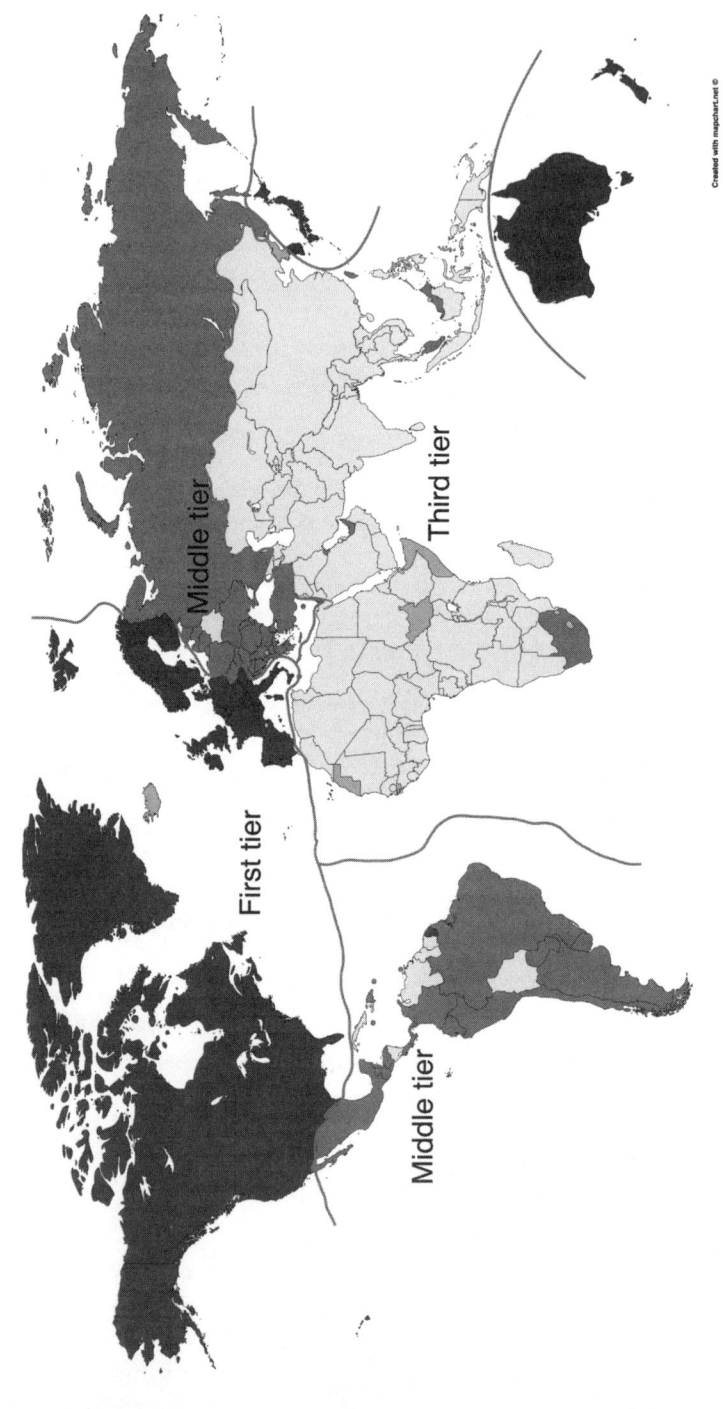

FIGURE 1.2. World map with citizenship tiers

Note: The map shows the world's countries according to their tier position. The dark-colored countries are first-tier and the light-colored ones are third-tier. Middle-tier countries are colored in medium grey. No data were available for Somalia, South Sudan, Western Sahara, North Korea, or Iceland.

Position in the citizenship hierarchy is expected to affect various individual-level behaviors and attitudes that pertain to global stratification, including, among others, the propensity to emigrate, constructions of identity, and patterns of consumption. Here, I focus on the way citizenship tier position shapes a specific behavior: attitudes toward the possibility of acquiring a second citizenship.

First-tier citizenship countries provide their citizens with the full package of citizenship entitlements in terms of security, opportunities, and rights. In addition, these countries' passports offer nearly unrestricted travel possibilities.[26] Most first-tier citizenship countries receive immigration from middle- and third-tier countries and most of them permit dual citizenship. Therefore, we can expect to find large numbers of dual citizens in first-tier countries who hold a secondary citizenship from lower-tier countries. However, demand for dual citizenship will be relatively low because the secondary citizenship will be of limited practical value.

Middle-tier citizenship countries provide their citizens with a package of security, opportunity, rights, and travel freedom that is above the global median, but falls short of the ideal set by the West.[27] Fourteen middle-tier citizenship countries in Central and Eastern Europe are members of the EU, meaning that their citizenship provides full rights in first-tier Western European countries. While Hungary, for example, remains far less prosperous than Germany or the Netherlands, EU citizenship compensates for this deficit in opportunities, providing access to the attractive labor and education markets of Western Europe. EU membership, and the settlement freedom that comes with it, boosts the value of these countries' citizenship. Even if they do not wish to emigrate to Western Europe, citizens of these Central and Eastern European countries benefit from the "backup plan" provided by EU citizenship, and may also use it for temporary, circular mobility. Therefore, even though Hungary, Romania or Poland are classified as middle-tier citizenship countries, for people outside the EU, their citizenship has the same practical value as first-tier citizenship.

Since 1990, most countries in Eastern Europe and Latin America moved to permit dual nationality. For historical and geographical reasons, many middle-tier countries host large numbers of people who have ties to Western and EU countries. These include descendants of European immigrants (mostly in South America and Israel) and coethnics of EU member countries (mostly in Eastern Europe), as well as populations with extensive migration ties to the West (especially in Mexico and East Asia). Many of these individuals have obtained EU citizenship through programs that offer citizenship to descendants of emigrants or coethnics including, for example, descendants of Italians in South America or ethnic Hungarians in Eastern Europe.[28] I will refer to this phenomenon as long-distance citizenship acquisition, paraphrasing Benedict

Anderson's concept of long-distance nationalism. Whereas Anderson focuses on emotional ties to the homeland, however, long-distance acquisition—as I will show below—does not necessarily involve sentiments or identity. In fact, it is usually free of such emotional ties.

We may expect to find relatively large populations in middle-tier countries that hold a highly desirable secondary citizenship from a Western or EU country. Moreover, demand for such citizenship will be high. At the same time, we do not expect to find large numbers of dual citizens produced by immigrant naturalization: not only because middle-tier countries receive small numbers of immigrants, but also because middle-tier citizens will only have a weak incentive to hold secondary citizenship from a middle- or third-tier country.

Third-tier citizenship countries occupy the bottom half of the world distribution in citizenship quality and travel freedom. The population of third-tier countries typically has few ancestral or ethnic ties to Europe. Moreover, these countries receive relatively little immigration and often do not permit dual citizenship. In third-tier countries, demand for higher-tier citizenship is presumably strong, but there are relatively few opportunities to obtain such citizenship. Wealthy individuals from third-tier citizenship countries are the most likely buyers in citizenship-by-investment programs, which will not be discussed in detail in this book.[29]

This model highlights the different dominant types of dual citizenship in the West and outside it. In Western countries, we would mainly find *sentimental dual citizenship* produced by ongoing immigration. In middle-tier citizenship countries, in contrast, we expect to find high levels of *compensatory dual citizenship* that will be more instrumental in nature. This chapter, and this book more generally, will not discuss third-tier countries. In the analysis below, I will compare patterns of dual citizenship in first- and middle-tier countries. Three propositions logically flow from the theoretical approach outlined above.

> Proposition 1: *Dual citizens in first-tier (Western) countries will typically hold a secondary citizenship from a lower-tier country and will consist primarily of first- and second-generation immigrants.*
>
> Proposition 2: *Dual citizens in middle-tier countries will typically hold a secondary citizenship from a Western country and will consist primarily of persons who have become dual citizens through long-distance acquisition.*
>
> Proposition 3: *Individuals in middle-tier countries who are potentially eligible for long-distance citizenship acquisition will exhibit higher demand and more instrumental motivations relative to eligible individuals in Western countries.*

Dual Citizenship Statistics: Evaluating Prevalence and Demand

The study of dual citizenship has long been hindered by the unavailability of comparative statistics. Here, I fill this lacuna by analyzing an original dataset that I constructed from administrative data and existing academic publications. The main dataset includes statistics on the prevalence of dual citizenship in thirty countries. In addition, I will analyze a second dataset, that includes statistics on the acquisition of ancestry- or ethnicity-based dual citizenship from eight European countries (a total of 2.66 million citizenship acquisitions).[30]

PREVALENCE OF DUAL CITIZENSHIP

In order to evaluate the prevalence of dual citizenship, I use an original dataset based on statistics from thirty countries with a combined population of 948 million. About 18.5 million of them—almost 2 percent—held dual citizenship. The countries in the sample include twenty-four European countries and four Latin American countries as well as Canada and Israel. In terms of citizenship tiers, the dataset includes nine first-tier countries and twenty-one middle-tier countries. For all countries but one, data pertain to years between 2010 and 2016 (for France, data were for 2008).

I compiled these data from a variety of sources, including national censuses, consular reports and academic publications (see methodological appendix for more details). The numbers given below should be treated as minimum estimates, because many persons with dual citizenship are unaware of their status or deliberately conceal it. Moreover, in some countries the data capture only part of the dual citizen population: in Switzerland, data only include persons over fifteen years of age; the figures for Israel, Brazil, Venezuela, Argentina, and Moldova rely on statistics from the major countries of secondary citizenship and are therefore incomplete by definition. Table 1.1 shows levels of dual citizenship in twenty-three countries that hosted fifty thousand or more dual citizens. It leaves out seven countries in Central and Eastern Europe where the number of dual citizens in 2011 was under fifty thousand: Czech Republic, Slovakia, Albania, Bulgaria, Armenia, Montenegro, and Lithuania.

The table presents levels of dual citizenship in different countries, making it possible to analyze them in the context of the global citizenship stratification. Column 2 shows the number of dual citizens in each country. In Germany and France alone, the number of persons with dual citizenship exceeds 7.5 million. Overall, the nine first-tier countries in the sample were home to 11.8 million dual citizens, who constituted 4.3 percent of their populations. Middle-tier countries also show a strong presence of dual citizens. There were a total of 6.7 million dual citizens in twenty-one sampled countries, equivalent to 1 percent

TABLE 1.1. Prevalence and Characteristics of Dual Citizenship in Selected Countries

1	2	3	4	5	6	7
Country	Dual citizens	% Dual citizens	Most common secondary citizenship	Tier of secondary citizenship	Main pathway to secondary citizenship	% Foreign-born
FIRST-TIER CITIZENSHIP COUNTRIES						
Germany	4,300,000	5.3%	Russia	II	Immigration	12%
France	3,300,000	5%	Algeria	III	Immigration	12%
Netherlands	1,306,274	7.7%	Morocco	III	Immigration	11%
Canada	944,700	2.9%	UK	I	Immigration	21%
Spain	863,000	1.8%	Ecuador	II	Immigration	14%
Switzerland	688,561	8.6%	Italy (EU)	I	Immigration	29%
Portugal	244,745	2.3%	Brazil	II	Immigration	8%
Finland	104,997	2%	Russia	II	Immigration	5%
Ireland	104,784	2.3%	US	I	Return migration	16%
Total: First tier	11,857,061	4.3%				13%
MIDDLE-TIER CITIZENSHIP COUNTRIES						
Brazil	880,000	0.4%	Portugal (EU)	I	Long-distance acquisition	<1%
Israel	840,000	10%	US	I	Immigration	26%
Bosnia-Herzegovina	800,000	20%	Croatia (EU)	I	Long-distance acquisition	<1%
Argentina	790,473	1.9%	Italy (EU)	I	Long-distance acquisition	5%
Mexico	778,000	0.6%	US	I	Return migration	<1%
Venezuela	587,555	2%	Colombia	III	Immigration	4%
Romania	441,331	2%	Hungary (EU)	I	Long-distance acquisition	<1%
Serbia	401,548	5.5%	Hungary (EU)	I	Long-distance acquisition	6%
Poland	327,500	1%	Germany (EU)	I	Long-distance acquisition	2%
Moldova	326,000	9%	Romania (EU)	I	Long-distance acquisition	11%
Greece	190,000	1.7%	Albania	II	Immigration	9%
Hungary	88,906	0.9%	Romania (EU)	I	Immigration	5%
Croatia	86,404	2%	Bosnia	II	Immigration	18%

TABLE 1.1. (*continued*)

1	2	3	4	5	6	7
Country	Dual citizens	% Dual citizens	Most common secondary citizenship	Tier of secondary citizenship	Main pathway to secondary citizenship	% Foreign-born
Russia	78,615	0.1%	Ukraine	II	Immigration	8%
Total: Middle tier	6,723,374	1%				*3.5%*
Total sample	18,580,435	2%				6%

Note: Columns 2 and 3 present the number of dual citizens in each country in absolute numbers and as a percentage of the total population. Column 4 presents the leading country of secondary citizenship and column 5 its citizenship tier. Column 6 presents the pathway that characterizes the leading country of secondary citizenship. Column 7 presents the percentage of foreign-born immigrants in the country's population. Totals also include low-prevalence countries (under 50,000 dual citizens) that are not shown in the table.

Sources: See methodological appendix.

of those countries' populations. While absolute numbers of dual citizens in first-tier countries are much higher, numerous middle-tier countries host substantial populations of dual citizens. The three countries with the highest percentage of dual citizens were middle-tier countries: Bosnia-Herzegovina, Israel, and Moldova. Overall, almost a third of the dual citizens in the sample were in middle-tier countries—demonstrating that dual citizenship is not restricted to the West.

Columns 4 and 5 list the most common secondary citizenship in each residence country and its tier position. In first-tier countries, the tiers of secondary citizenship countries were mixed, but tended to be middle- or third-tier. In the first tier countries that had the highest numbers of dual citizens—Germany, France, and the Netherlands—countries of secondary citizenship were middle- or third-tier. For example, the most common secondary citizenship in France was Algerian. Therefore, the practical benefits of secondary citizenship were minimal.

In middle-tier countries, the situation was very different: the leading country of secondary citizenship was typically an EU country or the United States. In nine of the ten middle-tier countries with the highest numbers of dual citizens, the dominant secondary citizenship was from an EU member country or the United States. Middle-tier countries where the dominant secondary citizenship was from a middle- or third-tier country (like Greece or Croatia) typically had very low numbers of dual citizens.

Columns 6 and 7 list the dominant pathways to dual citizenship in countries of different citizenship tiers. In Western European and North American countries, which receive large numbers of immigrants, dual citizenship is created in the context of immigration. It is mainly found among first- and second-generation immigrants who do not make any special effort to obtain a secondary (i.e., nonresident) citizenship, but instead have acquired it at birth. The leading countries of secondary citizenship in first-tier countries were often the countries that have sent the largest numbers of immigrants—for example, Algeria in France, and Morocco in the Netherlands.[31]

Most middle-tier countries, in contrast, typically receive little ongoing immigration. In most cases, dual citizens in middle-tier countries consisted of native-born citizens who have acquired a secondary citizenship from an EU country in a long-distance manner on the basis of descent or ethnicity. For example, Argentineans and Brazilians acquire descent-based citizenship from Italy, Portugal, and Spain; Serbians and Ukrainians acquire coethnic citizenship from Hungary, Romania, Bulgaria, and Croatia. Long-distance acquisition was the dominant pathway to dual citizenship in most of the middle-tier countries in the sample.

The exceptions were Israel and Venezuela, where dual citizenship was driven by immigration. Besides immigrant dual citizens, these two countries also host large populations of EU dual citizens that acquired their citizenship in a long-distance manner. In Mexico, secondary citizenship from the United States is produced in the context of circular migration, which includes voluntary return and deportation, but also strategic cross-border births.[32] Immigration also played a major role in Greece, Croatia, and Russia, but these countries hosted relatively small dual citizen populations.

The findings from this analysis of the prevalence of dual citizenship confirm propositions 1 and 2: in Western countries, the secondary citizenship of dual citizens is typically from a lower-tier country and has been produced through immigration; in middle-tier countries outside the West, persons with dual citizenship typically hold secondary citizenship from Western or EU countries that was produced through deliberate strategies of long-distance acquisition.

Long-Distance Acquisition: Evaluating Demand

The third proposition pertains to variation in demand and motivation. Given that potentially eligible individuals for, say, Italian or Hungarian citizenship are found in both first- and middle-tier countries, it is possible to compare levels of demand for ancestry-based dual citizenship. The compensatory citizenship approach predicts a gap in demand for dual citizenship. In first-tier countries, people will apply for long-distance acquisition only if they have a strong sentimental motive, resulting in small numbers of applications. Citizens in middle-tier countries, in contrast, will perceive first-tier citizenship as having practical value and will apply en masse even if they have no sentimental tie to the specific granting country.

TABLE 1.2. Long-Distance Citizenship Acquisitions in Eight European Countries

Granting country	Long-distance acquisitions	Applicants' leading source countries			Year range
Italy	1,003,403	Argentina	Brazil	Uruguay	1998–2010
Hungary	819,193	Romania	Serbia	Ukraine	2011–2016
Spain	491,101	Cuba	Argentina	Mexico	2009–2011
Romania	172,965	Moldova	Israel	Ukraine	2000–2011
Bulgaria	96,564	Macedonia	Moldova	Serbia	2000–2011
Germany	33,213	Israel	US	Argentina	2000–2011
Switzerland	25,092	France	Italy	Germany	1998–2012
Finland	18,372	Sweden	US	Canada	2003–2012
Total	2,659,903	Argentina	Romania	Brazil	

Note: The first column lists the countries that offer ancestry-based or ethnic-based long-distance citizenship. The second column details the number of long-distance acquisitions during the year range in the sixth column. Columns three to five list, in order, the three countries whose citizens have acquired the largest number of long-distance citizenships. For example, the largest national group that acquired Italian long-distance citizenship were Argentinians, and the second-largest group were Brazilians.

Sources: Author's calculation based on data from Harpaz 2015a; Izquierdo and Chao 2015; and Pogonyi 2017.

I took up this question in a 2015 paper that analyzed 1.1 million long-distance citizenship acquisitions on the basis of ancestry or ethnicity in six European countries: Italy, Germany, Romania, Bulgaria, Finland, and Switzerland.[33] The analysis demonstrated that the vast majority of long-distance applications for dual citizenship in European countries were made by individuals from middle-tier countries in Eastern Europe and Latin America; only a tiny minority of applications came from Western countries.

Here, I analyze an expanded dataset that includes the statistics used in that paper, in addition to two additional sources on Hungary and Spain.[34] The dataset includes 2.66 million citizenship acquisitions from eight granting countries. Table 1.2 presents a summary of the dataset, listing citizenship-granting countries and the three countries whose citizens were awarded the highest numbers of citizenships in each of them.

Table 1.2 highlights two patterns. First, long-distance acquisition creates surprisingly large numbers of EU citizens, which rival and even surpass the number of those who become citizens of EU countries through naturalization. For example, Italy gave out about an average of 84,000 ancestry-based citizenships each year between 1998 and 2010 (mostly to Latin Americans), while approving only 25,700 immigrant naturalizations a year during the same period.[35] Hungary approved over 160,000 coethnic citizenships each year from 2011 to 2016. This is not just higher than the number of immigrants

32 CHAPTER 1

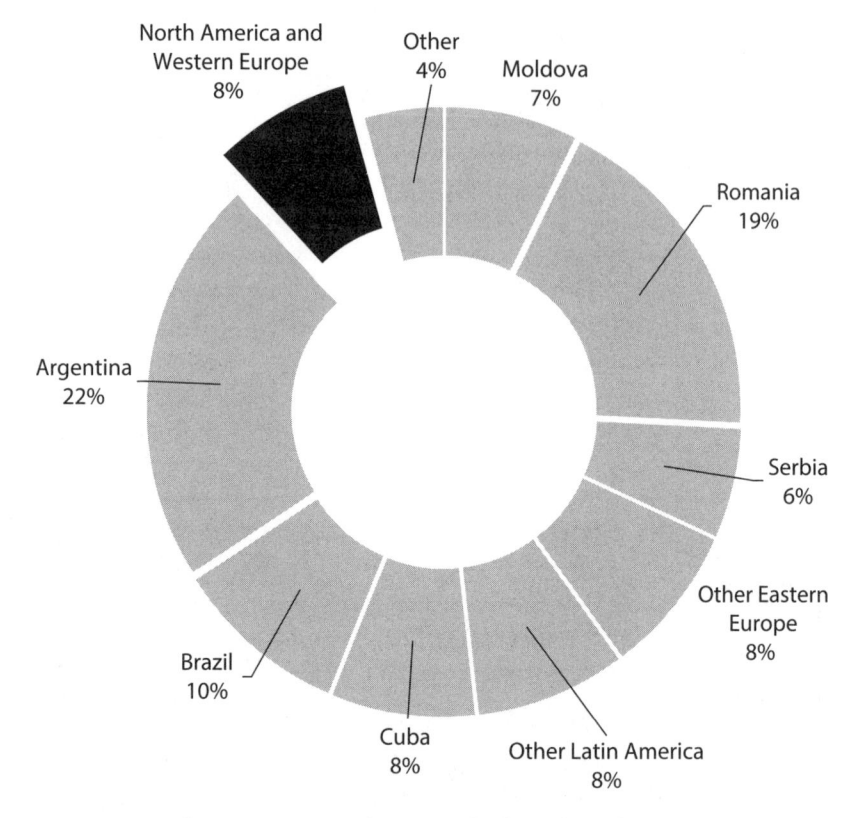

```
                North America and      Other
                 Western Europe         4%      Moldova
                       8%                         7%

                                                              Romania
                                                               19%

   Argentina
      22%

                                                              Serbia
                                                               6%

                                                         Other Eastern
                                                            Europe
                                                              8%
           Brazil
            10%
                            Cuba     Other Latin America
                             8%              8%
```

FIGURE 1.3. Long-distance acquisition of EU citizenship by applicants' origin country
Note: The figure shows the breakdown of 2.66 million applications for ancestry-based citizenship in eight European countries by applicants' country of origin (see table 1.2). For example, 6% of all applications in the sample were made by Serbian citizens.
Sources: See table 1.2.

who naturalized in Hungary; it is actually higher than the annual number of immigrant naturalizations approved by Germany or France.[36] Long-distance acquisition is a major pathway into EU citizenship that has not yet been properly studied.

A second pattern is the predominance of applicants from middle-tier countries. In the EU countries that gave out hundreds of thousands of citizenships, the leading origin countries for applicants were from the global middle tier. There are only two countries where citizenship applicants mostly came from the West—Switzerland and Finland—and these countries gave out a relatively minuscule number of citizenships. Figure 1.3 presents the distribution of the total sum of 2.66 million long-distance acquisitions in the sample by applicants' country and region of origin.

As the figure shows, at least 88 percent of all applications in the sample were made by citizens of Latin American and Eastern European countries.[37] Citizens of Western countries (e.g., Americans who applied for Italian passports or Canadians who applied for Finnish citizenship) were responsible for only 8 percent of all applications. This demonstrates that long-distance acquisition on the basis of ancestry or ethnicity is predominantly a phenomenon of the global middle tier.[38] Even though tens of millions of individuals in Western Europe and North America are potentially eligible for ancestry-based dual citizenship, remarkably few of them applied to recover their ancestral nationality.

A closer analysis of patterns in long-distance citizenship acquisition from two EU countries, Hungary and Italy, can help demonstrate this point. I will combine multiple sources to construct estimates of the relative size of the populations that are eligible for Hungarian and Italian citizenship in first-tier and middle-tier countries and use these estimates to compare levels of demand for secondary EU citizenship. I expect to find that demand for EU citizenship will be negatively correlated with the value of citizenship in potential applicants' original country of citizenship.

Hungarian citizenship. Since 2011, Hungary, an EU member country, offers dual citizenship to persons who are descended from former Hungarian citizens and can speak Hungarian (this case will be discussed in detail in chapter 2). Below, I compare levels of demand for Hungarian dual citizenship across a number of countries in Central and Eastern Europe, as well as the United States, Canada, and Australia. I used Hungarian citizenship statistics for 2011–14, together with census figures from the relevant counties that indicate the size of the eligible population.[39] The eligible population was defined as individuals whose mother tongue was Hungarian (in Central and Eastern Europe) or who spoke Hungarian at home (in the United States, Canada, and Australia).[40]

Acquisition rates varied widely across countries: from January 2011 to August 2014, Hungary approved 400,000 citizenship applications from Romanians: about 30 percent of Hungarian speakers in the country.[41] Over the same period, only 1,500 persons in the United States applied for Hungarian citizenship—under 2 percent of 93,000 Hungarian speakers.[42] Figure 1.4 plots the percentage of persons who acquired dual citizenship out of the eligible Hungarian-speaking population (an indicator of demand) against the origin country's citizenship value (represented by a country's passport index rank).

There was a very strong correlation (0.95) between origin countries' citizenship value and demand for Hungarian citizenship. The lower a country's passport ranking (which is very strongly correlated to its overall citizenship quality), the higher the demand for Hungarian/EU dual citizenship. The Hungarian passport is ranked tenth in the world in terms of travel freedom. Demand was practically nonexistent in countries that had a passport ranking that was

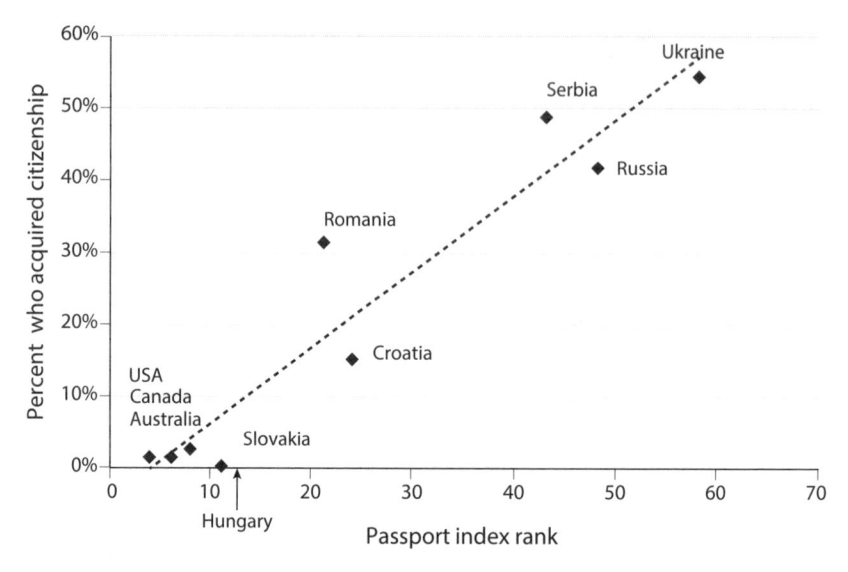

FIGURE 1.4. Acquisition of Hungarian citizenship and passport index ranking
Note: The y-axis represents the number of citizenship acquisitions between 2011 and 2014 as a percentage of the number of Hungarian speakers in each country. The x-axis presents the country's passport index rank.
Sources: Henley & Partners Visa Index 2016; Bálint 2014; ACS 2013; Statistics Canada 2012; Commonwealth of Australia 2014; Romanian National Institute of Statistics 2013; Schnellbach 2014; and national censuses of Serbia, Croatia, Russia, and Ukraine.

equal to it or higher. It was higher in countries that joined the EU later than Hungary and enjoyed more limited EU citizenship rights (Romania and Croatia) and reached peak levels in non-EU middle-tier countries (Serbia, Russia and Ukraine).[43] Note that other factors besides raw demand affect citizenship acquisition: in Slovakia—the only country in the sample that enforced a ban on dual citizenship—there was practically no long-distance acquisition of Hungarian citizenship. If we use the US acquisition rate as a baseline, the likelihood that a Hungarian speaker will obtain Hungarian citizenship was twenty times higher in Romania, thirty-one times higher in Serbia, and thirty-five times higher in Ukraine.

These results lend support to the hypothesis that decisions on whether to seek long-distance citizenship are shaped by instrumental calculations. Would-be applicants compare the value of the citizenship they already have and the one they stand to gain. Critics of this approach could counter that Hungarian ethnic identity is simply stronger in Eastern European countries that border Hungary. In those countries, ethnic Hungarians live in tight minority communities where national identity is strongly preserved. Moreover, cross-border Hungarians have become citizens of those countries as a result of border changes after World War I, and—especially in Romania and Slovakia—often experience discrimination, which consolidates their Hungarian identity. Therefore, the argument would go, it is no surprise that they are more attached to Hungary than people whose ancestors decided to emigrate to the United States or Australia. From this perspective, higher demand in Ukraine, Serbia, and Romania reflects a stronger Hungarian identity, rather than instrumental calculation.

There are various ways to respond to this counterargument (above all, by pointing to the fact that demand correlates citizenship value even when omitting Western immigration countries; see chapter 2). Here, I will provide further corroboration for the compensatory citizenship approach by conducting a similar analysis of demand that will compare uptake of Italian dual citizenship in Western countries and in Latin America.

Italian citizenship. To calculate demand for long-distance Italian citizenship, I use figures on the total number of acquisitions of Italian citizenship between 1998 and 2010, and historical statistics on Italian emigration.[44] The data pertain to the descendants of emigrants who have decided to leave Italy, and do not include cross-border coethnics.[45] I calculated an indicator of demand for dual citizenship by dividing the number of citizenship acquisitions in the total number of immigrants from Italy who settled in each country from 1861 to 1980. The figures on historical migration of Italians provide a rough sense of the relative size of the Italian "founder populations" in each country.[46] This measure provides a rough estimate of relative demand, even if it is impossible to determine the present size of the eligible population.[47]

Figure 1.5 plots the percentage of citizenship acquisitions out of the number of Italian immigrants who arrived before 1980 against countries' passport index ranking. Note that the percentage in the y-axis does *not* represent the actual share of the eligible population that took up citizenship but only a relative, ad hoc measure that is used for the sake of comparison.

As figure 1.5 clearly shows, demand for Italian citizenship varied widely between different countries that host descendants of Italian emigrants (all countries in the sample permit dual citizenship). Citizens of middle-tier countries with lower citizenship value exhibited much higher demand. The association of passport index rank and demand for Italian (EU) citizenship is again very high: a correlation of 0.96.

For example, the United States has received 3.1 million Italian immigrants between 1861 and 1980 but only 25,000 Americans applied for Italian citizenship from 1998 to 2010. Argentina received about 2 million Italian immigrants over the same period, but its citizens filed 452,000 successful applications for Italian citizenship. Demand in Argentina was about twenty-seven times higher than in the United States (the number of acquisitions is eighteen times higher, coming from an estimated eligible population that is about two-thirds the size).

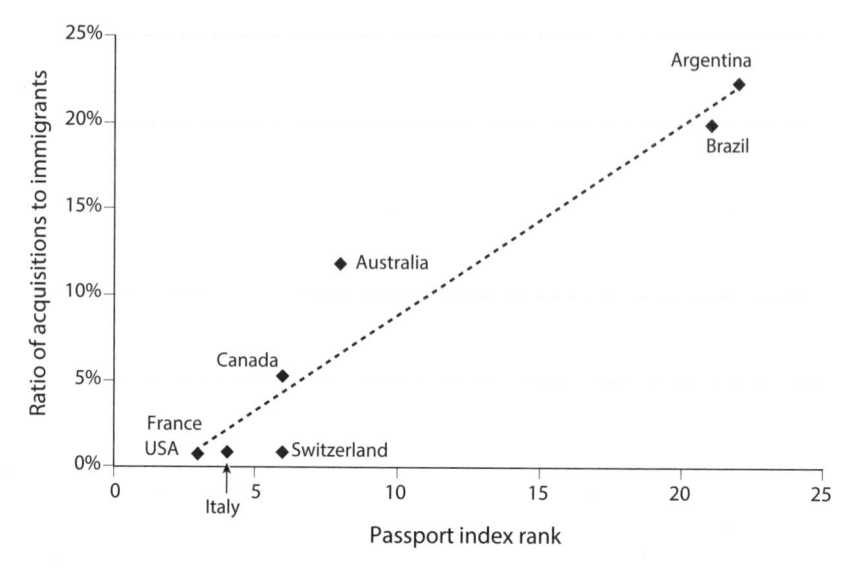

FIGURE 1.5. Acquisition of Italian citizenship and passport index ranking
Note: The y-axis represents the number of citizenship acquisitions between 1998 and 2010 as a percentage of the number of Italian immigrants before 1980. The x-axis presents the country's passport index rank.
Sources: Tintori 2012; Henley & Partners Visa Restrictions Index 2016; and AltreItalie 2014.

It is interesting to note that demand for Italian citizenship in Canada and Australia is higher than in the US and Western Europe. This might be explained by the fact that Italian immigration to these countries was more recent, as well as by the more extensive travel freedom provided by Italy's passport relative to those of Canada and Australia. The near-absence of interest in Italian citizenship in France and Switzerland is particularly telling. Had acquisition of Italian citizenship been driven by attachment to Italian identity, descendants in these countries that border Italy would likely have shown much higher demand than third- or fourth-generation Argentineans whose main connection to Italy is through their grandparents' home cooking. The fact is that French and Swiss citizens, who already enjoy access to the EU, feel no need for Italian citizenship, whereas Argentineans and Brazilians, conscious of their lower position in the global hierarchy, view such citizenship as a valuable asset.

This comparative analysis of the acquisition of Hungarian and Italian citizenship demonstrated that levels of demand for first-tier citizenship are mostly determined by the value of potential applicants' original citizenship. This is not intended to deny the impact of institutional factors, such as Slovakia's ban on dual citizenship. Overall, however, demand for citizenship is negatively correlated to the value of the citizenship that the potential applicant already holds.

The more general findings that were presented in table 1.3 and figure 1.3 give us reason to believe that the same pattern that was demonstrated in detail for Hungarian and Italian citizenship would be replicated whenever an EU member country offers ancestry- or ethnicity-based dual citizenship.

Furthermore, variation in demand for citizenship is expected to go hand in hand with variation in the motivations to acquire it. Low demand for dual citizenship in Western countries reflects its low practical value; those individuals who self-select into dual citizenship are more likely to have sentimental and symbolic attachments to the origin country. Outside Western Europe and North America, in contrast, individuals who were eligible for Western/EU citizenship expected practical benefits (enhanced opportunities, a high-prestige passport, an insurance policy, and more). This meant that demand for citizenship extended beyond the "ideological core" of people who had a strong attachment to their roots. Therefore, the motives of middle-tier applicants would be more instrumental.

In the paper mentioned above, I tested that hypothesis using statistical analysis of between-year fluctuations in the numbers of citizenship applications. I found that eligible individuals in first- and middle-tier countries responded differently to economic and political conditions.[48] Eligible individuals in Latin American or Eastern European countries were more likely to apply for long-distance citizenship acquisition when unemployment in their country of residence increased or when the country of eligibility joined the EU. This means that they engaged in a conscious or unconscious calculation of the practical value of their present citizenship relative to the one they stood to gain. In Western countries, demand for ancestry-based citizenship was not responsive to changes in economic or political conditions. These findings are consistent with the expectation that applicants from the West will be few and sentimentally motivated whereas middle-tier applicants will be numerous and instrumentally motivated. This corroborates Proposition 3.

Conclusion

This chapter laid out a new perspective on the phenomenon of dual citizenship that repositioned it within the context of global stratification. I pointed out the emergence of a new and understudied citizenship formation in the intermediate parts of the global citizenship hierarchy. The emergence of compensatory dual citizenship affects millions of individuals in middle-tier countries who obtain a second citizenship from a Western or an EU country.

The existing literature has mostly neglected the practical value of dual citizenship and the way its meaning is shaped by global inequality. Here, in contrast, I argued that individuals' attitudes toward citizenship are shaped by their position within the global citizenship hierarchy. In the West, dual citizenship is mostly a byproduct of naturalized immigrants' retaining their original citizenship. Few people actively apply for a second citizenship, and the demand for long-distance acquisition is very low. In middle-tier countries, dual citizenship is usually created through deliberate long-distance acquisition of Western/EU citizenship. Middle-tier citizenship is characterized by deficits in security, opportunities, mobility and/or rights. Consequently, individuals in middle-tier countries rush to take advantage of legal openings that allow them to acquire a second, higher-tier citizenship that will make up for those citizenship deficits. The acquisition of compensatory dual citizenship is an instrumental strategy of upward mobility in a stratified global system where rank is determined by citizenship.

Having established the general logic of demand for dual citizenship and the prevalence of compensatory citizenship in middle-tier countries, the next step is to explore the dynamics of the phenomenon on the ground. How do individuals obtain such citizenship and what do they do with it? The following chapters will offer in-depth analyses of three study cases that will analyze the dynamics of compensatory citizenship on the ground.

2

Serbia

BECOMING HUNGARIAN, RETURNING TO EUROPE

The European Union (EU) was conceived as an antidote against the nationalist conflicts that have wrecked the European continent twice over the past century. EU citizenship was celebrated as a new kind of membership that would replace primordial ethnic ties with an enlightened adherence to European universalist values.[1] In an ironic development, however, EU citizenship is now being used by some European countries to reinforce ethnic nationalism.

The legitimation of multiple citizenship has allowed numerous European countries to adopt policies that offer citizenship to coethnics and emigrants, and their descendants, without requiring residence or renunciation of former citizenship.[2] Countries that offer such programs include Spain, Italy, Hungary and Romania, among others. Demand runs high among eligible individuals living outside the EU—above all, in Eastern Europe and Latin America. Programs of citizenship "reacquisition" allow EU countries that suffer from population decline to attract new citizens that have been selected on the basis of their origin and ethnicity.

In Central and Eastern Europe (CEE), this kind of citizenship projects takes on a particular significance. In this region, the offer of dual citizenship is not aimed at descendants of emigrants living in faraway lands. Rather, they aim to reintegrate coethnics living just across the border, in territories that the granting country had once controlled and that it lost through war. Hungary offers citizenship to ethnic Hungarians in the territories that it had lost after World War I, while Romania targets Romanian speakers in parts of "Greater Romania" that had fallen to the Soviet Union in 1945, and Bulgaria creates new citizens in Macedonia, a territory on which it had its eyes set since the nineteenth century.[3] In the CEE region, then, coethnic dual citizenship policies open up ethnic questions that touch the root of national identity and sovereignty.

In this chapter, I examine Hungarian dual citizenship in Serbia as a representative case of compensatory citizenship that is created on the basis of coethnic ties. Hungary, a member of the EU since 2004, offers dual citizenship to citizens of neighboring countries on two conditions: descent from Hungarian nationals and command of the Hungarian language. Since its introduction in 2011, the Hungarian program met with enthusiastic demand: over one million persons have already acquired Hungarian dual citizenship.[4] By October 2018, about 180,000 Serbian citizens had obtained a second citizenship from Hungary.[5]

Most applicants come from Serbia's Hungarian minority, which numbers 250,000 persons. Serbia, meanwhile, has its own ethnic-kin citizenship policy aimed at ethnic Serbs in neighboring Bosnia-Herzegovina, Croatia and Montenegro. Hungarian-Serbian dual citizenship thus represents a juncture between two spaces where dual citizenship is harnessed in the service of ethnic nationalism: the former Hungarian territories and the former Yugoslav space.[6]

Thanks to Hungary's citizenship policy, speakers of Hungarian in countries like Serbia or Ukraine may gain full access to the EU—a tremendous opportunity for citizens of those low-income, high-unemployment countries. Members of the Hungarian minority, who constitute the large majority of applicants in Serbia, are driven by a mix of instrumental and sentimental motives: the younger generation take citizenship to expand their economic horizons and emigrate to Western Europe, whereas older applicants take a more sentimental approach, often shedding tears of joy at the moment they become Hungarian "once again." Alongside these coethnic applicants, thousands of would-be applicants study the Hungarian language specifically for the sake of citizenship. These are persons of Serb or mixed ethnicity who are not interested in Hungary as a second homeland or an alternative national identity; they are driven above all by the desire to secure EU citizenship.

Before proceeding, a terminological note is in order. In Central and Eastern Europe, the distinction between names of states and ethnic groups is often blurred: words like "Hungarian" or "Polish" usually denote both a citizenship and an ethnicity.[7] To avoid confusion, I will distinguish here between the terms "Serbian," which will refer to citizens of Serbia (regardless of ethnicity), and "Serb," which will pertain specifically to ethnic Serbs.[8] Given that no such ready distinction exists for "Hungarian," I will usually use "ethnic Hungarian" when referring to the ethnicity and simply "Hungarian" when referring to the state and nationality. I will use the term "non-Hungarians" to designate people in Serbia who are not of Hungarian ethnicity.

Legal and Historical Background

Hungarian-Serbian dual citizenship came into being in the context of two recent geopolitical shifts that have redrawn the map of Central and Eastern Europe: the fall of communist regimes in the 1990s and the expansion of the EU in the 2000s. The post-communist transition created the possibility to acquire dual citizenship (which communist regimes did not permit) while the expansion of the EU provided the incentive to do so. Since 2004, large gaps in citizenship value emerged between countries that joined the union and those that were left out.

In this chapter, I focus on dual citizenship in the Serbian region of Vojvodina (*Vajdaság* in Hungarian). This multiethnic region was part of Hungary from 1867 to 1918, and then became part of the Kingdom of Serbs, Croats, and Slovenes (renamed Yugoslavia in 1929).[9] Before 1918, Hungary subjected its non-Hungarian minorities to a policy of coerced assimilation or "Magyarization" (Magyar is another word for Hungarian). Serbs, Croats, and others living in Vojvodina were pressured to use the Hungarian language and to identify as Hungarian. Following World War I, the Treaty of Trianon tore away three-quarters of Hungary's territory and divided it among the neighboring countries. The territories lost by Hungary were ethnically mixed, but included three million ethnic Hungarians, who became minorities in their new countries of citizenship.

When it passed into Serbian-Yugoslav hands, Vojvodina was an extremely diverse region. Serbs and Hungarians made up a third and a quarter of the population, respectively. Other ethnic groups in the territory included Germans, Slovaks, Croats and Jews.[10] Northern Vojdovina—including the cities of Novi Sad and Subotica—fell under Hungarian control again in 1941 as part of Hungary's alliance with Nazi Germany. In 1944, Yugoslavia retook the region. While both Hungarians and Yugoslavs committed atrocities during World War II, interethnic violence was not as extreme as in other parts of Yugoslavia. Unlike in fascist Croatia, Hungarian authorities did not try to exterminate the Serb population under their control. When Yugoslav forces retook the area, they did not heavily persecute Hungarians either. On the other hand, Vojvodina's entire Jewish population, numbering 17,000 persons, were murdered by German, Hungarian, and Croatian forces.[11] During the Balkan wars of the 1990s, Vojvodina was again spared major interethnic violence.[12]

Today, Serbia's Hungarian minority enjoys cultural and linguistic minority rights, and Hungarian cultural and educational institutions receive financial support from both Serbia and Hungary.[13] Nevertheless, a century of Yugoslav and Serbian rule in Vojvodina has seen Hungarian demographic presence shrink in both absolute and relative terms. The number of ethnic Hungarians in Vojvodina dropped from 420,000 in 1910 to 254,000 in 2011—a result of assimilation, emigration, and low birth rates.[14] In relative terms, the percentage of Hungarians in Vojvodina's population shrunk dramatically: from 28 percent of the region's population in 1910 to only 13 percent in 2011. This is due to the large numbers of ethnic Serbs from other parts of Yugoslavia who settled in Vojvodina after World War II and the Balkan Wars of the 1990s.[15]

The Treaty of Trianon and the massive loss of territory are a lingering national trauma in Hungary. The dream of undoing Trianon has been a key factor in the country's foreign relations and citizenship policy. Revisionism was suppressed during communist times, but reemerged in the 1990s. Initially, Hungary provided cross-border Hungarians with social, educational and cultural rights but stopped short of citizenship.[16] Finally, in 2011, the government of Prime Minister Viktor Orbán offered dual citizenship to coethnics abroad, specifying two criteria: a) descent from citizens of Hungary (from before 1920 or between 1941 and 1944); and b) proficiency in the Hungarian language (demonstrated through an informal interview with a state official). Residence in Hungary or renunciation of former citizenship are not required.

In the same year, 2011, Orbán's government also approved a new constitution. The 2011 constitution states in its preamble (Article D): "Hungary shall bear responsibility for the fate of Hungarians living beyond its borders, and shall facilitate the survival and development of their communities; it shall support their efforts to preserve their Hungarian identity." This constitutional declaration provides the ideological context for the new citizenship law, which is the institutional expression of Hungary's commitment to "Hungarians living beyond its borders." Unlike the constitution, however, the citizenship law does not refer to "Hungarians" as a noun, and instead uses objective criteria of descent and language proficiency.[17]

These criteria create a façade of ethnic neutrality that is designed to circumvent criticism from neighboring countries and the EU, allowing Hungary to argue that the law expresses cultural affinity rather than ethnonationalist revisionism.[18] This cautious attitude reflects the increasingly controversial character of explicitly ethnic clauses in liberal democracies, as well as the growing readiness in EU institutions to criticize members' actions even in the traditionally sacrosanct field of citizenship policy.[19] These developments do not necessarily eliminate ethnic preferentialism in the field of citizenship, but push states toward certain legal forms that would withstand legal scrutiny. Szabolcs Pogonyi has argued that some EU countries, including Hungary, take advantage of European citizenship norms that were originally designed to protect minorities (including easy access to citizenship and the recognition of cultural and symbolic ties) in order to practice preferential policies toward cross-border coethnics.[20]

While the seemingly neutral phrasing of the law is designed to deflect accusations of ethnic discrimination, there is another criticism that was voiced in Western Europe about Hungary's citizenship policy. Some Western Europeans voiced concerns that Hungary's citizenship policy would open the door to mass immigration of Eastern Europeans. For example, the British *Daily Mail* ran a story under the headline "Passport Giveaway Opens UK Back Door: Two Million More Hungarians Will Have Right to Work Here."[21] Concerns about EU immigration were the biggest motive that drove UK citizens to vote "Leave" in the 2016 Brexit referendum.[22]

While the letter of Hungary's citizenship law avoids reifying "Hungarianness," the combination of criteria undeniably produces ethnic selection. If the descent criterion were used alone, millions of ethnic Serbs, Romanians, and Ukrainians would become eligible for citizenship. The language criterion excludes non-Hungarians without using provocative ethnic terminology. At the same time, the discourse used by the Orbán government when addressing the Hungarian public portrays the law as an overtly ethnic move that offers "positive discrimination" to cross-border Hungarians.[23] From a Hungarian nationalist perspective, the new law does late justice by redeeming cross-border Hungarians and healing the collective body of the nation by uniting all Hungarians in one state.[24]

Most analysts agree that there is another logic at work alongside the official ethnonationalist discourse. Numerous scholars, including Mária Kovács, Judit Tóth, and Kim Scheppele, posit that the creation of hundreds of thousands of new citizens was part of a plan to secure votes for Prime Minister Viktor Orbán.[25] New Hungarian citizens in Romania, Serbia, and Ukraine were granted the right to vote and even encouraged to do so. Indeed, 95 percent of the votes that were cast from outside Hungary in the 2014 elections went to Orbán and his party Fidesz, helping them secure a decisive majority in parliament, according to some analysts.[26] Apparently, rates of support for Orbán in the 2018 elections were equally high.[27]

Orbán's policy for recruiting "new Hungarians" should be understood in an additional context: demography. Hungary, like other CEE countries, has a very low birth rate. Its population has been steadily shrinking since the 1980s, exacerbating centuries-old fears about the very survival of the nation.[28] The state's official institutions stoke these anxieties: for example, in its 2018 demographic portrait of the nation, the Hungarian Central Statistical Office warned that Hungary's population could drop to 6 million by 2070.[29] In early 2019, Prime Minister Orbán declared his commitment to boosting the fertility rate of Hungarian women through a generous family benefit program.[30] Hungary's cross-border citizenship policy lies at the junction of "erasing Trianon" and "ensuring the nation's survival," making it hard for the opposition to resist it without sounding unpatriotic.

While some of Hungary's neighbors—above all Slovakia—protested its decision to hand out ethnic-kin citizenship, in Serbia the move met with no opposition.[31] This had to do with the relatively small percentage of Hungarians in Vojvodina and the good relations between the countries. It is also explained by the fact that Serbia has its own coethnic dual citizenship policy.

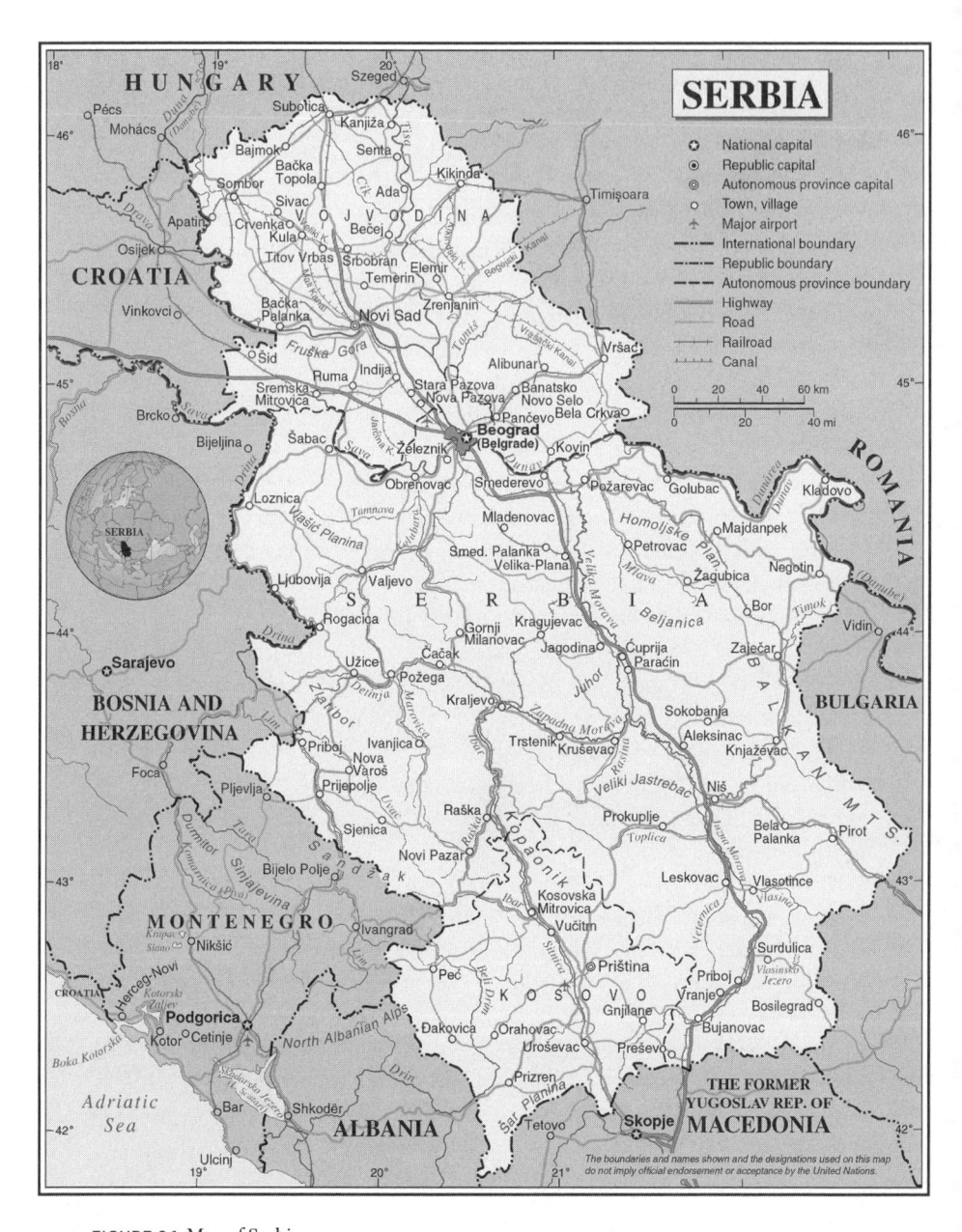

FIGURE 2.1. Map of Serbia

The dissolution of communist Yugoslavia created citizenship struggles, migrations of ethnic unmixing, and "accidental diasporas" that are comparable to those that Rogers Brubaker identified following the breakup of the Soviet Union.[32] As a result, the post-Yugoslav space contains complex configurations of dual citizenship.[33] In spite of the rivalry between Serbia and Croatia, there are over 120,000 Croatian-Serbian dual citizens in Serbia.[34] Since 2006, Serbia offers dual citizenship to coethnics abroad, focusing on ethnic Serbs in Bosnia-Herzegovina, Croatia, and Montenegro.[35] Hungarian-Serbian dual citizenship is part of an emerging region-wide regime in which ethnicity is translated directly into citizenship, without being dependent on territorial residence. This new logic has been described as "post-territorial nationalism."[36]

Hungarian Dual Citizenship by the Numbers

Hungary's offer of dual citizenship met with strong demand in neighboring countries: from January 2011 to July 2016, about 820,000 persons obtained Hungarian citizenship through simplified naturalization (as noted above, the total number reached one million in December 2017, but no statistical breakdown was available for the latter figure).[37]

The vast majority of applicants came from the four CEE countries that host significant populations of ethnic Hungarians: Romania, Serbia, Ukraine, and Slovakia.[38] Citizens of these countries alone were responsible for 98 percent of all citizenship acquisitions between 2011 and 2016. Consistent with the citizenship hierarchy approach, only a minuscule number of applicants came from countries like the United States, Australia or Canada, countries that are home to millions of people of Hungarian origin.[39] Figure 2.2 shows the number of people in each CEE country who obtained Hungarian citizenship, relative to the potentially eligible population of ethnic Hungarians in that country.[40]

Figure 2.2 shows that 38 percent of the total population of cross-border Hungarians in those four countries has obtained dual citizenship by July 2016. Romania hosts the largest Hungarian community in the region, and 40 percent of them have acquired dual citizenship. While Slovakia hosts the second-largest ethnic Hungarian population after Romania—460,000 persons—fewer than 1 percent of them obtained dual citizenship. This is mostly explained by Slovakia's ban on dual citizenship, which was adopted as a direct response to Hungary's coethnic citizenship law. It also has to do with the fact that Slovak citizens are already full members in the EU. In the remaining two countries, acquisition rates were much higher: 61 percent of eligible individuals in Serbia and 96 percent in Ukraine.

Scholars who have studied Hungarian cross-border citizenship—most notably, Szabolcs Pogonyi in his 2017 book on the subject—have often highlighted

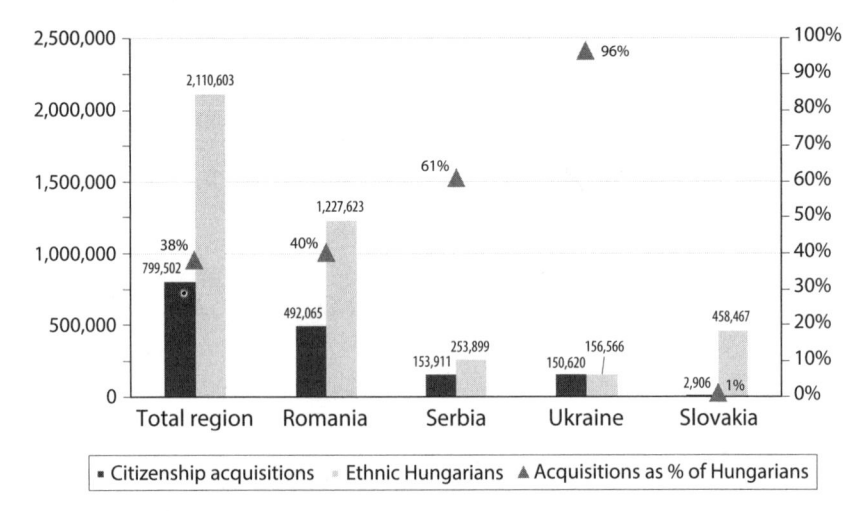

FIGURE 2.2. Citizenship acquisitions and ethnic Hungarians by country, 2011–2016

Note: For each country, the dark bar represents the number of citizenship acquisitions between January 2011 and July 2016, and the lighter bar is the number of individuals who identified as ethnic Hungarians in the 2011 censuses. Both bars refer to the axis on left. The floating triangle, which refers to the axis on the right, represents the number of acquisitions as a percentage of ethnic Hungarians.

Sources: Pogonyi 2017; and national censuses of Romania, Serbia, Slovakia, and Ukraine.

the role of symbolic and sentimental motives.[41] While such motives play an important role in shaping demand for citizenship, the comparative statistics demonstrate that an instrumental approach is effective in explaining acquisition patterns. Demand for Hungarian citizenship is extremely high in Serbia and Ukraine, which are not members of the EU.[42] Citizens of Romania and Slovakia, which are members of the EU, exhibited a smaller interest in Hungarian citizenship (demand in Romania was relatively high because it joined the EU later than Hungary and its citizens had only limited rights in the EU until 2014).

The regional comparison supports the citizenship hierarchy approach and suggests that demand in Serbia is generally high because of the gap in value between EU and non-EU citizenship. Additional statistical data that I have obtained from the Hungarian consulate in Subotica allow us to zoom in on the Serbian case and across levels of citizenship acquisition across different years from 2011 to 2014.[43] These figures show that demand in Serbia peaked in 2013. Combined with material from the interviews that will be presented later, I infer that the spike in applications came as a response to a threat made in 2013 by the EU to reimpose a visa requirement on Serbian citizens.

Since the early 1990s until 2009, Serbian citizens needed a visa to enter EU countries. This requirement was waived in December 2009. In 2013, however, EU officials threatened to withdraw Serbia's visa-free status, demanding that the country stop its citizens' "asylum system abuse" (mostly by Roma who entered EU territory with Serbian passports and then applied for asylum).[44] At a point when many Serbians feared losing their visa-free access to the EU, demand for Hungarian citizenship peaked. The Hungarian consul in Subotica reported that "when the EU threatened Serbia with visa restrictions, this led to a clear increase in the numbers of applicants." This shows that demand for dual citizenship is responsive to the EU's visa policy, providing an important indication about applicants' motivations. The Hungarian or EU passport is valuable because it guarantees travel freedom.

Demand for Hungarian citizenship is also connected with emigration. Many Serbians see the EU passport as a way to build a better life abroad. Indeed, migration statistics from Eurostat, the United Nations, and the World Bank suggest that emigration from Serbia has to Western Europe increased after 2011, which coincides with the year when Hungary started handing out passports.[45] Furthermore, the data show a growth in the number of Serbian-born in countries like Germany or Switzerland, that traditionally serve as destinations for Serbian immigration. The growth in the number of Serbian-born in those countries is significantly larger than the growth in the number of Serbian citizens. While some of this discrepancy is explained by the naturalization of Serbian immigrants in those destination countries, some of it is probably driven by the growing number of Serbian-born persons who enter EU countries with a Hungarian passport.

The great majority of the 154,000 Serbians who have acquired Hungarian dual citizenship by July 2016 were ethnic Hungarians. A sizable minority, however, were not. Hungarian consular officials estimated that 10 to 15 percent of citizenship recipients—about 15,000 to 23,000 persons—do not ethnically identify as Hungarian, but are ethnic Serbs or persons of mixed origin. Many of those strategic citizens have studied the Hungarian language just in order to secure a second citizenship. I will dedicate special attention to these non-Hungarian applicants for Hungarian coethnic citizenship.

Becoming a Dual Citizen

Hungary's decision to offer dual citizenship to its ethnic kin abroad has impacted society in northern Serbia in a number of ways. It increased the prestige of the Hungarian language and transformed understandings of nationality, while boosting emigration to EU countries. In the following sections, I discuss the everyday consequences of compensatory citizenship in Serbia. I mainly draw on interviews and fieldwork that I conducted in northern Serbia in 2014 (see methodological appendix).

Below, I present two short vignettes that illustrate the trajectories, motivations and discourses of three Serbians who seek Hungarian dual citizenship (none of them is an ethnic Hungarian). I will then describe the procedure of citizenship acquisition while focusing on the citizenship industry that emerged in response to Hungary's policy, and the family dynamics that surround applications. Then, I will analyze compensatory citizenship as a resource that provides opportunities and travel freedom.[46] Finally, I will discuss dual citizenship as an instrument of social closure and explore its interaction with class and ethnic identities in Serbia.

Vignette 1: Bojana, 24, and Jelena, 23, ethnic Serbs, applying for Hungarian citizenship[47]

Bojana and Jelena are sisters from a town in northern Vojvodina. They are ethnic Serbs; their father's family has lived in Vojvodina since Austro-Hungarian times and their mother's family immigrated from Bosnia after World War II At the time of the interview, both were students in Belgrade. Their father advised them to study Hungarian and apply for citizenship. He was inspired by the example of his nephew, who emigrated to Sweden after having obtained Hungarian citizenship through fraud.

Bojana, the older sister, presented two motives to apply for citizenship: "First, [Vojvodina] has always been closer culturally to Hungary and Austria. We prefer [Hungarian] goulash over pljeskavica [Serbian burger] . . . Hungarian citizenship was already in my family—so why not get it back? And, second, being a citizen of the EU would open a lot of doors for me, especially in terms of studying. . . . I want to do a second master's degree in Europe." At the moment, however, she has no concrete plans to leave Serbia.

The younger sister, Jelena, joined the application at Bojana's suggestion. She does not have any concrete plans to emigrate either, but would like to do so eventually. "I want this citizenship so I can have a normal life somewhere else," she said. Jelena complained about the incompetence and corruption in Serbia: "All people in Serbia ever do is drink coffee and smoke cigarettes. I don't fit within this system," She added that "[Hungarian citizenship] is just a paper that I need for a better life. . . . I would still feel Serbian in my heart."

Bojana and Jelena study Hungarian with a private teacher. "We try to speak with each other in Hungarian. Our teacher is sending us episodes of [the American sitcom] 'Love and Marriage' in Hungarian. It's perfect because it uses a simple vocabulary and it's all about family." They plan to file their applications in Budapest, where they heard that the required level of Hungarian is not as high. The total expenditure involved in obtaining citizenship, Bojana estimated, would amount to 500 Euros ($610) for each of them, including the language classes and the trip to Budapest.

Vignette 2: Mladen, 31, mixed ethnic origin, triple citizen of Serbia, Croatia, and Hungary

Mladen was born in Subotica. His father was Hungarian and his mother is Bunjevac, a small ethnic group that both Serbia and Croatia claim as coethnics.[48] His first language was Serbian and he went to Serbian-language schools. Until his father's death when he was twelve, Mladen would usually speak with him in Hungarian. In 1998, Mladen's mother applied for Croatian citizenship based on her Bunjevac ethnicity (she has never lived in Croatia). Mladen began his university studies in Croatia, where he received a special scholarship for students from the Croatian diaspora. At the time of the interview, he was living in Germany, where he was enrolled in a PhD program in physics. He and his mother applied for Hungarian citizenship in 2011. The application process was "very easy" because "we both speak Hungarian and have lived here for many generations." His total expenditure was under fifty euros (sixty-one dollars).

Mladen's motivation to obtain Hungarian citizenship, he says, was purely practical: "We have no emotional connection to Hungary ... Actually, I had no extra motive to get the Hungarian [citizenship] because I already had the Croatian [citizenship] which allows me to work outside Serbia. I have it just in case."

His mother, he said, had an additional motive to apply, which was "to distinguish herself from the Serbs, [to show] that she is not a Serb. She is a little bit nationalist, but not Hungarian nationalist—Bunjevac nationalist. . . . Plus, she might like to be able work somewhere in the EU when she retires, so she can live somewhere close to me [if I emigrate]." Mladen says that he does not identify with any nationality: "I don't have this ethnic thing and I don't feel like I am Serbian or Croatian or Hungarian or anything else . . . If you must ask me, I am Vojvodinian."

If he had to keep just one citizenship, he would keep the Hungarian "because of practical reasons." Emotionally, however, he feels closer to Serbia than to any other country. This is expressed, for example, in his support for the national team: "When Hungary or Croatia play against anyone else, I am for them. But whenever Serbia plays, I am always for Serbia."

Citizenship Industry: Strategizing Ethnolinguistic Identity

For ethnic Hungarians in Serbia, acquiring Hungarian citizenship is extremely easy. Hungarian authorities do not charge any fee for processing applications. To prove their descent from Hungarian subjects, applicants need only obtain their own and their parents' or grandparents' birth certificates. As native speakers of Hungarian, they have no difficulty filling out forms and passing an interview in that language. Moreover, staff from the consulate in Subotica regularly make the rounds in smaller towns in Vojvodina in order to reach potential applicants. It is also possible to file citizenship applications in many towns and villages around Hungary. For the "right" applicants, application is a straightforward and practically cost-free process.

Interest in dual citizenship, however, is not limited to ethnic Hungarians. Roughly half of Vojvodina's non-Hungarian population has roots in the region that stretch back before 1920, to Austro-Hungarian times. This makes these individuals—estimated at 750,000 to 900,000 people who are mostly ethnic Serbs—eligible for Hungarian citizenship based on the descent criterion.[49] All that stands between them and EU citizenship is the small technicality of passing a test in the Hungarian language (which, incidentally, is considered one of the hardest languages in the world). As a consequence, there is now lively demand for the instruction of Hungarian in Vojvodina and Belgrade.[50] To meet this demand, a local industry of citizenship-related services has emerged. This citizenship industry is analogous to the well-known concept of a migration industry, that includes immigration brokers, lawyers, and smugglers.[51]

Signs advertising local Hungarian teachers have sprung up in towns around Vojvodina. In the Serbian capital Belgrade, which has a large number of language schools focusing on languages that are useful for emigrants (e.g., English, German, or Swedish), many schools now also offer classes in Hungarian. The director of one Belgrade language school reported that, before 2011, the school employed one Hungarian teacher and only a handful of students studied the language. Now, he said, "We have three Hungarian teachers and fifty to a hundred persons are studying it at any given moment. 99 percent of them are in it for the citizenship."

Some companies explicitly state that their Hungarian classes are tailored for the citizenship exam at the Hungarian consulate. Rather than burdening students with the intricacies of Hungarian grammar, teachers in those companies present students with a list of questions that may appear in the interview, and encourage them to memorize the answers. When students are ready, the company arranges a minivan and takes them to file their application in small towns in Hungary, where the required level of Hungarian is rumored to be lower. Such companies also market their services to Serbian applicants who are already living in Western Europe. One of those companies, for example, operates a center in Vienna alongside its centers in Belgrade and Subotica.[52] Thus, a citizenship industry has emerged that focuses on the instruction of Hungarian to Serbians who seek EU citizenship.

The existence of this industry testifies to a degree of openness on the part of Hungarian authorities: it is possible (albeit difficult) to obtain Hungarian citizenship even if one has acquired the language by studying it as an adult—in other words, even if one is not ethnically Hungarian. This is surprising, given that the language criterion included in the law is aimed precisely at excluding non-Hungarians from citizenship. In practical terms, this openness is reflected in the effort of consular officials to keep the application process neutral in terms of ethnicity. Applicants as well as officials confirm that consular officials focus on evaluating applicants' level of Hungarian and disregard other indicators of ethnicity, such as names (Serbian and Hungarian names are easily distinguishable) and religion (Serbs are Orthodox and Hungarians mostly Catholic). Applicants are not asked whether or not they identify as Hungarian.[53]

This unexpected neutrality in the application of an overtly ethnic law can be explained, first of all, by a wish to avoid criticism from EU bodies for employing ethnic discrimination. According to a consular official in Subotica, "We only use language [as a criterion]. If you go any other way, you get lost"—that is to say, that decisions become legally indefensible and open to challenges.[54] Second, many respondents pointed out a common cultural assumption that "foreigners cannot learn Hungarian," which means that anyone who exhibits knowledge of the language is assumed to have learned while growing up.[55] Third—and most important—the Hungarian government has set target numbers of citizens that it seeks to create; they aimed to create half a million new citizens by 2014 and a million by 2018. Both targets were achieved.[56] Figure 2.3 shows Hungarian Prime Minister Orbán congratulating Miklós Lajkó, a farmer from a small village in Vojvodina who became the one millionth person to obtain Hungarian citizenship on the basis of the 2011 law.

Strategic applicants rushed to benefit from this openness. Some of them could not speak any Hungarian and used fraud to "buy" citizenship, most commonly by paying a native speaker to take the language test in their place. I will not discuss those cases here because it was not possible to interview a sufficient number of people who obtained citizenship in this manner. Other applicants had some knowledge of the language, which they have acquired in one of two ways: growing up with Hungarian relatives, neighbors, or friends (like Mladen in vignette 2) or studying the language from scratch (like Bojana and Jelena in vignette 1). Interestingly, the two latter types of strategic applicants—those who knew Hungarian from home and those who studied it—actually found their emotional ties to Hungarian culture strengthening during the process of acquiring citizenship.

Of particular interest in this context are strategic applicants who have studied the Hungarian language without prior background. Such applicants must first fulfill the criterion of descent from families that lived in Vojvodina when it was part of Hungary. This excludes Serb families that arrived in the region after World War II or during the 1990s and leaves only individuals from families with a long history in Vojvodina (and thus in Austria-Hungary).

FIGURE 2.3. The one millionth ethnic Hungarian who acquired Hungarian citizenship. In this photograph from December 2017, Hungarian Prime Minister Viktor Orbán (second from left) greets the one millionth person who received Hungarian dual citizenship through simplified naturalization. The recipient is Miklós Lajkó (third from the right), a farmer from Vojvodina, Serbia. He is photographed with his wife (third from the left) and their two children. Also present are the president of Hungary, his wife, and the speaker of the Hungarian Parliament. Photograph credit: Máthé Zoltán, MTI.

Eligible individuals who study Hungarian from scratch, without any prior knowledge of the language, will spend about 300 to 600 euros (375 to 750 dollars)—one to two average monthly salaries in Serbia. Beyond the monetary expenditure, they must also spend substantial time and effort to master what is considered to be one of the world's most difficult languages. Teachers of Hungarian reported that students had a high dropout rate. Tamara, who was teaching Hungarian at a language school in Belgrade, said, "The majority of people [who study Hungarian] don't get the passport because it takes like a year to master it, and they are impatient." Many Serbians who dream of Hungarian citizenship quit after failing the first application, or never even take the test.

Those who followed through all the way to citizenship—which usually required studying for over a year—were typically the most dedicated students. Such a commitment was much easier for individuals who developed an interest in Hungarian culture and language. Committed students would speak Hungarian in their free time and watch Hungarian music videos, cartoons, and TV shows. The case of Bojana and Jelena (vignette 1), who speak to each other in Hungarian and watch videos in Hungarian, is typical of successful applicants.

Other respondents said that they didn't mind studying Hungarian because they enjoyed learning foreign languages. For example, Milica, a twenty-six-year-old Serb who obtained Hungarian citizenship after studying the language, said, "I have a passion for languages so for me, it was like, why not. Plus, Hungarian is similar to Finnish and I really enjoyed my time [as an exchange student] in Helsinki." Another common attitude was that Hungarian culture was interesting and formed part of applicants' family heritage as Vojvodinians. While their initial motivation to study Hungarian was instrumental, successful applicants very often developed some sentimental attachment to Hungarian culture during the process. Some discovered that they had Hungarian ancestors and grew interested in learning more about their heritage. Whereas dual citizenship that is based on descent or place of birth may be entirely instrumental, citizenship premised on linguistic criteria must inevitably bear some relevance to personal identity.

Strategic applicants who study Hungarian draw on a composite of resources: a) an intellectual ability and academic disposition that make it possible to master a new language; b) a value orientation that would make such an endeavor normatively acceptable; and c) a cultural taste that enables them to enjoy the learning process. These characteristics—scholastic dispositions, cosmopolitan values, and a broad cultural taste—are mostly found among educated middle classes.[57] Indeed, many of those who stand to benefit from compensatory citizenship belong to Serbia's educated urban elites, who already possess a European self-understanding and a disposition to accumulate cultural capital.[58] Strategic applicants (those who started out the application procedure with no affinity to Hungary) often will have established some ties to Hungary by the time the process is complete.

Family Dynamics

The acquisition of Hungarian citizenship is legally defined as simplified naturalization. Therefore, it is a process that may be carried out by individuals, and family coordination is optional. The fact that family members are not functionally dependent on each other makes the Serbian case different from the Mexican case (where parents invest in citizenship for their children) or the Israeli case, where ancestry-based reacquisition depends on reconstructing the generational chain of citizenship all the way back to the original citizen. Furthermore, the procedure for proving ancestry is simple and straightforward. Vital records in most towns and villages in Vojvodina have been preserved since Austro-Hungarian times.[59] Birth registration archives are extant and in an easily accessible language, and visiting them requires nothing more than a short trip to the city center. This too makes cooperation between family members optional rather than mandatory.

Nevertheless, most ethnic Hungarians who applied for dual citizenship did so as a family. Members of different generations, however, had different motivations. Younger people were typically interested in the practical aspects of citizenship while older Hungarians focused on its symbolic and sentimental aspects. Older applicants were often extremely emotional during the citizenship ceremony and many of them were moved to tears. While they usually had few practical uses for citizenship, older applicants reported feelings of closure and completeness upon becoming Hungarian citizens.

Laszlo, a sixty-two-year-old ethnic Hungarian respondent, was born during World War II when his home village in northern Vojvodina was under Hungarian occupation. By the time he reached the age of four, the area was again part of Yugoslavia. Even though he speaks perfect Serbian, and his wife is an ethnic Serb, Laszlo feels strongly Hungarian. This is how he described the moment he acquired Hungarian citizenship: "I was born as a Hungarian. [So] when I took the oath, it was a wonderful feeling for me: at last, I am once again what I was earlier."

Hungarian citizenship connected older applicants not only to their former selves but also to their deceased parents and grandparents. This connection became especially powerful when those relatives suffered for being Hungarian. Edit, a fifty-nine-year-old ethnic Hungarian from Subotica, spoke of her Hungarian citizenship as a "memorial" (*spomenik* in Serbian) for her grandfather who, she said, was killed by Yugoslav partisans in 1944 for being "a great Hungarian patriot." She went on to say that "when I got the citizenship I was crying, it was as if I took a bouquet of flowers and put it on the grave of my mother and grandfather."

These sentimental expressions were mostly absent from the discourses of younger Hungarians in Serbia. Instead, they emphasized their practical motives for taking citizenship. The reluctance of young Hungarian respondents to portray their application as motivated by sentimental reasons did not mean that did not identify as Hungarian; typically, they described themselves as completely Hungarian. Instead, it reflected a view that saw citizenship and identity as two separate domains. A typical attitude was expressed by Agnes, a twenty-eight year-old ethnic Hungarian from Subotica: "Of course I am Hungarian. But identity was not part of my motivation. I don't belong [in Hungary]. . . . I just want the passport."

In many Hungarian families, applications for citizenship were initiated by the practically minded young generation, and older parents went along with it (keep in mind that, for ethnic Hungarians, citizenship is free of cost or effort). For example, Edit, who was cited above, did not apply for citizenship of her own initiative but rather followed her son, who applied because he plans to emigrate to the United States. In addition to the sentimental reasons mentioned above, she had a different reason to apply for citizenship: to make sure that she will be able to visit her son and future grandchildren in the United States without having to apply for a visa. This motivation is typical: in vignette 2, Mladen spoke about his mother, who obtained citizenship so that she will be able to live near him if he ends up settling in Western Europe. While many younger Hungarians obtained citizenship in order to emigrate (or at least have the option to do so), their parents applied for citizenship not only for symbolic reasons, but also to ensure that they had access to the EU, so that they do not become physically separated from their children by borders.

Many ethnic Hungarian families are driven to apply for citizenship for a mix of practical and sentimental motivations, but practical motivations take precedence. During the interviews, some respondents would say with great conviction that they became dual citizens to express their Hungarian identity, but would then let on that the initiative came from another family member who had practical motivations. This finding helps explain the two seemingly contradictory patterns: on the one hand, the prevalence of sentimental and symbolic discourses around Hungarian citizenship, and, on the other hand, the instrumental logic that was revealed by the acquisition statistics.[60] Most applications for coethnic dual citizenship involve both instrumental and sentimental components: an application that was begun with one type of motive often leads to the other as well.

In contrast to ethnic Hungarians, strategic applicants of Serb or mixed ethnicity typically acquire citizenship as individuals, not families.[61] Almost all of them were young people in their twenties and thirties, who sought the practical benefits of EU citizenship. Nevertheless, these applicants too often developed some sentimental connection to Hungary, and underwent a process that can be called "retrospective Magyarization." While studying Hungarian and preparing to apply for citizenship, those applicants developed a new interest in their Hungarian roots, sometimes even discovering that their own grandmothers had spoken Hungarian.

The initial motivation to dig into one's genealogy in search of Hungarians had to do with the biographical essay that applicants had to submit as part of their application. Applicants often felt that they had to emphasize any possible connection that they had to Hungary, whether historical, familial, or cultural. It should be made clear, however, that none of the strategic applicants underwent any kind of identity shift and reidentified as Hungarian. If these retrospective genealogical discoveries had an effect on identity, it had to do more with an increased sense of belonging to Vojvodina as a multiethnic and cosmopolitan region of Europe than to the ethnic nation-state of Hungary.

Putting Hungarian Citizenship to Use

OPPORTUNITIES

When asked to explain their interest in Hungarian citizenship, the first and most common motive offered by respondents was the desire to emigrate. There was a consensus among practically all respondents that Serbia's economic situation was hopeless and that emigration was the only real way to get ahead. Whatever good jobs that are available in Serbia, respondents said, are reserved to people with political or family connections. Indeed, the official unemployment rate in Serbia was about 22 percent in 2014 and the average household income was $600 per month.[62] Wages in Germany or Austria are about four times higher than in Serbia (this is roughly the same wage gap as between Mexico and the United States).

Respondents had a typical manner of talking about the gap between Serbia and Western Europe. While presenting their (often scathing) view of Serbia, they repeatedly brought up the concept of "normality." See the quotation from Jelena above (vignette 1): "I want [Hungarian] citizenship so that I can live a normal life somewhere else." Many respondents were of the opinion that it was impossible to live a "normal life" (*normalan život*) in Serbia. Zoran, a thirty-two-year-old engineer from Subotica, made a long list of everything that was wrong in Serbia: low salaries, bad health system, no social security, rampant corruption, and, in his words, a "small-town mentality." He concluded: "[Serbia] cannot provide me with a lifestyle like in normal countries . . . Therefore I will get the Hungarian passport and go to Sweden."

In these two declarations from Jelena and Zoran, the word "normal" is not used in its conventional sense of "ordinary, common, prevalent." What respondents saw as "normal" was not the economic and social standards that are common in Serbia, in former Yugoslav countries, or even in Central and Eastern Europe (some respondents said that "Hungary is not a normal country either"). Instead, "normal" to them meant "conforming to Western European standards." This raises an interesting question about Serbian respondents' self-perception: Why do they adopt a standard of normality according to which their own country and lifestyle are not normal?

On one level, evaluating one's own society as "not normal" is a rhetorical strategy of distinction: it posits the speaker as superior to the mainstream by implying that he or she has higher standards (e.g., morally or economically). Such a discourse was also found among Israeli respondents, many of whom adopted a Western vantage point to criticize Israeli society for being collectivistic, primitive, and oriental. Israeli respondents, however, did not actually believe that they were European and stressed their essential cultural difference vis-à-vis Europeans; their European self-identification was mostly rhetorical. The European identity of educated Serbians, in contrast, was not skin deep.

They deeply internalized a view of themselves as European and felt a deep disappointment with the failure of Serbia to live up to European (or, in their words, "normal") expectations.

To some extent, this incongruence between expectations and reality can be seen in the context of "Yugo-nostalgia."[63] The generation that was born in the 1980s and 1990s was exposed to nostalgic discourses about communist Yugoslavia, a land of (alleged) full employment, high standards of living, and Western, liberal attitudes. This form of nostalgia is particularly strong among Serbia's urban, educated middle classes. Part of the ideological justification of Yugoslav socialism came from its ability to offer Yugoslav citizens a Western-level quality of life, allow them to consume Western products, and nurture cultural ties with Western Europe.[64] Even though Yugoslavia was never on par with the West economically, the idea that it was a Western country powerfully shaped the self-understanding and the expectations of its citizens.

In most countries in Central and Eastern Europe, the post-communist transition and EU accession have created the possibility to catch up and become part of the West. Educated urban classes in countries like Poland or Hungary have become the most dedicated advocates of democracy, free markets, and EU accession. They expected that following the post-communist transition, they would be able to convert their cultural capital (university diplomas, cultural tastes, foreign language proficiency) into economic capital.[65] In Serbia, the transition was initially blocked: the communist regime remained in power until the year 2000 (when president Slobodan Milošević was ousted), and all throughout the 1990s the country was scourged by economic crises and international sanctions. As other CEE countries moved nearer to the West in values and lifestyle, Serbia grew farther from it. Avenues for economic advancement for educated Serbians—a chance to live a "normal" life—were extremely limited. Within this context, the possibility to acquire EU citizenship presents itself as an extremely attractive opportunity.

As an unintended consequence of Hungary's citizenship policy, educated persons from the most Europeanized parts of Serbia gained the possibility to convert their cultural capital into EU citizenship by strategically manipulating their ethnolinguistic identity. Some members of Serbia's educated classes a way to catch up with Western Europe and realize their aspirations for integration with the West. This is a historical irony: Milošević kept Serbia's educated elites out of Europe, and Orbán is now offering them a way in.

The idea that dual citizenship was above all a way to emigrate not only reflected Serbian applicants' actual motivations but was also shaped by the prevalent positive view of emigration. Respondents praised and envied family members and acquaintances who have emigrated. The act of emigration itself was seen as reflecting courage, wisdom, and a "winner" attitude. This perspective seemed to be typical of Serbian society more broadly.[66] There was far less resonance in Serbia with the kinds of negative stereotypes on emigrants that were found in Mexico (emigrants as lower-class "wannabes" or "rotten persons" [*pochos*]) or Israel (emigrants as weaklings and defectors). Indeed, the proliferation of Hungarian dual citizenship coincided with a growth in emigration from Serbia.

The vast majority of Serbian citizens who emigrate thanks to their Hungarian dual citizenship are ethnic Hungarians. Informal evidence of different kinds suggest high rates of emigration among the Hungarian minority. Leaders in Serbia's Hungarian community complained in interviews that dual citizenship was leading to a depopulation of their communities.[67]

The mayor of a Hungarian-majority village near the Hungarian border complained that his village was shrinking rapidly: "All the young people obtained citizenship and left for abroad." The mayor's own son, who studied medicine in Hungary, left for Sweden, where wages are much higher. An official at the National Council of the Hungarian National Minority reported that the number of students entering Hungarian-language primary schools in Serbia has dropped by 15 percent between 2011 and 2014, which, she explains is a result of the emigration of young parents.[68] Similar reports about mass emigration of Hungarians appeared in the Serbian media.[69] The sense of local depopulation is translated to a national concern. As the village mayor put it: "In 2050 there will not be even 100,000 Hungarians in Vojvodina, I can sign you that!"

There are several reasons beside EU citizenship that make ethnic Hungarians especially prone to emigrate and less likely to return from abroad. In recent years the number of emigrants from Hungary to Western Europe has dramatically increased. The presence of Hungarians in Western European destination countries makes it easier for Hungarian speakers to make job connections and social ties, and even to find Hungarian food and entertainment.[70] Moreover, many of the Hungarians in Vojvodina are weakly integrated into Serbian society and speak poor Serbian. After living with Hungarian passports in EU countries, integrating into Hungarian social networks, and working hard to master the German or English language, most emigrants are unlikely to ever return to Serbia.

This finding adds an interesting dimension to an argument made by the sociologist Rogers Brubaker, who claimed that the countries of Central and Eastern Europe are undergoing "nationalization without nationalism." Even after those countries abandoned the coercive nationalistic policies of the past, which sought to impose the majority language and culture on minorities, the process of ethnic homogenization continues. In the absence of ethnonational tensions that reinforce social boundaries, ethnic minority populations diminish through peaceful processes of intermarriage and reidentification.[71] My findings suggest yet another powerful agent of national homogenization: emigration propelled by coethnic dual citizenship. Ethnic minorities in Serbia now have an easy way out. Thus, in an ironic development, Hungary's 2011 citizenship law—putatively aimed to fulfill the promise of Hungary's new Basic Law and "facilitate the survival and development of [cross-border Hungarian] communities"—is actually contributing to the shrinking of those communities through emigration.

TRAVEL FREEDOM

The global hierarchy of citizenship value that was described in chapter 1 is also a hierarchy of travel freedom. In Serbia, the issue of travel freedom resonates powerfully as a metonym for Serbia's standing in the world. Dual citizenship is experienced as an opportunity to liberate oneself from the limitations placed on ordinary Serbians.

From 1992 to 2009, Serbian citizens were required to obtain a visa before they could visit EU countries. These restrictions were seen as a clear, everyday reminder of the dramatic decline in the value of their citizenship. Communist Yugoslavia had a high-value passport that allowed free movement around both the capitalist and communist blocs. Citizens of Yugoslavia often used that freedom to travel to Western Europe as tourists, shoppers, and guest workers. In the early 1990s, however, Serbia was plunged into a decade of wars, economic crises, and high emigration. EU countries responded by requiring visas from all Serbian visitors. Since 1992, Serbians who wanted to travel abroad have had to wait for hours outside foreign embassies and provide extensive documentation on their financial, personal, and medical condition, as well as their travel plans.[72]

For Serbians, this regime of "global immobility" was a source of painful humiliation. Many people responded by avoiding travel abroad altogether. In the mid-2000s, only about 10 percent of Serbians had a passport.[73] At the same time that Serbians were becoming increasingly restricted in their movements, citizens of neighboring ex-communist countries such as Hungary—which, during communism, was poorer and more oppressive than Yugoslavia—were enjoying ever-greater freedom to visit the West. To add insult to injury, the EU was quick to offer visa-free access to citizens of Croatia, Serbia's bitter enemy in the wars of the 1990s.

As the anthropologist Stef Jansen points out, Serbians did not view European travel restrictions as a rational policy move meant to deter immigration; instead, they saw them as a malicious attempt to punish and humiliate Serbia and the Serbs.[74] This view was widely promoted by the Milošević regime because it strengthened Serbs' sense of victimization and discouraged domestic challenges to his rule.[75] One of its lasting effects is that people still refer to EU visa requirements as "sanctions" (*sankcije*).[76] Jansen described this situation as "geopolitical entrapment" in the "immediate outside" of the EU.

Starting in December 2009, Serbian citizens enjoyed visa-free access to Schengen countries (they still need a visa to visit Britain). This means that

Serbians who are in their mid-twenties to early forties have spent seventeen years—most of their lives or at least its adult portion—"trapped" in Serbia. This experience produced a trauma that bears heavily on the minds of urban and educated elites, who used to travel abroad under communist Yugoslavia and who treat visits to Western Europe as constitutive of their identity. The fear of renewed entrapment helps explain the uptick in citizenship applications in 2013, when the EU threatened to reimpose a visa requirement on Serbian citizens.

The topic of cross-border mobility came up in many interviews as a central motivation for obtaining Hungarian citizenship. Respondents often said that they were determined never to be subjected to such restrictions again, and that the Hungarian passport was their way of making sure of that. In the words of one respondent from Subotica, "I just want [the Hungarian passport] to travel more easily and not be in big shit again."

To illustrate the experience of travel restriction, consider the following statement by Gabrijela, a twenty-seven-year-old local government official from Novi Sad of mixed Serb-Hungarian origin. She brought up travel freedom to explain why she had applied for a Hungarian passport: "I visited the Czech Republic in 2008 and I had to wait for a whole day in front of the embassy [to get a visa]. It was so humiliating. . . . You had to prove that you had money, say where you will sleep, and pay up front. And then—maybe you will get [the visa], maybe you won't. . . . I hope we don't have to live through this again." In this typical account, the seemingly mundane procedure of applying for a visa is experienced as an extreme humiliation.

The humiliation of visa application is expressed in terms of time ("a whole day"), space ("in front of the embassy"), and information ("maybe you will get it, maybe you won't"). It is exacerbated because it is delivered by the embassy of the formerly communist Czech Republic. When Serbians must request a visa to visit a country that they used to look down on, this provides a powerful illustration of their loss of status.

In the final sentence, Gabrijela switches to the plural form: "I hope *we* don't have to live through this again." The humiliating experience of visa application is not just her personal experience; instead, it is the collective experience of an entire generation. More precisely, it is the collective experience of a group within her generation: those who viewed travel to Europe as a central part of their identity and lifestyle but were barred from doing so. One reason that the EU's imposition of visa requirements was so humiliating for Serbia's educated elites was that it robbed them of one of their key strategies for social distinction.

Gabrijela continued: "After 2009, we could travel with the Serbian passport everywhere, so I didn't need a Hungarian passport. But [in 2013] was some political problem . . . and they said Serbians might need visas, and I panicked and ran to do the [Hungarian] passport." She is referring to the EU threat to return the visa requirement that was discussed above. She describes the feeling that drove her to acquire Hungarian citizenship as "panic," even though it would be equally logical to say that she made a rational, calculated decision. The choice of terms has to do with the trauma that was described in the previous paragraph: the experience of life under visa restrictions was so bad that she would do anything to avoid it being repeated. Thus, attempts to avoid it have an irrational element to them.

Respondents who have acquired a Hungarian passport and use it for travel report a sense of liberation and ease. When traveling with a Hungarian passport, they are no longer asked any questions when crossing borders in Europe. Moreover, they have a sense that their travel freedom is secure and not dependent on political relations between Serbia and the EU. These responses provide evidence of the importance that Serbians attribute to freedom of movement. A range of powerful emotions (humiliation, panic, liberation) is associated with the mundane act of crossing borders. These findings demonstrate the manner in which global mobility acquires subjective value—not only for its practical implications, but as a marker of status, dignity and belonging.

Social Closure: Ethnic Hierarchies Upended

Serbian society is characterized by relatively low levels of economic inequality—lower than most Western European nations, and much lower than the United States, Mexico or Israel.[77] This is not just a product of Serbia's recent communist history. It also results from the country's slow economic development since the nineteenth century, which did not create the conditions for the kind of encompassing economic stratification that is found in the West.[78] At the same time, Serbia is an ethnic nation-state that has been shaped by dynamics of ethnonational competition, exclusion and violence.[79] Today, ethnic minorities make up 14 percent of Serbia's population. Status hierarchies strongly interact with ethnic hierarchies. I will discuss here two aspects of social closure through dual citizenship: individual prestige defined by cultural capital and prestige tied to collective ethnic identity.

On the individual level, we have seen that most strategic applicants belong to the educated urban strata of northern Serbia, a group that prides itself on having a special connection to Europe and being agents of "Europeanization" in the Balkan country. The boundary between Vojvodina and central Serbia parallels the historical border between Habsburg-dominated Central Europe and the Ottoman-dominated Balkans. Given the high prestige of European culture in Serbia, we would expect to find EU citizenship operate as a status symbol, as it does, for example, in Israel and Mexico. There were no indications, however, that Hungarian dual citizenship was a status symbol. Respondents in Serbia typically discussed their second citizenship in a detached, almost apologetic, manner that was very different from the excited attitude of Israeli respondents toward their EU citizenship.

How to explain this unexpected finding? Part of the explanation has to do with the communist legacy and a strong egalitarian tradition that makes Serbians less attuned to the acquisition and display of status symbols, relative to Mexicans and Israelis. Another key reason has to do with status hierarchies. In Mexico and Israel, European-origin elites are economically and politically dominant in society. Therefore, they are in a position to impose their views and values—what Pierre Bourdieu has called the "vision of divisions"—on other, less dominant, social groups.[80] As a consequence, having EU citizenship denotes elite membership ipso facto. The association with dominant groups (Ashkenazi Jews, European-origin Mexicans) means that EU dual citizenship is to some degree impervious to criticism.

The situation in Serbia is very different. Ethnic Hungarians are usually worse off than the general population and Vojvodina is not significantly more prosperous than the rest of Serbia. Hungary itself is perceived in Serbia as a low-status country, and there is no special pride in having a Hungarian passport. Moreover, Serbia's liberal, European-oriented educated classes do not have any clear economic or political advantage over the rest of society and are not in a position to impose their vision on them.[81] The dominant group that has power to define the agenda remains the communist-turned-nationalist elites that have thrived since the time of Milošević. These elites—led by current Prime Minister Aleksandar Vučić (who at one point served as Milošević's Minister of Information)—promote a nationalist-collectivist ideology that might potentially mark seekers of dual citizenship as targets for criticism.

At the time of the study, there were no significant negative responses in Serbia to Hungarian dual citizenship policy. Nationalist politicians and intellectuals mostly kept silent on the topic. Nonetheless, ethnic Serb respondents who strategically sought dual citizenship often expressed concerns that they would be criticized by nationalists. To understand the basis for that criticism, we should keep in mind that the principle of nonassimilation has been the hallmark of Serbian identity for centuries. It is credited with guaranteeing the survival of Serb identity as a discriminated and beleaguered group within the Ottoman and Habsburg empires.[82] In fact, many Serb nationalists believe that (Catholic) Croats and (Muslim) Bosniaks are descended from disloyal Serbs who converted to Catholicism and Islam, respectively. Serbian folk culture provides a ready vocabulary of criticisms against Serbs who adopt other identities for the sake of expediency.[83] Wary of such criticism, strategic applicants often kept a low profile.

Bojana, who was quoted above (vignette 1), did not tell people in Belgrade that she was seeking dual citizenship. While nobody has ever actually criticized her for applying, she had no difficulty imagining what hypothetical critics—people she described as "conservative and closed"—would say. The criticism would be "that you're acting elitist because you're from [Vojvodina], that you don't like Serbia, even that you don't like Russia. [They would say] that you're not a real Serb, you're giving up your Serbian identity." In the context of Serb-nationalist discourse, Serbs from Vojvodina are seen as lesser Serbs than people from central Serbia: less proud of being Serbian, less committed to preserving Serbian traditions, suspected of being elitists, and having a pro-German instead of a pro-Russian orientation. By taking up Hungarian citizenship, Vojvodina Serbs confirm these suspicions and expose themselves to censure.

Furthermore, numerous respondents pointed out that Hungary's policy of giving out passports in Vojvodina raises concerns that it might have territorial designs on the region. Biljana, a thirty-two-year-old Serb engineer from Belgrade, said: "Some people say that Vojvodina will end up like Kosovo. I will not support such a thing." The reference to Kosovo alludes to the region's 2008 declaration of independence from Serbia after decades of bloody conflict, which included NATO intervention against Serbia in 1999. There is nothing fantastic about the fear that Hungary might someday use coethnic citizenship as a pretext to try and seize parts of Serbia; such a strategy was actually used by Russia to justify invasions of Georgia and Ukraine. Moreover, in recent years, as Russian attacks on eastern Ukraine have weakened its state capacity, Hungary has been infringing on Ukrainian sovereignty by financing a growing number of institutions, handing out citizenships, and promoting Hungarian cultural presence and public displays of the Hungarian flag.[84] At the time of writing, no such provocative acts have been conducted vis-à-vis Serbia.

In spite of her concerns about a Kosovo-like scenario, Biljana went ahead with the citizenship application because "I am selfish . . . I always tell myself that one more passport won't make a difference." This response was typical in the sense that many strategic applicants thought that there was something selfish or fake involved in taking dual citizenship. Usually, they would justify their decision to seek another citizenship by criticizing Serbia and the substandard "citizenship package" that it provides, rather than defending dual citizenship in principle. The insistence that Serbia is not a normal country is a form of self-justification that is inseparable from the sense of shame that is associated with Hungarian dual citizenship.

Aside from putting in question the relation of individual Serbian citizens to Serbia, Hungarian dual citizenship also has the potential to upend collective status hierarchies between ethnic groups. While Hungarian dual citizenship never became a status symbol at the individual level, it does have a tangible effect on power relations between Hungarians and Serbs in Vojvodina. Officially, Vojvodina is a multicultural region with a well-developed system of minority language and cultural rights that was passed down from communist Yugoslavia.[85] For example, all official signs in Subotica are written in Serbian,

Hungarian, and Croatian, and the state provides public support for media and culture in the Hungarian language.[86] In practice, however, the Serbo-Croatian language has dominated public life and public spaces in communist Yugoslavia as well as in present-day Serbia. All Hungarians had to speak some Serbian to gain access to employment and government services; the use of Hungarian was usually restricted to the ethnic community and to private and domestic settings.

The most important mechanism for the preservation of the dominance of the Serbian language has been the fact that the vast majority of Serbs could not speak any Hungarian and had no interest in learning it. Given that most local and state officials—including police, municipal staff, magistrates, and so on—cannot provide services in Hungarian, the official policy of multilingualism remains on paper only. The linguistic opportunity structure was such that children who did not acquire a high level of Serbian would be disadvantaged for the rest of their lives. This led couples of mixed ethnicity to send their children to schools where the language of instruction was Serbian (Serbo-Croatian, in Yugoslav times); when they grew up, those children usually identified as Serbs or Yugoslavs.[87] The Hungarian language had low social status and Hungarians were assimilating into the majority even in the absence of any assimilationist policy.

Hungary's citizenship policy reshuffled the linguistic opportunity structure in Vojvodina, in a way that cannot but have an effect on ethnic power relations. Today, the Hungarian language acquires practical value because it provides access to a political-economic entity that is incomparably larger and richer than Serbia: the EU. The Hungarian language has become associated with opportunities, freedom and wealth.[88]

Above, I discussed the surge in demand for the study of Hungarian by non-Hungarians who hope to secure EU citizenship. Remarkably, even individuals who are not making a systematic effort to learn the language are developing a new appreciation for and interest in Hungarian.[89] Some Hungarian respondents were even approached by Serbs who asked them for Hungarian lessons, and some of them—especially retired teachers—began offering such classes. Hungarian shopkeepers are surprised to find longtime customers, with whom they always communicated in Serbian, suddenly asking them to speak to them in Hungarian "so I can practice." Even the educational choices of mixed couples seem to be affected: according to an analysis made by the Hungarian National Council, there has been an increase of 25 percent in the number of children from mixed families who attend schools where the medium of instruction is Hungarian.[90]

The higher visibility (perhaps we should say audibility) of Hungarian is not just a function of citizenship policy: Hungary has dramatically increased its financial support for Hungarian-language education and culture in Serbia. It also provides funds for projects that would increase the accessibility of public services in the Hungarian language. Local Hungarian leaders report relatively high responsiveness on the part of Serbian public servants to this policy, which they attribute in part to the newfound prestige and usefulness of Hungarian. Hungary's dual policy of offering dual citizenship conditional on language while putting funds into cross-border Hungarian culture has been successful in stopping the drift toward Serbianization of the Hungarian and mixed-origin population in Vojvodina. This development, however, is highly ironic: with one hand, Hungary is bolstering the prestige of Hungarian language and culture in its Habsburg-era territories. Meanwhile, with the other hand, it is facilitating a large-scale emigration of the actual Hungarians living in those same territories.

Conclusions

In this chapter, I analyzed how Hungary's dual citizenship policy is received on the ground in Serbia. This case exhibits the basic characteristics of the global phenomenon of compensatory citizenship: a granting state that permits external dual citizenship as a result of domestic political processes; an eligible population in a middle-tier country that rushes at the opportunity to acquire EU citizenship; and a population of strategic applicants who tweak relevant characteristics (in this case, language) in order to gain citizenship. It can be seen,, moreover, that the opportunity to obtain compensatory citizenship interacts with domestic structures of inequality: there are specific types of preexisting capital that can be converted into a second citizenship.

The case of Hungarian-Serbian dual citizenship is characterized by an ethnolinguistic evidentiary regime, which is consistent with the dominant mode of population classification in Central and Eastern Europe. This means that the resources that can be converted into dual citizenship are ethnicity (being a native Hungarian speaker) or cultural capital (being able to learn Hungarian). Hungarian citizenship policy is formulated in strongly ethnic terms. In practice, however, institutional gatekeepers exhibit surprising openness toward individuals who have studied the language, even if they do not identify as Hungarians. This highlights the inherent paradox in the way ethnicity is politicized in Central and Eastern Europe. On the one hand, ethnic identities provide the taken-for-granted principle of political legitimacy. Multiple times in the nineteenth and twentieth centuries, this principle has led governments to brutally pursue projects of ethnic homogenization and persecute persons who spoke the "wrong" language. At the same time, ethnolinguistic identification is a performative practice that individuals may refashion and modify in a flexible and strategic manner.

In terms of its interaction with local structures of inequality in Serbia, we can identify two effects of Hungarian citizenship policy. On the level of ethnic identities, the availability of dual citizenship for Hungarian speakers has bolstered the prestige and practical value of the language. One could say that this constitutes a soft return to the policy of Magyarization that Hungary enacted when the area was under its control. This time, however, the rising status of Hungarian coincides with a decline in the number of actual Hungarians living in the territory, as many use their citizenship to emigrate.

There is another effect of Hungary's citizenship policy, which is the emergence of unintended beneficiaries—that is, non-Hungarians who strategically study the Hungarian language For those individuals, who are mostly drawn from Serbia's northern urban elites, the opportunity to obtain citizenship as a reward for studying a foreign language seems as a way out of their predicament at the margins of Europe. By obtaining EU citizenship as individuals, they rejoin the ranks of "normal" Europeans, compensating themselves for Serbia's failure to become a member of the prestigious Union.

Furthermore, the findings contribute to the literature on ethnic minorities and disputed territories in Central and Eastern Europe. In recent years, there has been growing interest in the role that citizenship policy—and especially coethnic dual citizenship—play in these dynamics.[91] While that literature focused on the impact of nationalism in those policies and the ways that they are received on the ground, my findings highlight the role of the EU, which is a silent but extremely powerful partner in many of those cases. The EU membership of some countries allows them to bolster the status and attractiveness of "their" ethnicity (whether Hungarian, Romanian, Bulgarian, or Croatian) in all of the neighboring countries, reshaping ethnic hierarchies across borders. The bottom-up responses to such policies illustrate the surprisingly flexible, even strategic structure of ethnolinguistic identity in the region, which stands in striking contrast to the reified discourses and violent struggles that surround it.

3

Mexico

STRATEGIC BIRTH AS ELITE INVESTMENT

Immigration from Mexico to the United States is one of the largest and longest-lasting migrations in the contemporary world. It is also one of the most thoroughly studied; research on Mexican immigrants in the United States has played a crucial role in sociological theories on immigrant integration, transnationalism, and immigration policy.[1] One key dimension, however, has been mostly overlooked in this extensive literature: citizenship and nationality.[2] This analytic neglect is explained by the fact that, until recently, not much was happening in that domain. The United States grants automatic birthright citizenship to anyone born in its territory. Mexico, for its part, traditionally had limited interest in offering citizenship to US-born children of Mexican emigrants. As a consequence, for most of the twentieth century, the population of North America was neatly divided in terms of nationality. Migration between Mexico and the United States produced few dual nationals, no instances of statelessness, and little of the struggles over political boundaries that have fueled the contested politics of citizenship in Europe.[3]

In recent years, however, two trends have combined to reshape the citizenship constellation involving Mexico and the United States.[4] The first change is legal: in 1998, Mexico moved to permit dual nationality and invited former citizens, and their children who were born abroad, to regain Mexican nationality. The second is demographic: since 2007, Mexican immigration to the United States leveled off, and record numbers of Mexicans are moving back.[5] Return migration to Mexico—some of it voluntary and some coerced through deportations—means that there are now millions of people in Mexico who have spent extended periods in the United States or were born there. Together, these legal and demographic changes are blurring the once-solid boundary between the citizenries of the United States and Mexico. Pablo Mateos estimates that over fifteen million persons in the United States and Mexico may be potentially eligible for dual nationality.[6] As of now, we know remarkably little about the dual national population that straddles the political boundary between the two countries.[7]

American-Mexican dual nationals are divided into three major categories: a) immigrants and their children in the United States; b) returnee and deportee families in Mexico; and c) elite Mexican parents who strategically give birth in the United States.[8] In this chapter, I set aside the first two groups and focus on the latter group and the practice of strategic cross-border births. This practice, colloquially called "birth tourism," refers to parents who travel to the United States with the express purpose of giving birth there and securing citizenship for their children; following the birth, they return to their countries of origin.[9] Between 1990 and 2017, there were 178,000 births in the United States to mothers without a US address, who presumably have come from abroad in order to give birth. Of these births, 144,000 were to Mexican mothers.

Cross-border birth is a citizenship strategy used by individuals from middle-tier countries to secure compensatory citizenship from the two first-tier countries that offer automatic *jus soli* (right of soil) citizenship: the United States and Canada.[10] This strategy does not require ancestral or ethnic ties to the citizenship-granting country. It is theoretically open to anyone who holds a visa and can afford the rather hefty costs of travel and the delivery, which run from $7,000 to over $50,000. There is evidence that strategic birth is practiced by individuals of many diverse nationalities, including Turkey, Russia, China, Taiwan, Nigeria and others.[11]

This chapter analyzes the phenomenon of strategic cross-border birth among elites in northern Mexico. Studying strategic birth by Mexicans rather than, say, by Chinese or Russians, provides an opportunity to analyze the practice within the context of Mexican migration and the dynamics of the US-Mexico border. At a time when immigration is becoming increasingly contested and the lives of immigrants ever more precarious, it is important to examine how US citizenship operates as a valuable resource for persons both inside and outside the national territory. Class plays a key role in shaping the desired stake and the way to achieve it: while millions of working-class Mexicans expose themselves to risk and uncertainty by living in the United States without legal status, thousands of middle- and upper-class Mexicans manage to secure dual US citizenship while continuing to live in Mexico.

The typical Mexican birth strategizer is a person coming from the north (*norteño*) and belonging to the middle or upper classes. Families that practice birth strategies use the resources at their disposal—economic capital, physical location, practical know-how, and even culture and phenotype—to secure extra rights from the United States. Elites in northern cities like Monterrey, Tijuana and Ciudad Juárez have intricate transnational ties with the United States that do not typically involve immigration, but rather focus on consumption, tourism and education.[12] In the present period, as northern Mexico is plagued by extreme insecurity, US territory also provides a safe haven. Dual nationality and strategic cross-border birth are integrated into this complex pattern of border-crossing practices.

Legal and Historical Background

Over the past two decades, a new citizenship constellation has emerged between the United States and Mexico that allows individuals to belong to both countries simultaneously. Unlike the Serbian and Israeli cases of dual citizenship, which involve the awakening of ancestral or ethnic ties, the American-Mexican case represents the active creation of new ties. The United States does not encourage long-distance acquisition of its citizenship. And yet, in an example of equifinality (different conditions that lead to a similar outcome), compensatory dual citizenship appears here as well. It is an unintended consequence of individuals' taking advantage of a new opportunity structure that emerged at the crossroads of the United States' birthright citizenship with Mexico's recent acceptance of multiple nationality.

The United States' legislation on citizenship is tied to its self-definition as a country of immigrants.[13] According to the principle of birthright citizenship— "right of soil" or *jus soli*—anyone born in US territory automatically becomes a citizen.[14] This principle was enshrined in the Fourteenth Amendment (1868), which was adopted in order to end the exclusion of African Americans. It is continuous with a regime of easy access into US citizenship that has prevailed since colonial times, and was initially limited to Europeans.[15] By ensuring full membership to second-generation immigrants, birthright citizenship precludes the creation of large populations of noncitizens. Immigration scholars, most notably Richard Alba, have argued that birthright citizenship plays a key role in explaining the United States' greater success in integrating immigrants relative to Western European countries.[16]

For most of the twentieth century, the regime of easy entry into US citizenship was complemented by a regime of easy—and often involuntary—exit. Patrick Weil has shown that, from 1906 to 1977, nearly 150,000 Americans have been stripped of their citizenship for various reasons, including serving in a foreign military, voting in foreign elections, or just being away from the United States.[17] In 1967, however, the Supreme Court limited the State Department's authority to expatriate Americans against their will, leading to a gradual elimination of the practice. Patrick Weil has argued that this change reflects a new legal doctrine that he called "the sovereign citizen."[18] The retreat from citizenship stripping entailed the informal acceptance of dual nationality in the United States. Dual nationals, however, remain subject to some restrictions and are barred from sensitive government positions.

As the United States' citizenship regime grew more flexible, new opportunities emerged for foreigners who wished to acquire citizenship strategically. Here, I focus on strategic birth, which takes advantage of the combination of automatic *jus soli* and the principle of nonexpatriation.[19] It is impossible to determine precisely when foreigners began to practice strategic birth in the United States and which origin countries produce the largest numbers of "birth tourist" parents. Chinese strategic birth in particular has gained notoriety because of controversies over maternity homes for Chinese women in California and elsewhere.[20] While Mexican strategic cross-border births are not as conspicuous as Chinese birth tourism, Mexico still counts as one of the leading origin countries.

Mexico, like the United States, automatically grants nationality to anyone born in its territory. Until 1998, however, Mexican law did not tolerate dual nationality. Moreover, only native-born Mexicans enjoy full political rights, while Mexicans by naturalization are excluded from positions of power in politics, the economy, the military, and even academia.[21] The restrictive approach toward naturalized citizens is a product of Mexico's troubled history: Spanish colonialism followed by a French invasion followed by the traumatic loss of vast territories (half of Mexico's original territory) to the United States in 1848. This series of setbacks has left a legacy of suspicion: those who were born in another country or hold another nationality are traditionally seen as potentially disloyal.

In 1998, the reality of mass emigration finally pushed the Mexican government to permit dual nationality. While immigration from Mexico to the United States has a long history, going back as far as the 1880s, for many decades it mostly consisted of circular and short-term movement. Only since the 1970s did large numbers of Mexicans begin to settle in the United States.[22] Douglas Massey has argued that the shift from circular migration to mass settlement is a response to changes in US policy. The Immigration Reform and Control Act (IRCA) of 1986 led to the legalization of two million undocumented Mexican immigrants, opening a path to naturalization; this was followed in 1996 by a tightening of border controls and by legislation that stripped noncitizens in the United States of various entitlements. By blocking circular movement and penalizing nonnaturalized immigrants, this policy pushed many Mexican immigrants to apply for US citizenship. Whereas in 1995, only 20 percent of Mexican immigrants who were eligible to naturalize had done so, by 2011 this

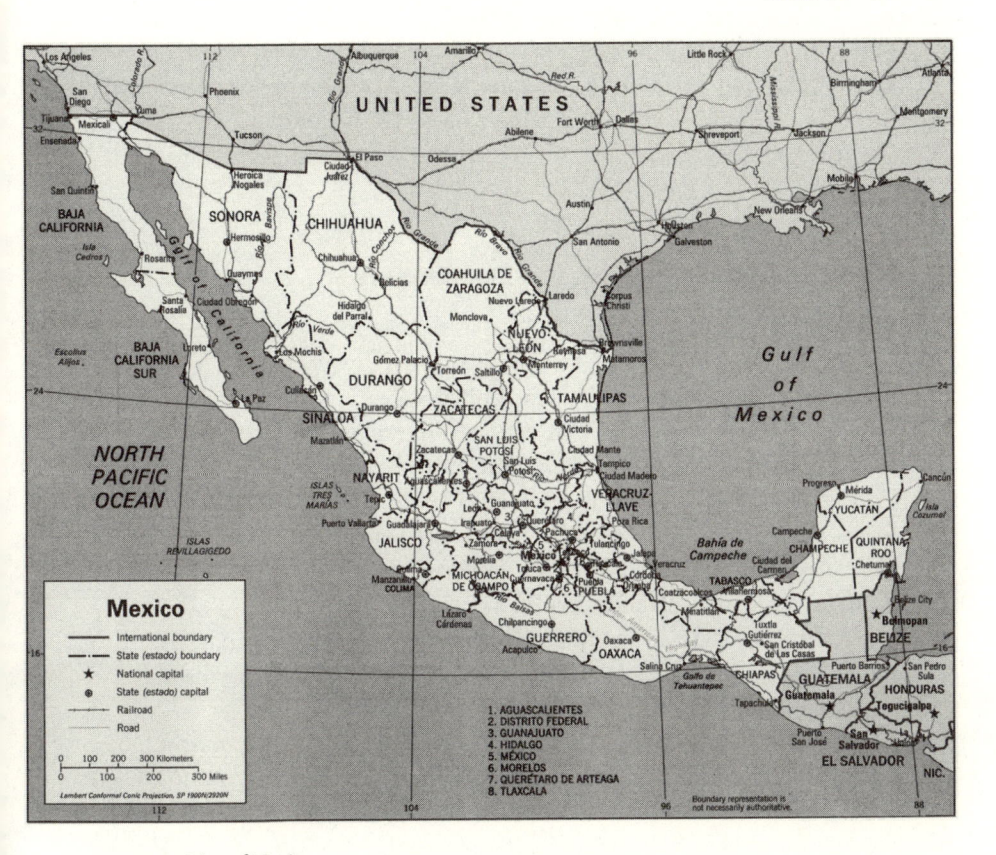

FIGURE 3.1. Map of Mexico

percentage climbed to 36 percent. Even so, Mexicans remain the immigrant group that is least likely to naturalize in the United States.[23]

This was the context that led the Mexican government in 1998 to dramatically retreat from its traditional position and permit dual nationality. Also referred to as the "law of no-loss" (*ley de no pérdida*), the new nationality law allowed Mexicans to naturalize in another country without losing their nationality.[24] The law aimed to encourage Mexican immigrants to naturalize in the United States while facilitating the retention of political and economic ties to Mexico. This inclusive intention did not stop Mexican legislators from stipulating a long list of restrictions that limit the access of dual nationals to most sensitive or influential positions. Political scientist Henio Hoyo has argued that Mexico treats its dual nationals as suspicious "half-citizens."[25]

As I will show below, Mexico's 1998 law of no-loss was not a major success in terms of promoting dual nationality among Mexican immigrants in the United States; it did, however, have the unintended consequence of increasing the legitimacy and the prevalence of dual nationality among (mostly upper-class) Mexicans *in Mexico*. This chapter will explore this phenomenon while focusing on the experiences and perspectives of residents of northern Mexico (*norteños*) and especially individuals from the city of Monterrey (often called *regios*).

US Nationality in Mexico, by the Numbers

Mass immigration from Mexico, which was a taken-for-granted aspect of US society for over a generation, is winding down. In recent years, more people have been moving to Mexico from the United States than the other way around: a million Mexicans and their family members returned to Mexico between 2009 and 2014, compared with only 870,000 new arrivals in the United States. In 2013, China replaced Mexico as the top sending country of immigrants to the United States, and India might soon push it to the third place. In 2016, for the first time in five decades, the majority of undocumented immigrants apprehended at US borders were not Mexican nationals.[26]

This decline in Mexican immigration to the United States can be traced to societal changes in Mexico, including reduced fertility, improved education and intensified industrialization. The country has moved past its "migration hump"—a period of peak emigration that ensues as a society moves along the path to higher development and lower fertility, in the terms of Ronald Skeldon.[27] This means that the volume of Mexican immigration to the United States is not expected to bounce back up (except in the event of a major crisis in Mexico). We are entering a new phase in the history of Mexico-US migration, that will be marked by new demographic, economic and political dynamics that connect the two nations. The proliferation of dual nationality is a key element in this new, post–mass immigration constellation.

In this chapter, I focus on American-Mexican dual nationality on the Mexican side of the border and set aside dual nationality in the United States. With over fifteen million first- and second-generation immigrants from Mexico in the United States, the potential for dual nationality is huge. At the present moment, however, Mexican immigration does not seem to produce a massive dual national population in the United States: the first generation typically live in the country for many years (legally or illegally) without naturalizing, while second-generation Mexican Americans rarely seek Mexican nationality.[28] In contrast, when we move south of the border, we find a large and growing number of American-Mexican dual nationals living in Mexico. They can be divided into two categories.

The first category of dual nationals consists of *returnee and deportee families*. Children in these families are involuntary dual nationals: they were born in the United States and grew up there until their parents were deported or decided to

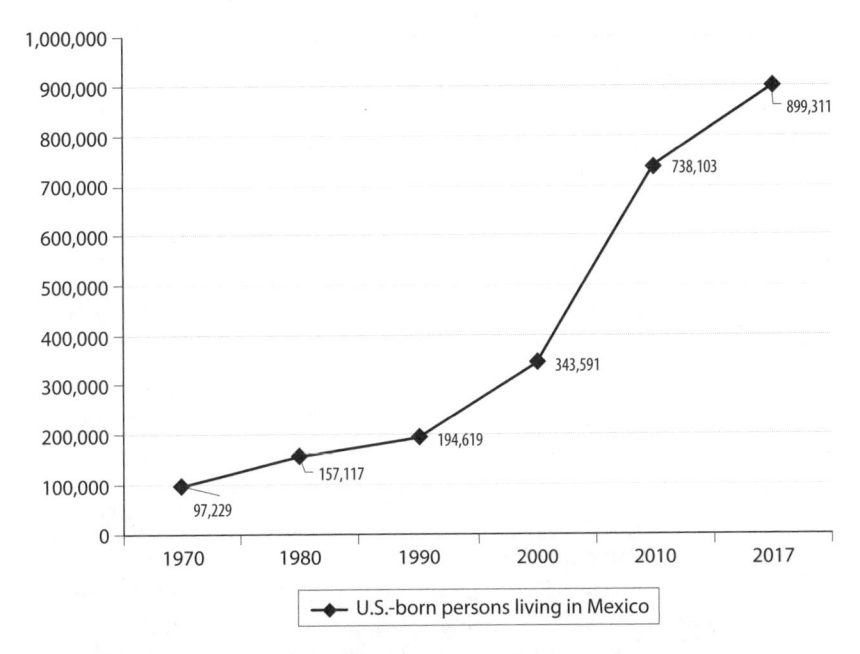

FIGURE 3.2. Number of US-born persons in Mexico, 1970–2017
Note: The figure shows the number of persons living in Mexico who were born in the United States, based on data from the Mexican census (for 1970 to 2010) and the UN Population Division (for 2017).
Sources: 1970–2010 data from Chavez 2010, 2013; 2017 data from United Nations Population Division 2017.

return to Mexico. Such families are mostly lower-class and rural; they typically do not have the resources (money, education, connections) to derive benefits from their status as dual nationals.[29] In this chapter, I focus on a second group: nonimmigrant parents from middle- and upper-class backgrounds who practice *strategic cross-border birth* in the United States. Such parents enter the United States legally with a tourist visa, give birth there, and secure US nationality for their children. They then immediately return to Mexico.

The available data are not detailed enough to determine the precise number of persons in each category, but they provide a general sense of the trends. Data from the Mexican census show that there has been a dramatic growth in the number of persons who were born in the United States and are now living in Mexico.

Figure 3.2 illustrates the dramatic growth in the number of US-born individuals in Mexico since 1970. This number reached 900,000 persons in 2017—almost triple the figure for 2000 and more than nine times the number in 1970.[30] We can use these figures to learn about dual nationality. Anyone who was born in the United States can safely be assumed to be a US citizen. How many among them are dual nationals? The Mexican National Institute of Migration (*Instituto Nacional de Migracion*) lists 60,000 US citizens who are living in Mexico with some kind of immigrant visa (data are for 2009).[31] They are presumably mononational Americans; all the others can be assumed to hold both American and Mexican nationalities.

Note that the figure for US-born persons in Mexico—900,000 in 2017—does not capture the full number of dual nationals in Mexico, which also includes immigrants who returned after having naturalized in the United States, and people who received US citizenship from their parents *jure sanguinis*.[32]

Returning to the almost 900,000 US-born in Mexico, the census reveals that 80 percent of them are under the age of twenty.[33] This means that the growth in US citizens in Mexico is not the result of hundreds of thousands of American adults (presumably retirees) deciding to leave for Mexico. Instead, this growth is driven by the US-born children of Mexicans who follow their families back to Mexico, whether as a result of return migration (including deportation), or strategic cross-border birth. In order to disentangle these two different pathways to dual nationality, is helpful to examine the distribution of dual nationals by region.

The map in figure 3.3 shows the prevalence of US-born dual nationals around Mexico's territory. It is reproduced from a recent paper by the geographer Pablo Mateos, which shows the distribution of the.US-born in Mexico in 2010, by *municipio*, an administrative unit that is roughly equivalent to a U.S. county.[34] Darker areas have a higher proportion of US-born persons in the population relative to the national average, whereas lighter ones are below national average (see index under the map). For the sake of simplicity, in this analysis I ignore the small percentage of US-born who are American mononationals.[35]

As the map illustrates, the large majority (75 percent) of the US-born in Mexico were concentrated in two regions: the central-western part of the country, which is a traditional emigration-sending region; and the area along Mexico's border with the United States. The analysis of data from official Mexican sources provides evidence of the different pathways that produce dual nationality in each region. The central-western region—an underdeveloped part of Mexico where incomes are significantly lower than the national average—is overrepresented in terms of emigration: home to 36 percent of Mexico's population, it is responsible for 47 percent of the country's emigrants and 40 percent of return migrants (many of them have been deported). This region is home to 29 percent of the US-born in Mexico.[36] The large majority among them would logically be the children of returnees and deportees.

Mexico's northern border states are marked by much higher level of economic development (average income is 70 percent higher than in central-western

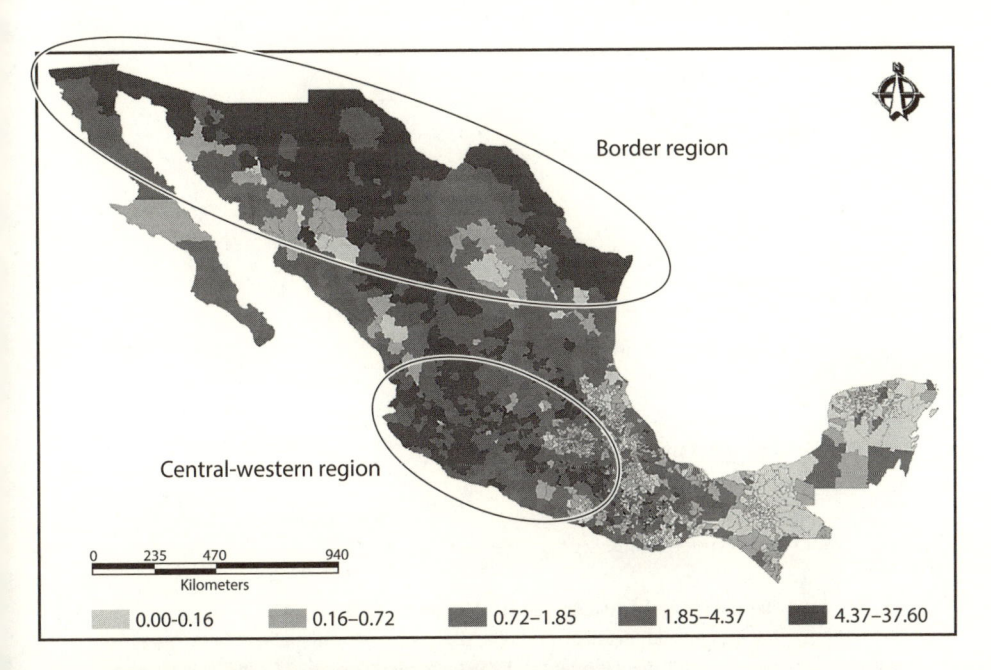

FIGURE 3.3. US-born population in Mexico, by *municipio*, 2010
Note: Each *municipio* is colored to represent the proportion of the population that was born in the United States, relative to the national average. The darker ones have the largest number of US-born persons relative to their population.
Source: Mateos 2019, prepared from Mexican Census of Population longform microdata.

states). In spite of its proximity to the border, the northern region is not a hot spot of emigration: the share of northern states in emigration is proportional to their share in the national population. The six border states are home to 17 percent of Mexico's population, have sent 20 percent of emigrants, and received 19 percent of return migrants. The presence of dual nationals in this region, however, is disproportionately high: the border is home to 45 percent of the US-born in Mexico, or 330,000 persons. Roughly 1.6 percent of Mexicans in the border region were born in the United States and hold American nationality—three times higher than the share in central-western Mexico or in the nation as a whole. Furthermore, since 2000, the border region has seen a much faster growth in the number of US-born persons than any other part of Mexico.[37]

Given the border region's relatively modest and stable contribution to emigration, the high and growing presence of US-born dual nationals in the border regions cannot be explained simply as a consequence of return migration and deportation. This suggests that strategic cross-border births play a growing role in producing dual nationality along the US-Mexico border.

76 CHAPTER 3

```
[Chart: Line graph from 1990–2017 showing births to nonresident mothers, with vertical line at 1998 labeled "Mexico permits dual nationality". Y-axis 0–12000.]
```

— Total births to non-resident mothers   - - - Non-resident mothers: Mexican
— — Non-resident mothers: Non-Mexican

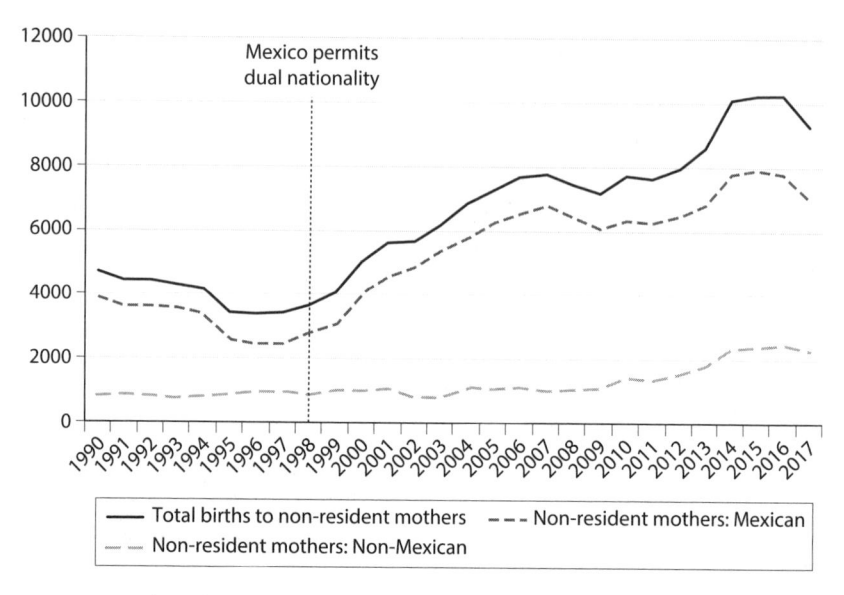

FIGURE 3.4. Births in the United States to nonresident mothers, 1990–2017
Note: The graph shows the number of births in the United States by mothers who did not provide a US address. The black line represents the total number of nonresident births, while the dotted lines represents births to Mexican mothers (the upper line) and non-Mexican mothers (the bottom line).
Source: Author's calculation based on NCHS statistics for 1990–2017.

Statistics from two sources provide further evidence of this trend. First, I analyzed data on births from the US National Center for Health Statistics (NCHS). These data show that births to nonresident mothers, who did not provide a US address when registering their child's birth, represent a very small percentage of the total number of births; however, the numbers have grown since 1990, and the growth was driven by Mexicans.[38] The data are presented in figure 3.4.

As the figure shows, in the period leading up to Mexico's approval of dual nationality in 1998, there were about 2,500 births a year to nonresident Mexican mothers and another 800 to 1,000 births annually to nonresidents who were not Mexican. After 1998, the number of births to nonresident non-Mexican mothers remained constant (until 2012), while the number of births to Mexican mothers began to climb, reaching 6,000 to 8,000 births a year after 2005. This increase is most likely attributable to Mexico's acceptance of dual nationality. Since 2012, the number of births to non-Mexican foreign-resident mothers began to increase, while in 2017 there was an overall drop in the number of foreign-resident births. I do not have sufficient data to explain these trends in detail, but the latter change might reflect a tougher attitude at the US border during the Trump administration, or greater caution on the part of prospective birth strategizers.

Between 1990 and 2017, there were 178,235 births in the United States to mothers without a US address (143,957, or 80 percent, were to Mexican mothers). The total figure of strategic births in the United States can be estimated to be higher, because it is not difficult for foreign mothers who give birth there to provide a US address even if it is not their permanent domicile. Even when acknowledging that this is an undercount, it should be clear that such births represent a tiny fraction of the number of births in the United States. From 1990 to 2017, a total of 113 million persons were born there; births to foreign-resident mothers represent just 0.16 percent of this figure.[39]

The trend of growth after Mexico's 1998 dual nationality law is also evident in a second set of statistics, that I obtained from the Mexican Ministry of Foreign Affairs. These data pertain to registration of Mexican dual citizenship at the Mexican consulate in El Paso, Texas, between 1994 and 2014. These data show a growth in the number of US-born persons who registered as dual nationals in El Paso (a known destination for strategic birth). Mexican citizenship registrations increased from under 100 in 1994 to 503 in 1998 (when Mexico permitted dual nationality) to over 1,500 a year after 2011.[40]

Citizenship registrations provide an indication of cross-border strategic births because parents who wish to secure dual nationality for their children would usually register them as American as well as Mexican in the United States before returning to Mexico with them (see the next section). There was a strong correlation between the trends in US births to nonresidents (according to NCHS data) and registrations at the consulate in El Paso. This strengthens the hypothesis that these indices are measuring the same phenomenon.[41]

These figures, coming from three different sources (the Mexican census, the United States' NCHS, and the Mexican Ministry of Foreign Affairs), lend significant support to the hypothesis that the growth in the number of US-born dual nationals in Mexico is driven in part by a growth in the number of strategic cross-border birth. This growth, in turn, can be attributed to the legitimization of dual nationality in Mexico since 1998. I should note, however, that these figures cannot yet provide a full picture of strategic cross-border births—a phenomenon that is very difficult to measure precisely.

The growing impact of strategic birth on dual nationality adds an important element to the extensive writing on the US-Mexico border as a binational region. Previous authors have explored cross-border interaction in the domains of language, economics, consumption, status hierarchies, and governance.[42] The analysis given here shows that the border region is increasingly home to a large population that is binational not just in its language or culture, but in terms of its actual citizenship status.

Obtaining US Nationality

The new legal structure of American-Mexican dual nationality has significant consequences across the border region. It allows thousands of Mexican families to convert their socioeconomic privilege into a new form of global resource, while at the same time tightening the integration between the two nations and creating a large American citizen population in Mexico. In the following sections, I discuss the everyday consequences of this case of compensatory citizenship.

I will first present two short vignettes to illustrate the life circumstances, motivations, and pathways of birth tourists and dual nationals. Then, I will discuss the procedure of citizenship acquisition, while focusing on the citizenship industry of births in the United States, and the family dynamics around it. I will then analyze compensatory citizenship as a resource that provides opportunities, security, and travel freedom. I will highlight the way dual nationality is integrated into preexisting social and economic ties between *norteño* elites and the United States. Finally, I will analyze US nationality as an instrument of social closure and a status symbol.

Vignette 1: Ricardo, 37, upper-class, from Monterrey, had his children in the United States[43]

Ricardo was born in Monterrey and lives there with his wife and their three daughters, who were all born in the United States. An entrepreneur from a wealthy family, he spent four years in the United States studying for a master's degree in business administration and working for a US firm. "My eldest daughter was born in Michigan because we were there at the time, and the younger ones, now 5 and 3, were born in McAllen [in Texas] of our own choice. . . . My wife is now pregnant with our fourth child and he will be born in McAllen too."

Each birth in McAllen cost $18,000 to $20,000, including regular trips across the border for check-ups during the pregnancy and a month-long stay for the birth itself. Ricardo lists three motives for giving birth in McAllen: "First, to give them equal status with [the eldest]; second, to give them optionality [*sic*; originally in English] so that they can choose where to live, study and work. . . . And, third, we had a big security crisis here, and many people went to live abroad. So we wanted to give [our daughters] more flexibility, so they can move between the territories seamlessly."

Ricardo was never interested in obtaining a US green card or citizenship for himself because "it implies stringent fiscal liabilities and you're taxed on your global income." The family has no plans to leave Monterrey in the foreseeable future. Ricardo's daughters attend a bilingual American school but, he explains, this has nothing to do with their citizenship: "English is necessary for anybody who lives in Monterrey, [because] this city is so connected to the US."

Vignette 2: Carmen, 30, middle-class, from a border town, born in the United States

Carmen was born in 1984 in Harlingen, Texas, a small town on the US-Mexico border. She grew up in a small Mexican border town, where her father grows corn and cotton. She now lives in Monterrey with her husband and works in finance. Carmen is the eldest of four siblings; all of them were all born in the same Harlingen hospital and all are dual nationals. Carmen's mother said that they had decided to have her in Harlingen because it had the nearest modern hospital and also "so that [Carmen and her siblings] could study in the United States without problems, [so] that they won't need a visa, [and] that they will never stay without work."

Carmen originally planned to study in the United States. However, she was offered a scholarship at a prestigious university in Monterrey and ended up studying and working there. In 2011, as violence in the border region escalated, Carmen moved to McAllen, Texas, and lived there for several months in order to sponsor US residency for her parents. Carmen's parents now spend two days a week in Mexico and five in McAllen. Her three younger siblings live in McAllen.

Carmen has an authentic US birth certificate but her Mexican birth certificate is fake: it says that she was born in Mexico. "My identity is completely Mexican, but I have no legal way to prove that I am Mexican," she says. She is trying to fix her status in Mexico with the help of a lawyer. She has a US passport and uses it for international travel. When she will have children, she plans to give birth in the United States "for the same reasons [that my parents had me there]: so that if things are bad here, [my children] can go live there."

STRATEGIC BIRTH AS A CITIZENSHIP INDUSTRY

Cross-border strategic birth is a pathway to compensatory citizenship that developed in response to openings in the United States' system for determining individuals' eligibility for citizenship (in other words, its evidentiary regime). In a *jus soli* citizenship regime, place of birth is the master principle that provides automatic, undisputed membership in the national community. The US birth certificate is the key document that establishes US nationality. Strategic birth is aimed at securing this document, which is produced at the intersection of two kinds of authority: a medical professional at the hospital or birth clinic, who supplies the certificate of live birth, and an official at the county's vital statistics office. After having obtained a birth certificate, parents must also secure their child's Mexican nationality. This procedure may be done either in Mexico or at a Mexican consulate in the United States. It is crucial because children without Mexican nationality do not have full rights to public education and health services in Mexico.[44]

Some *norteño* families practiced strategic birth in the United States before dual nationality became legal in 1998. In those times, fraud was the norm, but it was directed mostly toward Mexico.[45] Parents would travel to the United States and give birth there; they would then show up at their local civil registry (*registro civil*) office in Mexico and use connections—or a bribe—to obtain a Mexican birth certificate that specified that the baby had been born in Mexico. Carmen's account in vignette 2 is typical of those dynamics. With the acceptance of dual nationality and the tightening of control over personal identification in Mexico, this kind of fraud is becoming less common. However, many dual nationals (including Carmen in the vignette above) still have two distinct legal personalities: a legitimate one in the United States and a fake one in Mexico. Ironically, it is their primary citizenship, the one they use in their everyday lives, that is fraudulent, while their secondary citizenship from the United States is genuine. In recent years, many US-born *norteños* who have lived their entire lives with fake birth certificates are turning to lawyers to legalize their status. The Mexican government is encouraging this regularization. For example, in 2015, the city of Tijuana put up posters that implored residents to register as dual nationals, under the slogan "Become Mexican!" (*¡Hazte Mexicano!*).[46]

Today, dual nationality is a legitimate status that is usually produced in a legal manner. There are two ways for parents to secure Mexican nationality for a baby that was born in the United States. The first is to register the child at a Mexican consulate in the United States. This registration (called *inscripción*) is done on the spot and carries a very low cost. Nonetheless, it requires planning ahead and some bureaucratic know-how. Parents who follow this method—including most middle-class parents who practice strategic birth—return to Mexico with their child already fitted with three crucial documents: a US birth certificate, a US passport, and a confirmation of Mexican nationality. The dual national status of such children is undisputed.

In contrast, most Mexican immigrants who give birth in the United States do not visit the consulate to register their children as Mexican. This population consists mainly of low-income, uneducated persons who are often in the United States illegally. Due to their unstable economic situation, they are reluctant to take a day off work for a procedure that carries no immediate benefit; moreover, they often lack the bureaucratic know-how.

This means that the large majority of deportee and returnee families come to Mexico with children that are US mononationals. Those children must then confirm their Mexican citizenship from inside Mexico. This is a challenging endeavor. Since Mexico's *registro civil* does not accept documents in English, the US birth certificate must be apostille-approved in the United States and then translated. This procedure takes an average of five months and costs over $130—a hefty sum in rural Mexico.[47] The process becomes even more challenging when applicants cannot enter the United States—the typical situation for deportees—in which case they must go through the procedure by mail. Often, children of deportees must wait for months in a state of effective statelessness before Mexico recognizes them as nationals.[48]

The gap between two kinds of dual nationals, who share the same legal status but diverge in their ability to realize their citizenship rights, highlights the class aspect of strategic birth. Middle- and upper-class individuals secure official recognition for dual nationality through a relatively simple and painless procedure; working-class individuals find themselves in far more complicated situations, often spending months or years in a state of uncertainty. Access to dual nationality depends not just on ties to the United States or financial ability, but also on bureaucratic know-how and planning ahead—two skills that are common among middle-class individuals but not those of a working-class or rural background.[49]

The most significant barriers facing parents who wish to practice strategic cross-border birth are the requirement to hold a visa to the United States and the ability to pay for the birth out of pocket. A US visa in itself is a mark of privilege in itself in Mexico: the US consulate only issues visas to applicants who can prove that they have solid economic means and strong ties to Mexico. Often, they own real estate or hold a steady, well-earning job.[50] Moreover, giving birth in the United States is expensive. The typical expenditure—including the birth itself, doctor visits, check-ups during pregnancy, and accommodation in the United States during the final months—ranges between $6,000 and $20,000. These sums represent a huge expense, given that average yearly salaries in northern Mexico range from about $7,500 to $9,000.[51] Strategic birth is an exclusive strategy that is only open to middle-class and elite *norteños*.

For these elites, strategic birth is part of a broader pattern of border-spanning status-oriented consumption. High-income residents of Monterrey (*regios*) regularly visit the United States for shopping and vacations. Some locations in Texas—McAllen, San Antonio, South Padre Island—figure on the mental map of *regios* as designated locations for high-prestige conspicuous consumption.[52]

The economy of US border towns is strongly dependent on Mexican shoppers, who frequent their malls, restaurants, outlet stores, and even grocery chains (the Trader Joe's in San Diego is a favorite among residents of Tijuana). For many norteña mothers, giving birth in the US is yet another form of cross-border consumption. Mexican parents engage in "birth tourism" not only to secure US citizenship for their children, but also in order to enjoy high quality medical service and a gratifying consumer experience.

The decision by thousands of Mexican families each year to invest in acquiring US citizenship for their children has led to the rise of a citizenship industry. The professionals who are positioned to take advantage of these opportunities include ob-gyn specialists in US hospitals and birth clinics, as well as lawyers and insurers in Mexico. All of the people that I interviewed picked a doctor based on personal acquaintance or reputation. Besides the natural tendency to rely on personal networks when seeking trust-sensitive services, this preference also reflects the high degree of integration of the two sides of the border, which made it possible for *norteños* to locate clinics in the United States with relative ease.

The industry of cross-border births in northern Mexico is relatively informal. There are indications that the citizenship industries that offer maternity services to parents coming from farther abroad—for example, those catering to Russians or Chinese—are more formal and rely more heavily on organized service providers and online advertising. Often, the websites of maternity companies openly promise US citizenship as one of the benefits of giving birth in the United States. For example, the Spanish-language website of a company called *Doctores Para Ti* invites parents from outside the United States to give birth in El Paso, assuring them that their children will have a guaranteed constitutional right for citizenship.[53] Another company, *Deluxe Childbirth Services*, seems to cater mostly to Nigerians and promises a US birth at a cost of about $6,000.[54]

For Russians and Russian speakers, the company Аист (Russian for "stork") invites parents through its Russian-language website to give birth in Houston, Texas. Parents can choose between an "optimal" package ($12,890) that includes all medical services and the formalization of the baby's second nationality, and a "premium" package ($18,900) that also includes trips around Texas, a professional photo shoot with the newborn, and other perks.[55] I did not investigate these websites and the companies behind them, but there is enough scholarly research and journalistic reporting to show that such firms do exist and that they arrange a certain number of US births each year (while precise data are unavailable, the biggest market seems to be Chinese).[56]

The citizenship industry that developed in northern Mexico is more local and informal than these global companies. From the point of view of the consumer, strategic birth (or birth tourism) is remarkably similar to other kinds of cross-border consumption and tourism. There are, however, special complexities involved in this practice—above all, its controversial and legally dubious nature. There is no law that prohibits nonresidents from giving birth in the United States, and the US government has not seriously carried out a systematic effort to eliminate strategic cross-border births.[57] Nonetheless, would-be birth tourists must cross an international border, where they undergo heightened surveillance and may easily be denied entry.[58]

Respondents reported that US Customs and Border Protection (CBP) agents occasionally refuse entry to visibly pregnant women. Mexican mothers who intend to give birth in the United States usually take precautions to conceal their pregnancy, including crossing the border before the final months of their pregnancy, wearing a loose coat, or holding a bag on their knees. This is possible because *norteños* usually enter the United States through land borders, seated in their cars; they do not typically undergo the rigorous scrutiny that airline passengers are subjected to.

Mexican parents who cross the border with a baby that was born in the United States are often asked to provide proof that they have paid for the birth and vaccinations out of pocket. If CBP agents find that they have drawn on government assistance—for example, by having Medicaid pay for the birth—their visas might be revoked.[59] Cross-border birth is a risky endeavor.

These elements of risk and illegality are absent in other cases of compensatory citizenship, where eligibility is based on ancestry or ethnicity. They lead us to consider the parallel between strategic birth and undocumented immigration—in other words, between a citizenship industry and a migration industry.[60] *Coyotes* (human smugglers) that guide undocumented immigrants across the border in the United States charge fees that are not much lower than the prices charged by the medical professionals that offer birth services to upper-class Mexicans. Estimates from 2013 and 2014 put the cost of a single undocumented crossing at between $3,000 and $10,000.[61] Besides the economic cost, lower-class, uneducated Mexicans who illegally cross the border are exposed to serious risks: they might die of thirst and exposure in scorching deserts, be abused or kidnapped by criminals, or face arrest and incarceration.

While lower-class undocumented immigrants put their life savings—and often, their life itself—on the line in order to enter the United States and work there precariously, upper-class birth tourists invest a much smaller proportion of their wealth and take on much smaller risks to gain a secure link to the United States through their children. Socioeconomic status not only stratifies Mexicans within Mexico but defines divergent modes of access to the United States.

Family Dynamics

Strategic cross-border birth is a form of intergenerational transfer of wealth, like an investment in children's education or the purchase of real estate. It is an investment that would only pay off in the long run. The large majority of Mexican parents who engage in cross-border birth will most likely never benefit personally from the act in which they invested so much time and money. That is because US citizens may only sponsor their relatives for an immigrant visa after they have turned twenty-one. Contradicting the pejorative and misleading expression "anchor babies," children born in the United States cannot provide any "anchor" before that age. There is no legal clause that protects foreign parents of American citizens under the age of twenty-one from deportation (in fact, hundreds of thousands of such persons have been deported since 2008) or offer them privileged access to immigration visas. Typically, the middle- and upper-class *norteños* who practice strategic birth have no intention to emigrate from Mexico.

All respondents who strategically gave birth in the United States explained their decision in terms of the future usefulness to the child—above all, the general formulation that he or she "will have more opportunities." None of them said that they expected a direct personal benefit from their children's citizenship. Nevertheless, there were cases where the parents of adult dual nationals did benefit directly from their children's US citizenship, when they sponsored their immigration. This scenario usually unfolded when conditions in their places of residence in Mexico became dangerous, and they moved to the United States for security. Such immigration was usually temporary or part-time, and follows the pattern described in vignette 2 above: in towns that have become unlivable due to rampant crime, dual national children move to a US border town and then the parents obtain a "green card" and split their time between Mexico and the United States. I will discuss this kind of mobility in greater detail below.

In most cases, then, cross-border birth is a free gift from parents to children. By offering such a gift, Mexican parents are strengthening the cohesion of the family unit: the act of giving citizenship performs the parents' commitment to their children, instills a reciprocal obligation on the part of the children, and creates a new family asset. This resonates with the insights of sociologist Viviana Zelizer, who argues that money and intimate relations are not "separate spheres," as the dominant ideology of our time decrees; rather, money is a central instrument in creating and maintaining relations.[62]

There are two additional, unexpected family values that came up in the interviews and were associated with strategic birth and dual nationality. The first is equality between siblings: several respondents (including Ricardo from vignette 1) wished "to give all children equal [citizenship] status." Often, these were parents whose first child was born while they were studying or working in the United States and then decided to give birth to all their other children there. Such decisions are conditioned by social class: equal treatment of older and younger siblings and of boys and girls may serve as a performance of parents' enlightened values and their elite identity. This sets them apart from lower-class Mexican families, where between-sibling favoritism (based on gender, birth order, certainty of paternity, or looks) is common. It also sets them apart from migrant families, where mixed citizenship statuses are the norm.

A second value that was associated with dual nationality was personal freedom. Many interviewees contrasted Mexican and American systems of values and conduct. They viewed Mexican culture as marked by rigid codes that governed gender and family roles, class-appropriate behavior, and personal opinion. In contrast, Americans were seen as more free, independent, and efficacious than Mexicans. At the same time, many respondents preferred the Mexican system because they viewed it as warmer, more human, and more forgiving. For example, respondents typically said that children who were raised in Mexico are more respectful and committed to their parents, and have a lower chance of getting in trouble. Within this context, US nationality provides children with greater personal freedom in a sense that extends beyond its practical advantages: it is a bridge to another culture that is more individualistic and achievement-oriented. These two points—equality and freedom—suggest that strategic birth is also used as a medium for performing and transmitting elite identity and values.

US citizenship is an asset that does not come free of liabilities. The chief liability is being subjected to global taxation: US citizens who live abroad are required to report their income and their assets, and higher-income individuals may have to pay additional taxes. In 2010, in the wake of the economic crisis, the US Treasury Department tightened its taxation regime, requiring foreign banks to report on the accounts of US citizens. As a result, record numbers of Americans living abroad have renounced their US citizenship.[63]

Remarkably, dual nationals in Mexico—especially those from working-class and middle-class backgrounds—were mostly unaware or indifferent to their potential tax obligations as Americans living abroad. When asked about the potential tax implications of US citizenship, most respondents reacted with surprise. Most of the adult dual nationals that I interviewed have never filed a US tax report.

Some respondents formed an exception to this rule: individuals from the most affluent and business-savvy families in the sample were keenly aware of all the liabilities that came with dual nationality and frequently consulted their auditors about them. Several wealthy individuals had decided to renounce their US citizenship in order to protect their assets or their privacy.

A few elite Monterrey families reportedly employed a strategy of differentiated citizenship by gender: girls would be born in the United States and boys in Mexico, and all taxable assets would be registered under the name of the men in the family. This careful division of ownership allows families to enjoy the security provided by US citizenship, without exposing their property to the US tax collector. One respondent from an upper-class family (whose wife, also of elite background, was born in the United States) explained, "My wife was born in Texas, but she is not worried, because she has nothing on her name.... She has no income. Everything she buys, signs or pays is on my account.... So if they want her to pay taxes, what can they charge? She has nothing."

Sociological research on elites has shown that they carefully plan how to distribute their wealth across different kinds of assets—including, for instance, real estate and stocks—in a way that would maximize benefits and minimize tax liability and exposure to risk. The strategy described in this quotation illustrates that a second citizenship has become yet another asset that is integrated into elites' investment portfolio, one that comes with its own particular composition of benefits and liabilities. In this case, this strategy also had the added effect of reinforcing male domination in the family.

Putting US Nationality to Use

OPPORTUNITIES

American-Mexican dual nationals, like all American citizens, have an unqualified right to reside and work in the United States. Given that the United States is the world's top immigrant destination, that one in ten Mexicans already lives there and that US wages are on average four times higher than in Mexico, we might expect strategic birth to be closely tied to emigration. In other words, acquiring dual nationality could reasonably be seen as the first step toward moving to the United States. However, as the statistics above already showed, there are large and growing numbers of dual nationals living south of the border, and the interviews I conducted confirmed that emigration is not particularly attractive to middle- or upper-class *norteños*. This raises a puzzle: Why would Mexicans invest significant resources in securing US citizenship and then refrain from using it to emigrate?

National identity and sentimental attachments to people and places play a huge role in keeping people from emigrating, and they are central to this case as well. Interestingly, however, respondents often presented practical-economic reasons to explain why they preferred to live in Mexico even with US citizenship. They referred to two main themes: quality of life and business opportunities.

First, many respondents explained that from their perspective Mexico offered superior quality of life relative to the United States: housing was cheaper, domestic help was more affordable, and there was much more leisure time. Saul, a twenty-eight-year-old dual national from Monterrey who works in a successful family business established by his grandfather, explained (text in Italic was originally said in English): "Some people have the *American Dream* . . . but I have the *Mexican Dream*. Compared to the middle class in the US, I live much better. As middle-class here, I earn a lot more relative to the country. And I enjoy luxuries that [Americans] do not have [or] that are expensive there, like servants, personal drivers, [better service at] restaurants and bars." This explanation was typical of upper-middle-class respondents, who emphasized the affordability of luxuries and high-quality services in Mexico.

Affordability of service is closely tied to extreme income inequality. The top decile of earners in Mexico enjoy an average income that is twenty-nine times higher than the bottom decile—almost double the ratio in the United States (sixteen to one), which is itself very high compared to the gap in EU countries (seven to one).[64] Such vast income disparities allow members of the elite in Mexico to purchase personal services at ridiculously low costs and enjoy a very high quality of life.

A second reason for preferring Mexico was that it offered more extensive opportunities for profit that capitalize on know-how and social connections. A big part of the wealth of Mexican elites takes the form of connections, friendships, and a reputation—social capital, in Pierre Bourdieu's terms.[65] This is a resource that does not travel well across borders.[66] The more entrepreneurial among the respondents argued that Mexico offered more lucrative opportunities because of its high growth rate and flexible rules. Saul continued: "In Mexico, if you have contacts, it's much easier to do business here. You can avoid paying taxes, you can do things 'incorrectly' [use bribery] and you can start many businesses that don't exist here yet." This attitude was typical of elite *regios*, who seemed to view Mexico as a high-risk business environment, rife with crime and corruption, but one in which they could reap high profits, thanks to their advantageous starting position.

Alfredo, a thirty-one-year-old real-estate developer whose children were born in the United States, said: In terms of opportunities, "Mexico is now where the US was fifty or a hundred years ago. Things are less expensive so there are more opportunities . . . Here I can get much higher returns on my investment than in the US, where there is more competition and more information on the market." According to this account, business in Mexico is more profitable not only because the country is less developed (and therefore has more potential for growth) but also because the market is more skewed in terms of information and less carefully regulated than in the United States. From this perspective, US citizenship is seen as a valuable risk-mitigating strategy. Having both nationalities is comparable to holding a diverse investment portfolio that has both high-risk, high-yield stocks and more solid, low-risk stocks. I will discuss this point further in the next section.

While *norteño* elites were mostly uninterested in immigrating to the United States for work, they saw dual nationality as valuable because it facilitated their children's access to education in the United States. In fact, educational opportunities were the main motive that parents cited when asked why they opted for strategic birth. The possession of American nationality made studying there easier in several ways: dual nationals did not have to apply for a student visa and could work during their studies. Those born in Texas were even eligible for reduced in-state tuition in that state.

Some birth-tourist fathers had lived or studied in the United States without citizenship—an experience that left them with a keen sense of the value of nationality. Pedro from Monterrey, who studied for a year in Houston, recalled a tough experience. He was not allowed to work during his studies and had to deal with strict visa rules: "This made the whole issue of studying more difficult, because [US authorities] required proof that I will come back here. . . . I had to keep a large sum of money frozen in my bank account. . . . I don't want my daughter to have to fight [to study in the United States] in the same way that I did."

The concept of dual nationality as a pathway to a US education was part of a broader pattern of admiration for the US educational system. In northern Mexico, having an American or at least an English-language education was an indispensable part of being elite. Some of the most prestigious private schools are bilingual; teenagers from elite Monterrey families often spend a year in the United States or Canada as exchange students or au pairs; and many children in border towns commute every day to schools on the US side of the border. Even as many Americans are anxious about the level of public education—a concern fueled by the unimpressive performance of the country's fifteen-year-olds in the international PISA examinations—Mexico's middle and upper classes maintain a very high opinion of US schools and colleges. In this context, having an American or English-language education was not necessarily an avenue for emigration or a source of greater income; instead, it was first and foremost an enhancer of educational opportunities and an indicator of high social status.

SECURITY

Security is another public good that is included as part of the package of US citizenship. True to Max Weber's definition of the modern state, the United States maintains a very effective monopoly on legitimate violence in its territory. Mexico, in contrast, suffers from endemic criminal and political violence. This violence has worsened in recent years, with the government occasionally losing control over large parts of the country's territory.

The security situation in Mexico deteriorated in 2006, when then-president Felipe Calderon launched an attempt to quench drug smuggling. This led to a frontal confrontation between the state and powerful drug cartels, which for decades were integrated into local institutions of governance. Northern Mexico and the border areas were hit especially hard. In town after town in the north, law and order broke down. Drug-smuggling gangs would wage gun battles on central streets in broad daylight, occasionally skirmishing with the police or the military; decapitated bodies would be left hanging from bridges, often with menacing handwritten notes pinned to their torsos; and residents often became the target of indiscriminate killings, kidnappings, and robberies.

This "insecurity" (*inseguridad*), as it is usually referred to, temporarily pushed many residents away from the affected areas. Youth from other parts of Mexico who were planning to study in Monterrey headed to Guadalajara or Mexico City instead; international visitors and tourists stayed away; affluent *regios* began looking for a way out. Many elite families temporarily moved to San Antonio, Texas; if they did not have dual nationality, they stayed there by obtaining an investor's visa or buying real estate.

Statistics from the American Community Survey (ACS) provide clear evidence of these movements. While the overall number of Mexican immigrants in the United States as a whole remained constant between 2007 and 2014 (at 11.7 million), trends diverged in different parts of the country. Traditional immigrant destinations like Los Angeles and Dallas saw the number of Mexicans shrinking, as a result of mass deportations and return migration to Mexico. At the same time, the number of Mexican-born living in towns and cities along the border with Mexico surged.

The timing of the increase in each border county is synchronized with the onset and decline of mass violence in the Mexican state across the border. For example, the Mexican state of Baja California was hit by insecurity around 2008 and levels of violence declined by 2011; the number of Mexicans in San Diego across the border shot up by 40,000 from 2007 to 2010, then went back down. Violence in the Mexican border states that border Texas peaked after 2010, and the result was a spike in the number of Mexicans living in Texas.[67]

In this context of semicoerced, temporary movement across the US border, dual nationals found themselves in a much better position relative to their mononational neighbors. Not only could they cross the border at will and set themselves up in the United States (for border residents, "immigrating" to the United States may mean moving no more than an hour's drive away), but they could also sponsor their parents, siblings and partners for US residency.[68]

This practice was particularly common in the border towns of the state of Tamaulipas, which were hit hard by drug-related insecurity. Twenty-seven-year-old Guadalupe was born in Brownsville, Texas, grew up in a small Mexican border town, and now resides in Monterrey. Some of her family members recently moved across the border to the United States. She said: "Many people from [my town] moved to Brownsville [around 2011]. My aunt, both of her sons were born in the US. So she moved there ... because of the drug gangs, the gun fights, and the curfews." A similar picture emerges from an interview with a resident of another Tamaulipas border town (the mother of Carmen, the respondent cited in vignette 2): "When the shootings and kidnappings started here," she said, "many people left for the US. . . . Those who had children [in the US] benefited from the possibility to become residents. The others had to immigrate illegally."

Compensatory dual citizenship is often a form of "insurance policy" against some undefined future catastrophe. In Israel, people acquire EU citizenship as insurance in response to general fears about the country's continued existence and prosperity (see chapter 4). In northern Mexico, the catastrophe against which US nationality was meant to insure has actually materialized, and compensatory citizenship has proven its usefulness.

TRAVEL FREEDOM

Many respondents said that a major consideration in deciding to give birth in the United States was the wish to provide their children with greater travel freedom . As Ricardo (vignette 1) said, "We wanted to give [our daughters] more flexibility, so they can move between the territories seamlessly." Many Mexicans from the northeast do not see Texas as a foreign country exactly; not only is it geographically close and topographically similar, but it is also home to many Mexican-origin people and Spanish is widely spoken. Moreover, Texas was part of Mexico until 1836, as reflected in the many Spanish-language place names. Popular shopping and vacation destinations in south Texas like McAllen or San Antonio are experienced by middle-class *regios* as closer than Mexico City or Guadalajara. Against this background, it is easy to understand why *norteños* experienced the border as a somewhat arbitrary check on their movement. Many felt that they were entitled to cross this border freely, and dual nationality guaranteed this freedom of movement.

All dual national respondents held a US passport and most of them have used it every time they entered the United States. Dual nationals reported that they crossed the border with greater ease than Mexican mononationals and faced less questioning. This fact was rarely discussed as a major advantage of US citizenship, only mentioned in passing as a kind of side benefit. The low interest in border crossings can be contrasted to the attitudes of Israelis and Serbs with EU citizenship, who were enthusiastic about owning a "European passport" and were eager to use it when crossing borders. Why is there relatively little enthusiasm about the mobility provided by the US passport in Mexico?

The power of the passport as a marker of nationality becomes most visible at border crossings. Passport control checkpoints are usually designed to demonstrate, even exaggerate, the difference between nationals and foreigners. In most border crossings around the world, foreigners use a separate line which is slower-moving and more unpredictable than the line for nationals.

In the next chapter, I will describe the excitement that EU-Israeli dual citizens experience when they are allowed to use the line for EU-nationals.[69] The same national-foreigner distinction is also experienced by travelers who arrive in US airports.

When entering the United States by land, however—and this is the most common mode of entry for *norteños*—nationality plays a more minor role. In border crossings such as San Diego or McAllen, Americans and foreigners wait in the same line. US citizens have an easier time entering the country, but they share the same line as Mexicans, making their advantage invisible to others and therefore less subjectively significant. At US land borders, access to the privileged, faster-moving lane is not allocated on the basis of nationality; instead, the special lane is reserved to persons of any nationality who signed up for programs like Global Entry and SENTRI. These programs offer a fast and easy crossing, in exchange for providing a great deal of personal information and paying a hefty fee. Through these programs, well-to-do Mexican mononationals can cross the border faster and with greater ease than less affluent US citizens, reflecting a prioritization of class over nationality. For elite Mexicans who hold a visa to the United States, having a US passport does not dramatically change the experience of entering the United States.

When traveling to destinations outside North America—above all, to Europe—dual-national respondents did not exhibit a preference for either of their passports. Since Mexicans may enter EU countries without a visa and are not treated with any special suspicion, the US passport did not provide any concrete advantage there. Some respondents reported that they have used their US passports in Europe but were ashamed of it, admitting that it was an act of "*malinchismo*" (Mexican admiration of foreigners).

Other respondents told stories about their travels whose moral was that people around the world liked Mexicans more than Americans. For example, Bernardo, a twenty-seven-year-old dual national from Nuevo Laredo, said, "When traveling abroad, I use a US passport but I always present myself as Mexican." He went on to tell about a visit to Honduras, when "the customs guy was very hostile at first when he thought I was a *gringo*, but then I spoke to him in Spanish and he started liking me." This statement was typical: other respondents said that they preferred to use their Mexican passports when entering Brazil, France, or Spain, explaining that people in those countries didn't like Americans.

In contrast, respondents said, "nobody has any problem with Mexicans" ("except in the US," one respondent added after a moment's reflection). Such narratives align with a Mexican self-image as a peaceful and globally well-liked nation, which was contrasted with a view of the United States as aggressive, imperialistic, and globally unpopular.[70] On the other hand, numerous dual national respondents said that in case of need while abroad, they would prefer to turn to the US embassy, because the United States was more committed to protecting its citizens.

Overall, travel freedom was not a central consideration of upper-class Mexicans when seeking compensatory citizenship. They accepted the requirement for a visa to enter the United States as natural and did not consider it a humiliation or hindrance; moreover, everyone in their elite social circles typically held a tourist visa so the US passport was not experienced as a major upgrade. As for global travel beyond the United States, the Mexican passport was seen as entirely satisfactory. This stands in contrast to the situation in Israel and Serbia. In those countries, securing extra travel freedom was one of the key incentive to obtain a second, EU passport as a way to avoid being stigmatized when traveling abroad.

Dual Citizenship as Social Closure: Consumer, Not *Migrante*

Mexico is a country of extreme inequality in wealth as well as social status. Moreover, status inequality in Mexico is closely tied up with a cultural characteristic commonly called *malinchismo*: the admiration of anything foreign.[71] Numerous analysts of Mexican society—above all, the famous writer Octavio Paz—identified *malinchismo* as a key feature of the Mexican national psyche and a powerful legacy of colonialism.

Respondents frequently made references to this trait during interviews.[72] Above, I discussed the way *malinchismo* is expressed in the high value that *regios* attached to shopping and consuming in the United States, to US schools and universities, and to the English language. Given those characteristics, one might expect US nationality to become a prominent status symbol among middle-class Mexicans. However, the interviews I conducted provided few indications that this was the case. In everyday life, dual nationals rarely mentioned to others that they were US citizens; and, during interviews, they spoke about their second citizenship with little excitement and usually downplayed its personal importance to them. Clearly, it was not a source of pride.

To understand why US citizenship is not perceived a sign of higher status in Mexico, a key clue is provided by a remark that was repeated by several respondents: "Anybody can get it." The notion that US citizenship is not exclusive enough sounds strange, given the high economic costs involved in cross-border birth. In fact, the exclusiveness implied in this statement is drawn from another system of social stratification: race and origin.

More precisely, it refers to the hierarchical ordering of Mexican society by degree of European ancestry and phenotype. The sociologist Edward Telles has described Latin American countries, including Mexico, as "pigmentocracies."

In those societies, social status is powerfully connected with whiteness.[73] European colonialism, which officially ended two centuries ago, retains an influence on Latin American societies in the form of deeply internalized hierarchies that posit white as prestigious and beautiful, and indigenous or black as inferior.

In the wake of the Mexican Revolution, in the 1920s and 1930, elites attempted to create an alternative national ethos that depicted Mexico as a uniform *mestizo* (mixed-race) nation. Mexicans, according to this view, constitute a unique "cosmic race" that has been created through the union of all human races.[74] On the ground, however, a Eurocentric racial hierarchy continues to have a major impact on Mexican society. This bias is expressed, for example, in the everyday discrimination experienced by dark-skinned and indigenous-looking individuals and in the consistent tendency of Mexican media to cast fair-skinned actors or models for any role that conveys prestige and high status.[75] The preoccupation with whiteness is particularly strong in northern Mexico, where many families claim descent from Spanish or other European settlers.[76]

Given this social context in which European ancestry equals high status, we should not be surprised to find that dual citizenship from any European country is a formidable status symbol: a Spanish, French or German passport provides an undisputable demonstration that one has European ancestry. A recent study on Euro-Mexican dual nationals by Pablo Mateos suggests that Euro-Mexican dual nationals almost all belonged to the upper class. European citizenship was widely perceived as a mark of high status. For example, one of Mateos's Euro-Mexican respondents mentioned a (mononational Mexican) partner that she had dated: "He thought it was great that I was Spaniard, but I felt very uncomfortable that he could see this as attractive not because of the possibility of getting a job and moving to Europe [but simply for] being European, only for having a nationality from the First World."[77]

US citizenship, in contrast to European citizenship, says nothing about the origins of its bearer—European, indigenous, or otherwise. This is the sense in which "anybody can get it." American dual nationality could even have a negative impact on its owner's status because of its association with Mexican immigrants in the United States (*migrantes*) and their children.

Many middle- and upper-class *norteños* hold negative views of Mexican-Americans. *Migrantes* are stereotypically seen as poor, uneducated persons from Mexico's less developed states. It is an image that middle-class individuals wish to distance themselves from. At the same time, there is also widespread condemnation of people of Mexican origin who have become Americanized— including immigrants who settled in the United States permanently, as well as their children who were born there. As David FitzGerald has shown, such individuals are pejoratively described as *pochos* (roughly meaning "rotten") or *gabachos*.⁷⁸ Respondents in the Monterrey area usually referred to Mexican-Americans as *chicanos*, a term that carried connotations of lower-class origins and a *malinchista* mentality.

Some respondents would accuse *chicanos*—especially those employed in border control and the police—of treating Mexicans from Mexico in a discriminatory manner. They attributed this hostility to the resentment that those *chicanos* supposedly inherited from their lower-class immigrant parents. Sometimes, upper-class *norteños* would even point out the "Mexicanness" of *chicanos* in a derogatory (even racist) manner: for example, "He has the cactus on his forehead" (*tiene el nopal en la frente*). The cactus (*nopal*) represents Mexico, and this phrase describes a person who tries to hide his lower-class Mexican origins ("they pretend that they are American") but is given away by his indigenous phenotype.

Considering this view of Mexican Americans, it becomes clear why US nationality did not become a status symbol for middle- and upper-class Mexicans. To put it crudely, from their perspective a Mexican with a European passport is a member of the white elite; a Mexican with a US passport is a *chicano*.

The very act of strategic birth is an ambivalent practice in terms of status and prestige. On the one hand, it is a form of conspicuous consumption that demonstrates that one has substantial economic means and a visa to the United States. Recounting the experience of having given birth in McAllen can be compared to talking about one's last vacation in South Padre Island or shopping trip to San Antonio. On the other hand, strategic birth may symbolically lower one's status because of its apparent similarity to the practices of lower-class *migrantes* who seek to enter the United States and make a living there. In 2011, it was reported that the wife of the notorious drug lord Joaquin Guzman ("El Chapo") traveled to Los Angeles to deliver her daughters there—another illustration of the maxim that "anybody" can get US citizenship, regardless of background or origins.⁷⁹

In response to this ambivalence, many respondents took pains to distance themselves from *migrantes*. One such self-distancing strategy included proclaiming their commitment to and love of Mexico, and avowing lack of interest in the United States. Indeed, dual nationals who have acquired their American nationality through strategic birth never presented themselves as American or Mexican-American. Instead, they saw themselves as Mexicans who also had American nationality. This self-presentation strongly resembled that of EU-Israeli dual citizens, who usually described themselves as "100 percent Israeli" that happened to carry a "European passport."⁸⁰ Dual nationals in Mexico typically exhibited little interest in the political aspects of American citizenship. None of the respondents I interviewed had voted in American elections from Mexico.⁸¹

Another distancing strategy came up when discussing the future uses of citizenship: elite *regio* parents emphasized that they only wanted to give their children opportunities to study in the United States, while dismissing the possibility that they would work or settle there. Respondents also made it clear that they had paid for the births themselves and that they regularly spent money on shopping and vacations in the United States. In other words, the bid for US citizenship as an act of consumption that will facilitate additional acts of consumption, rather than an attempt to secure benefits from the US government.

Roberto, an entrepreneur from Monterrey whose wife has given birth in the United States, said: "[My family and I] contribute a lot to the US economically. We travel there, shop there and engage in tourism. . . . And in the final count, we don't use any of the benefits of US citizenship. We don't use the infrastructure, don't saturate the roads or the health system." Pedro, another respondent whose wife gave birth in the United States, stressed that he was very different from lower-class immigrants who sought welfare benefits: "In general, the Mexican [immigrant] in the US works lot and does difficult jobs. . . . [But] some people are nothing but parasites. If you don't contribute then you don't have the right to demand anything." This statement intends to distance the speaker from "parasites" who do not contribute, and to place his family's citizenship strategy within a legitimizing framework.

These responses hint at the hierarchy of worth that is associated with different types of economic transactions, and on the place of the United States within the moral universe of *norteños*. The complicated moral meaning of ties to the United States reflects more generally Mexicans' ambivalent relation to the neighbor from the north. On the one hand, the United States is seen as the bully that has invaded Mexico, conquered its capital city, and took away half the national territory. The rhetoric and actions of President Trump act as a continuous provocation and remind many of Mexicans of their country's many humiliations at the hands of the United States. On the other hand, many Mexicans are attracted to the "American Dream"—this term came up in many interviews, and was always said in English—and seek to emulate American lifestyle and culture. The affinity with the United States is particularly strong in northern Mexico, which is a border region in the cultural as well as the political sense.

The relation to American nationality among middle- and upper-class respondents mirrors this ambivalence: it may ennoble or degrade, and sometimes seems to be doing both at the same time. Having American nationality may signal high class and privilege, but it can also indicate that one is the *pocho* son or daughter of a lower-class *migrante*. Spending money in the United States on shopping and tourism is a mark of high status; working there is not particularly prestigious, and receiving money as welfare is degrading.[82]

Conclusions

In this chapter, I explored the growing phenomenon of strategic cross-border births practiced by middle- and upper-class families in northern Mexico. Paradoxically, those individuals and families who possess the resources and the motivation to practice cross-border birth often have the least incentive to emigrate to the United States. They perceive US nationality as an insurance policy and an opportunity enhancer (especially for education), and have little interest in the traditional contents of citizenship, such as residing in the United States, or voting.

The growth of strategic birth represents a new patterns of transnational interaction between Mexico and the United States. The massive immigration flow that started in the 1980s settled down in 2007–2008. The post–mass-immigration age will presumably be marked by a greater overlap in the countries' citizenries and by more short-term and short-distance mobility. These changes will be driven by the presence of large numbers of US dual nationals in Mexico—elite beneficiaries of cross-border births as well as the US-born children of returnees and deportees. Future studies should go beyond the traditional focus on Mexican labor migration and examine transnational dynamics of consumption, mobility and class formation.[83]

Second, this study of strategic US dual citizens highlights a population of growing importance: American citizens who live outside the United States. The number of US citizens abroad has more than doubled over fifteen years: from 3.8 million in 1999 to about 8 million in 2015.[84] Studies of Americans abroad have focused on "classic" expatriates who grew up in the United States before emigrating and have a strong national identity as Americans.[85] However, there are strong grounds to assume that many nonresident US citizens—living in Mexico, China, the Philippines, and elsewhere—are dual nationals who have much stronger ties to their countries of residence. They include the US-born children of return migrants and deportees, as well as beneficiaries of strategic birth in the United States. While some preliminary studies have begun to examine these "accidental" or strategic Americans, there is still much to be learned about the novel ways in which these individuals understand and use their US citizenship.[86]

4

Israel

EUROPEAN PASSPORTS AS INSURANCE AND RESTITUTION

The expansion of the European Union, coupled with member countries' citizenship outreach policies, have created new opportunities for people outside the Union's territory. In chapter 2, I explored the dynamics of cross-border EU citizenship in Serbia. The pull of the EU, however, extends far beyond the European continent. In middle-tier countries that have historically received immigration from Europe, the children and grandchildren of those immigrants are now drawing on their ancestry to acquire dual citizenship. Hundreds of thousands of Argentineans and Brazilians obtain Italian citizenship, Cubans and Venezuelans secure Spanish citizenship, and many Israelis acquire citizenship from their countries of origin in Central and Eastern Europe (CEE), such as Germany, Poland, Hungary and Romania.[1]

In this chapter, I analyze EU-Israeli dual citizenship as a case of compensatory citizenship that is produced on the basis of ancestry. This case has a special place within the book's comparative framework. Israel's high income level and low emigration rate set it apart from Serbia and Mexico and make dual citizenship less obviously useful. Many Serbians dream of immigrating to Western Europe, and many *norteños* are closely tied to the United States. Israelis may visit Europe frequently as tourists, but there is very little Israeli immigration to the EU.

Moreover, European-origin Israelis are hardly nostalgic about the countries where their families have been persecuted and murdered. Several Israeli politicians and intellectuals have condemned the quest for German and Polish citizenship as a disgrace for Holocaust survivor families and an affront to Zionist ideals.[2] Israelis, these critics argue, should have neither a practical nor a sentimental reason to seek EU citizenship. And yet they do so—and in large numbers.

In this chapter, I argue that the motives that drive Israelis of European origin (or *Ashkenazim*) to acquire dual citizenship are thoroughly embedded in culturally specific, noneconomic logics of action. Many applicants acquire dual citizenship as an "insurance policy" in case Israel is destroyed. This reflects an attitude toward citizenship that is conditioned by a Jewish family habitus—a set of behavioral dispositions and value orientations, in the terms of Pierre Bourdieu—that was shaped by centuries of diasporic existence as an ethnic minority. Another important motivation to obtain an EU passport is that it is perceived as a "cool" thing to have, talk about, and show at border crossings. For many younger Israelis of European origin, the EU passport also serves as a status symbol.

The particularity of this case is also reflected in the way Israelis speak about the phenomenon. The term "dual citizenship" and the name of the granting country are almost never used. Instead, Israeli dual citizens say that they have obtained a "European passport." This phrasing tiptoes around the provocative term "dual citizen" while also minimizing the connection to origin countries like Germany and Poland, whose name usually evoke negative associations in Israel. Instead, the focus is on Europe—with the global prestige that goes with that name—while citizenship is reduced to the physical object of the passport.

Citizenship from CEE countries is just one of multiple types of dual citizenship in Israel. Nearly a quarter-million Israelis hold dual citizenship from the United States, and many are dual citizens of Russia (see methodological appendix). In 2015, Spain and Portugal passed laws that offer citizenship to the descendants of Jews who were expelled by Spanish and Portuguese kings at the end of the fifteenth century (called Sepharadim). This move expanded potential eligibility for EU citizenship to all Jews who have roots in the Balkans, North Africa, and the Levant—about 2.5 to 3.5 million persons in Israel alone. As of late 2018, about 10,000 persons have already acquired Spanish and Portuguese citizenship, but only about 2,000 of them were Israeli: many applicants hailed from Jewish communities in Turkey, Venezuela, Argentina and elsewhere.[3] The eligibility criteria are essentially ethnic: applicants must prove their membership in the Sepharadic community rather than direct descent from a former citizen (it cannot be otherwise, given that the loss of citizenship took place more than five centuries ago).[4] Here, I focus on the more longstanding and common phenomenon of EU citizenship acquired on the basis of descent from CEE immigrants.

Legal and Historical Background

The emergence of EU-Israeli dual citizenship reflects deep geopolitical and societal changes in both CEE countries and Israel. Like Hungarian dual citizenship in Serbia, EU-Israeli dual citizenship became possible and attractive thanks to the legal acceptance of dual citizenship and the admission of post-communist CEE countries to the EU. At the same time, the phenomenon also reflects changes in Israeli society—above all, a generational shift that has created a new understanding of national identity.

Today, seven decades after the Nazi destruction of European Jews, Jewish presence in Central and Eastern Europe is negligible. Across most of the region, all that remain are old synagogues and abandoned graveyards. Historically, however, the region was home to the majority of the world's Jews for centuries, from the late middle ages up until the Holocaust.[5] Ashkenazi Jews from Central and Eastern Europe provided a large share of the immigrants who came to Israel. Between 1920 and 1970, about one million European Jews arrived in Israel (before 1948, the Mandate of Palestine). Most of them came from Poland, Romania, and Germany.[6]

Today, those immigrants (*Olim* in Hebrew) and their descendants number an estimated 2 to 2.5 million persons and form roughly a third of Israel's Jewish population.[7] Ashkenazi Jews are Israel's most advantaged group, enjoying higher socioeconomic status and symbolic prestige compared to Jews of Middle Eastern or Russian-speaking origins, not to mention the country's discriminated Arab minority. To date, all of Israel's prime ministers and all but two of its presidents were Ashkenazi.[8]

Most Ashkenazim in Israel descend from immigrants who arrived shortly before or soon after World War II. They came as refugees and have lost most of their families—and whatever property they had—in the Holocaust. In some CEE countries, including Poland, Hungary, and Romania, anti-Jewish policies and actions began long before the Nazi occupation and continued into the postwar years.[9] Jews were never accepted as full members of those nations, even when they were formally citizens. This defines a key difference between EU-Israeli dual citizens and other cases of ancestry-based citizenship acquisition. When Italian descendants in Argentina apply for dual citizenship, they are also reconnecting with their ethnic roots.[10] EU-Israeli dual citizens, in contrast, typically have no ethnic or national identification with their countries of origin.

How did dual citizenship become available in this case? Israel has always permitted toward dual citizenship. It is explicitly permitted in the country's citizenship law, which was passed in 1952 and has undergone only minor revisions since then.[11] The main logic driving this tolerant attitude is ethnonational. As Patrick Weil has argued, Israeli law is premised on a legal construction whereby

Jewish immigrants (*Olim*) are defined as returning emigrants and thus *already* members of the nation.[12]

This conception lies at the root of Israel's 1950 Law of Return, which offers automatic citizenship to Jewish immigrants without imposing any of the requirements that are associated with immigrant naturalization. The toleration of dual citizenship is aimed to encourage *Olim* to become Israeli while allowing them to keep their former nationality.[13] In the early 1950s, when Israel's citizenship regime was taking shape, the right to dual citizenship was irrelevant for the majority of Israelis, who arrived stateless from Eastern Europe or the Middle East. The tolerant policy was mainly intended to attract Jews from Western Europe and North America. Dual citizenship, which was originally designed as an exception for elite immigrants, is now common among native-born Israelis.

In CEE countries, in contrast, the acceptance of dual citizenship is a new development that dates from the 1990s (see introduction). The newly permissive citizenship laws in CEE countries were not designed to facilitate the integration of immigrants, for the simple reason that these countries (except Germany) receive very little immigration. Instead, they were primarily aimed to facilitate the inclusion of descendants of emigrants and coethnics living abroad.

All countries in Europe allow the transmission of citizenship *jure sanguinis* to the children of citizens born abroad. Moreover, most European countries now permit the descendants of emigrants to reacquire dual citizenship from abroad even if they had not received it at birth.[14] What makes the citizenship policy of many post-communist CEE countries remarkable is its restitutive function.

Dual citizenship laws in Central and Eastern Europe are a mechanism of restitution in the sense that they reclaim for the nation these territories and populations that had been lost through war. This is the logic that guides the Hungarian policy that was discussed in chapter 2, and the dual citizenship policies of other countries including Romania, Bulgaria, and Croatia. Some countries' citizenship laws also seek to reverse the emigration of conationals during communism. In the nationalist historical narratives now accepted in most CEE countries, the communist period was a time of antinational repression that pushed countless patriots to emigrate to the West. The offer of dual citizenship is an invitation to those émigrés and their descendants to rejoin the nation.

Even when these individuals do not immigrate back to their ethnic homelands (and this is usually the case), the citizen diaspora is still valuable as a source of foreign investment, a political lobby, and a symbol of the nation's perseverance. In the words of Constantin Iordachi, "In Central and Eastern Europe . . . dual citizenship has not served as a way of integrating alien residents, but mostly as a way of reconstructing the national 'imagined communities.' "[15]

Jews were never members of those imagined national communities, and the laws offering citizenship restitution are not aimed at them. Therefore, Israelis who obtain EU dual citizenship are accidental beneficiaries of policies that are actually aimed at reinforcing ethnonationalism. This is ironic because ethnic nationalism in countries like Poland, Hungary and Romania was—and often still is—marked by strong anti-Jewish sentiments.

The case is different for Germany, where there is an explicit and deliberate policy of restitution for Jews. The German Basic Law from 1949 decrees the return of German citizenship to those who have lost it due to Nazi persecution, and to their descendants. Israelis have had the possibility of regaining German citizenship since 1965, when the two countries established diplomatic relations.[16] In recent years, additional CEE countries began to enact a deliberate policy of citizenship restitution vis-à-vis their Jewish former citizens—most notably, Poland.[17]

The growth of EU-Israeli dual citizenship, then, is mostly an unintended consequence of citizenship policies that are aimed to achieve very different aims. The rise of aggressive ethnic nationalisms in the 1920s and 1930s has led to the destruction of European Jewry and made Israel into a haven for Jewish refugees. In the 1990s, however, the children and grandchildren of those refugees became eligible for dual citizenship from the countries that their families had escaped decades before. After 2000, with the expansion of the EU, such citizenship also became useful and desirable. This development is ironic in a double sense. First, the descendants of Jews who narrowly escaped destruction in Europe are now looking back to their origin countries for protection. Second, Israelis are now acquiring citizenship on the basis of laws that were not intended for them, and that draw on the same ethnonationalist ideas that previously justified their exclusion.

EU-Israeli Dual Citizenship by the Numbers

The number of EU dual citizens in Israel has increased dramatically over the past two decades. As of 2015, it can be estimated at about 380,000 (including British and Swiss), or almost 5 percent of Israel's population.[18] Out of this total, approximately 200,000 Israelis held dual citizenship from countries in Central and Eastern Europe: 125,000 from Germany and another 75,000 from Poland, Romania, Hungary, Bulgaria, the Czech Republic, and Austria. Based on an estimate of 2 to 2.5 million Israelis of CEE origin, between 8 and 10 percent of the potentially eligible population have acquired EU citizenship.

Dual citizenship in itself is not new in Israel, and there have always been some Israelis with dual citizenship from the United States or other Western countries. However, citizenship from CEE countries other than Germany is a new phenomenon. Data that I have collected from embassy records and various administrative sources show that before the year 2000, there was practically no demand for citizenship from Poland, Romania, Bulgaria, and Hungary. Between 2000 to 2017, over 85,000 Israelis have acquired EU citizenship from

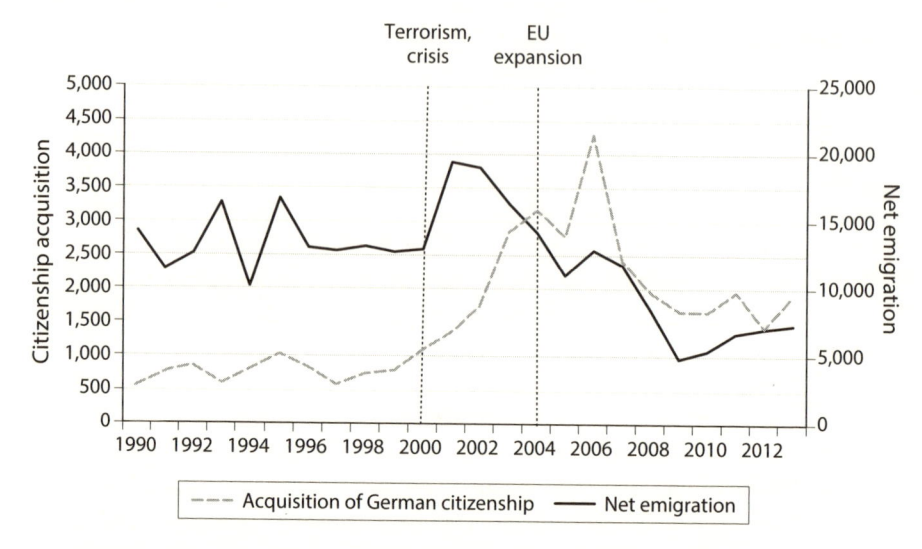

FIGURE 4.1. Acquisition of German citizenship and emigration from Israel, 1990–2015
Note: The dashed grey line represents acquisition of German citizenship by Israelis and refers to the axis on the left. The solid black line represents net emigration from Israel and refers to the axis on the right.
Sources: Data received upon request from German Statistical Office; data from Israel's Central Bureau of Statistics (CBS).

Germany, Poland, Bulgaria, the Czech Republic, Romania, Hungary, Greece, and Austria. This includes 33,321 acquisitions of German citizenship, about 28,000 acquisitions of Polish citizenship, and between 3,000 and 6,000 citizenship acquisitions in each of the following countries: Romania, Bulgaria, Greece, Hungary, Austria, and the Czech Republic.[19]

The timing of citizenship applications shows that the citizenship of postcommunist Eastern European countries only became attractive to Israelis once these countries were on their way to join the EU.[20] This is consistent with the compensatory citizenship approach: conscious of the value of actual and potential citizenships, eligible individuals only file applications when they stand to gain a higher-tier passport. There are, however, other logics at work beside instrumentality. In order to learn more about the forces that drive citizenship acquisition, I will analyze data from the only granting country that has made detailed statistics available: Germany. Figure 4.1 displays statistics on the acquisition of German citizenship between 1990 and 2015, alongside figures on emigration from Israel.

The graph shows that levels of German citizenship acquisition (the dotted gray line) were relatively low during the 1990s, punctuated by minor spikes in 1992 and 1995. In 2001–2, acquisition begins to increase dramatically, alongside a temporary increase in emigration from Israel. After a peak in 2006, citizenship acquisition settled down to a level that is almost double the level in the 1990s. Net emigration was relatively high during the 1990s, spiked in 2001–2, then gradually declined. The graph allows us to analyze the connection between citizenship acquisition and (1) the security situation in Israel, (2) EU expansion, and (3) emigration. I will discuss these elements in order.

First, the spikes in citizenship acquisition in 1992 and 1995 most likely express Israelis' response to security events: Iraqi missile attacks in 1991 and Palestinian suicide bombings in 1993–95 (the delay is explained by the processing time of applications, which is at least 6 to 12 months). Likewise, the dramatic increase after 2000 is partly explained by the wave of terrorist attacks that began that year and went on until 2003. In interviews with consular officers and citizenship lawyers, they repeatedly mentioned that security-related events—the Palestinian suicide bombing campaign in 2000–2002 and the conflicts with Hezbollah and Hamas in 2006, 2008, and 2014—led to spikes in citizenship applications.

I corroborated this point through a separate analysis of statistics that I obtained from a citizenship lawyer on the number of phone inquiries about German citizenship received by his office. Phone inquiries provide a more direct indicator of raw demand than acquisitions, because there is no processing delay. That analysis showed that between 2008 and 2014, interest in citizenship was strongly correlated with the number of Israeli casualties of war and terrorism. In years with more casualties, more people inquired about German citizenship.[21] This shows that security concerns are one of the key forces that drives demand for dual citizenship.

The second factor is the expansion of the EU, which affected citizenship acquisition both directly and indirectly. The direct effect has to do with the citizenship of CEE countries beside Germany, including Poland, Romania, and others. Israeli demand for citizenship in those countries only appeared when they were about to join the EU. Indeed, the statistics show that the acquisition of Polish citizenship began to increase in the years leading up to 2004—the year that the country joined the EU. Demand for citizenship from Romania and Bulgaria, which became EU members in 2007, started increasing one to two years before their accession.

Beside the direct influence of EU expansion, which made citizenship from Poland or Romania attractive overnight, it also had an indirect effect on German citizenship. Germany has been a member of the EU from its very beginnings, and the practical value of its citizenship did not increase in 2004–6, the years when acquisition reached its peak (see figure 4.1). This suggests that one of the factors driving the popularity of German citizenship has been destigmatization. As ever more Israelis acquired citizenship from countries like Poland or Hungary, it became increasingly legitimate and socially acceptable to have a "European passport"; this effect spilled over into the most controversial and provocative citizenship.

German citizenship has been available to Israelis since 1965, when the two countries established diplomatic relations. For a long time, however, it was seen as an "abomination," and Israelis who took it were subjected to harsh criticism.[22] Until the 1980s, many Israelis boycotted German products on principle.[23] Against this background, EU integration increased the legitimacy of German citizenship by minimizing its association with Germany. In contrast to the idea that individuals seek dual citizenship because it is associated with a particular nationality or ethnicity, in the Israeli case, German citizenship became desirable precisely because it had been disassociated from a specific national identity. It changed from "abominable" German citizenship into a prestigious European passport. This demonstrates the key role that conceptions of honor and shame play in shaping demand for dual citizenship.

The third aspect connected with EU citizenship is emigration. Did citizenship uptake lead to an increase in emigration, as was seen in the Serbian case? The figure shows that it did not. The proliferation of EU citizenship did not lead to an increase in emigration. The spike in emigration in 2001–2 was a response to the security situation in addition to an economic downturn in Israel. Since 2003, emigration levels went down in spite of the greater ease of emigrating with the help of the EU passport. In fact, the rate of emigration from Israel is now significantly lower than it was in the 1990s or the early 2000s, when far fewer Israelis had dual citizenship.[24]

In general, Israel is not an major emigration-sending country (only about 4 percent of the persons who were born in Israel now live in other OECD countries, compared with 9 to 12 percent for Serbia or Mexico).[25] While the emigration rate has declined, there is some evidence that a slightly larger proportion of Israeli emigrants head to Europe. There has been a modest growth in the number of Israelis who emigrated to EU countries in the period between 2000 and 2015 relative to the period between 1990 and 2000.[26] Some Israeli immigrants in Europe settled in a new destination: Germany, and especially Berlin. I will discuss this interesting development later in this chapter.

Acquiring EU Citizenship

The proliferation of EU citizenship has attracted a great deal of attention in Israeli society. This is no surprise, given that the phenomenon opens up provocative questions about identity and history. It also leads families to engage in a collective effort to uncover documents from past lives and provides a new set of global resources and opportunities. In the following sections, I discuss the everyday consequences of EU dual citizenship in Israel.

Below, I will present two short vignettes to illustrate the life circumstances and motivations of Israelis who seek EU dual citizenship. Then, I will discuss the citizenship industry that emerged in Israel and the dynamics of family cooperation. Next, I will describe how Israelis use EU citizenship to secure opportunities, security, and travel freedom. Finally, I will analyze dual citizenship as an instrument of social closure, exploring its place within the Israeli system of ethnic and class stratification.

Vignette 1: Shiri, 37, German-Israeli dual citizen, lives in Tel-Aviv

Shiri was born in Tel-Aviv to parents who were also born in Israel. Three of her grandparents were born in Poland and one grandfather was born in Berlin. In 1992, her grandfather applied for German citizenship. "Back then, it was mainly about [getting back] the property and less about the citizenship—we had several buildings and a factory in East Berlin," she said. Soon afterward, Shiri's mother took her to get her first German passport. "I realized that there was some conflict around it because my aunt said to my mother: 'Why would you take a Nazi passport?'"

At twenty-one, after completing her military service, Shiri moved to Europe and lived there for eight years. She studied cooking in Paris and completed a master's degree in European Studies at Maastricht. When living in Europe, she discovered that her German citizenship gave her extensive rights, including reduced tuition fees, a work permit, and health insurance. She became friends with many Germans there ("I feel close to them in my mentality because my grandfather was very German"). At the same time, she said she was often treated like a token Jew. "Once, on a class trip, we visited [the Nazi concentration camp] Theresienstadt. There I really felt like a monkey in the safari. All the Germans wanted to have their picture taken with me."

Shiri returned to Israel in 2007 and now works at organizing collaborative projects between the EU and Israeli municipalities. "Living in Europe has not made me more European or more German but it has made me less Israeli. . . . My biggest insight from this sojourn abroad is that we [Israelis] are not the best or the most beautiful or the most just. . . . I want to be cosmopolitan, to keep away from any kind of nationalism."

When traveling abroad, Shiri uses her German passport exclusively. She is married and has a young son, whom she registered as a German citizen when he was two months old. "As an Ashkenazi Jew, you always feel persecuted and you want to know that you have other options."

About her right to German citizenship, she said, "Well, my grandfather was German so if there had been no Holocaust, I would have been German. But if anyone asked me to justify [my citizenship], I wouldn't justify. It just happened. Karma. . . . It's like winning the Green Card lottery. I won a Green Card to Europe and I am very grateful for it. It's tragic that it's involved in the complex history of Ashkenazi Jews, but that's how things turned out."

Vignette 2: Nadav, 31, eligible for Hungarian and Spanish citizenship, lives in Tel-Aviv

Nadav was born in a village near Tel-Aviv to parents who were born in Israel. His father's parents were born in Austro-Hungarian territories that now belong to Poland and Slovakia, and his mother's parents were Sepharadic Jews from Turkey and Greece. After completing his undergraduate studies in Israel, he completed a graduate degree in government at an elite US university. At the time of the interview, he was working at a research institute in Tel-Aviv. "I started [my quest for EU citizenship] at the Polish embassy. But I discovered that my grandfather was briefly drafted to the IDF in 1948 so I was ineligible. . . . Then, I tried the Czechoslovak side but [my grandfather's town in Silesia] changed hands several times and now it's not part of the Czech Republic. So that didn't work either. I also contacted the Turks and the Greeks but nothing came out of that."[27]

Nadav temporarily gave up on his dream of a second citizenship, until two years ago, when new opportunities surfaced: "In 2013, my sister discovered that we might be eligible for Hungarian citizenship. It would cost us 10,000 shekels ($2,800) and I would need to study Hungarian—but only to a basic level. . . . So I bought some books from Berlitz and at some point I will sit down and learn Hungarian." Several months before the interview, he discovered he could get another, more attractive citizenship: "My mom read in the newspaper that Spain was giving out citizenship and her parents' last names are on the list of Sepharadic names. . . . She was initially against the dual citizenship thing but now that it's Spain she got excited."

The main reason that Nadav is interested in dual citizenship is "freedom of movement. . . . [With another passport] I can go to Jordan and from there, theoretically, anywhere I want. [I will be able to] go to Indonesia, Malaysia, Dubai . . . United States without a visa. Freedom." He added, "There is this global elite that is very mobile. And you can't get into it unless you're in that small group of Israelis who have two passports.... Having another passport, together with my connections from the time I spent in the US—that would open up many opportunities for me".

Dual citizenship, he said, is also a form of insurance: "For my [future] kids, so they have more options. If [Israel] stops being prosperous or becomes insecure for any reason, they can leave." A final motivation was that "with another passport, you tell a story [about yourself] that's more complex and unique.... It's like some cool gadget that you install in your car and you can tell people about."

Nadav defines his identity as exclusively Israeli. He does not feel connected to any of the countries from which he tried to obtain citizenship ("except maybe Greece, because of the food my grandmother used to make"). Furthermore, he says, "the passport I would have really liked to have is American. Europe is not attractive for me. But I'll take whatever I can get."

Citizenship Industry: Capitalizing on European Ancestry

Eligibility for EU citizenship is determined on the basis of a single criterion: descent from a citizen.[28] Applicants are not officially required to demonstrate language skills or any other kind of affinity with the granting country.[29] Ancestry, in this case, can be described as genealogical capital. Once applicants have established the citizenship of the original European-born immigrant, eligibility for citizenship flows down to his or her descendants, thanks to the *jus sanguinis* laws of CEE granting countries, most of whom set no generational stopping point for citizenship transmission.[30] Therefore, the key to EU citizenship is locating the documentation that provides proof of the original immigrant's citizenship.

In chapter 2, I described the ease with which applicants in Vojvodina established their ancestors' Hungarian nationality: this requires nothing more than a trip to the nearby town where they could find the relevant records written in Serbian or Hungarian. Israeli citizenship applicants are in a very different situation. Most of them have never visited their country of origin and cannot speak its language. The typical immigrant grandparent has left his or her origin country fifty, sixty, or seventy years ago and has never visited it since. Moreover, many immigrants were sole survivors from families and communities that were wiped out and many have spent long years in Nazi concentration camps and then in resettlement camps for displaced persons. Jewish life throughout Central and Eastern Europe was extinguished in the Holocaust, meaning that no local communities remained there. In many cases, the Nazis destroyed the official records of Jews, seeking to wipe out the bureaucratic persona alongside the physical person.[31] In other cases, records were destroyed in the context of wartime chaos. Therefore, obtaining proof of the original citizenship is often a major challenge.

The first step in the quest for citizenship is digging up decades-old documents in the original citizen's home. A surprising range of documents may provide the required proof, including passports, travel permits, identity cards, birth certificates, or even a high-school diploma from the European country of origin. In many cases, however, this search does not produce anything. When applicants cannot locate a document that testifies to the immigrant's citizenship, their families must somehow reconstruct the grandparents' "paper trail" in their origin country and locate some documentary evidence of their past lives there. Often, they have only vague family anecdotes to guide them.

At this point, many families turn to citizenship specialists, who facilitate applications by locating necessary documents and pushing applications through the bureaucratic pipeline. Whereas demand for American-Mexican dual nationality produced an industry of cross-border births and Hungarian-Serbian dual citizenship created an industry of foreign language instruction, in Israel the availability of EU ancestry-based citizenship gave rise to an industry of experts who specialize in navigating through the bureaucracies of CEE countries. This industry has grown rapidly after the year 2000, to the point that there are now dozens of lawyers, translators, and *machers* (Yiddish for "fixers," who cut through red tape).

What kind of expertise do these citizenship specialists sell? The first and most important asset is knowledge: they are proficient in the relevant country's language, familiar with its citizenship laws, and they possess bureaucratic contacts and know-how. Every lawyer or *macher* specializes in one or two countries, usually based on their origins (e.g., Romanian-origin lawyers specialize in Romanian citizenship).

A second and less obvious way in which specialists make applications accessible to Israelis goes beyond resolving bureaucratic and linguistic difficulties. It has to do with the moral or normative aspect of dual citizenship. Citizenship specialists are agents of destigmatization, who play a key role in constructing EU dual citizenship as a legitimate commodity, one that is "good to think." They do this by informing Israelis about their eligibility for citizenship and by serving as intermediaries who buffer applicants from direct contact with their would-be countries of citizenship.

First, citizenship lawyers contributed to the dramatic increase in the public awareness about the possibility of applying. In 2001, Israeli bar regulations changed to allow lawyers to advertise their services. Citizenship services proved ideal for advertisement, and soon there were many newspaper advertisements inviting eligible Israelis to reclaim German, Austrian, or Polish citizenship. Up to that point, most eligible Israelis had no idea that they could become citizens of CEE countries. The appearance of advertisements led to an increase in awareness that led to an increase in demand, and that in turn led to a further increase in public awareness, as the media took up the subject.[32]

Today, the vast majority of European-origin Israelis are aware of their potential eligibility for citizenship. In this process, biographical trivia—a grandmother from Łódź in Poland; a father born in Cluj, Romania—turned overnight into a valuable resource. It is interesting to compare this to the situation in Serbia, where the main actor that spreads information about eligibility for citizenship is the Hungarian government itself. Whereas demand for Hungarian citizenship is promoted through top-down campaigns by a vote-seeking government, in Israel it is a bottom-up marketing effort by profit-seeking individual entrepreneurs—in other words, a business.

Second, citizenship specialists act as buffers between applicants and the countries from which they seek citizenship. They insulate applicants from the negative associations and traumas that are associated with their origin country, and from feelings of shame and discomfort. The fieldwork I conducted at embassies suggested that many applicants felt extremely uncomfortable when interacting with officials from "their" European country. Officials typically insisted that applicants use only the national language (e.g., Polish or Hungarian) and refused to speak English. This created a stressful situation, as second-generation applicants typically spoke the language poorly and first-generation immigrants associated it with painful memories. Furthermore, consular officials often displayed a hostile and uncooperative attitude and the embassies themselves—especially the Romanian and Polish—were experienced as disorderly and chaotic spaces, creating an experience of bureaucratic humiliation.[33]

Many applicants instinctively linked this unwelcoming treatment to the experiences of persecution that they or their parents experienced in Europe, and to anti-Jewish prejudice. The following episode took place outside the Polish embassy during an observation session:

> Ruth, a Polish-born Israeli woman in her seventies, was waiting outside the Polish embassy, which was scheduled to open in ten minutes. She told me that she had come to apply for the sake of her grandchildren. It started raining, and she asked the security guards to allow her to enter the embassy for shelter before the official opening time. After the security guards refused to let her in, she came back looking shocked and said: "They told me 'Out!' They dared to tell me 'Out!' They did not change one bit. They just want to humiliate us." She then walked away from the embassy in anger.

The extreme sensitivity expressed in this vignette reveals the deep trauma that many Israeli Holocaust survivors carry, and which is also shared by many second-generation and even third-generation applicants. Thus, many people find the procedure of citizenship application too painful or humiliating even when they have all the documents. Citizenship specialists handle most of the required embassy visits for their clients, thereby greatly reducing the emotional cost of application, and the sense that this is something other than the purchase of a good.

There were many indications of this commodified approach to citizenship. Applicants often used terms that explicitly compared citizenship acquisition to investment. For example, Ya'akov, a fifty-eight-year-old Romanian-born Israeli who applied for Romanian citizenship for himself and his daughter, explained: "[The European passport] is like a luxury article that you buy, a fine watch or a laptop computer. You will not use all of its features. Possibly, you will never use more than five or ten percent of its capacities. But you are willing to pay extra for the potential." In this description, national membership is translated into the language of market consumption. EU citizenship is a "luxury article"; it is "bought" rather than acquired on the basis of origin and identity. This citizenship-reimagined-as-product does not confer rights (let alone impose duties); instead, it has "features" and "capacities." In a similar vein, Nadav in vignette 2 compares EU citizenship to a high-tech gadget and admits that he would have preferred US citizenship, but "I'll take whatever I can get." In those discourses, citizenship is envisioned as a form of private property. It obeys the logic of instrumental rationality: it is a means to an end (and therefore interchangeable) rather than an end in itself.

Another variant of the property discourse revolves around restitution. Many respondents argued that their parents' or grandparents' citizenship was a piece of family property that was illegally taken away, and that they had a natural right to demand its return.[34] Respondents often appealed to their right to restitution and historical justice when justifying their right for citizenship. Sharon, twenty-nine, a German-Israeli dual citizen, said: "My great-grandfather was from a bourgeois family that owned a big department store [in Germany]. Everything was taken away from them. They came [to Israel] and started everything anew and never received any compensation. So there is no reason why there shouldn't be some indirect restitution to their descendants." Another respondent, Shoshana, a second-generation Hungarian-Israeli, said: "We are not asking for any favors—we just want what is ours."

Such conceptions are understandable when considering the losses of life and property suffered by Israeli Jewish families in the Holocaust. But there is also a hint of irony: until recently, when lawyers and the media began informing Israelis that they could acquire citizenship, most applicants had no idea that they possessed such a right.

The material from the interviews suggests a strong tendency among Israeli applicants to conceive of citizenship in economic terms: many of them spoke of their EU citizenship as an investment or a product, something that they received as restitution and passed on as gift. At the same time, we must stress that applicants did not view citizenship acquisition as a purely economic transaction. Instead, it was an economic exchange that was mixed up with moral and emotional values: love, commitment, nostalgia, and a sense of vindication, but also discomfort and shame.

Many dual citizens felt that citizenship restitution offered late justice to their persecuted parents and grandparents, and, moreover, it displayed love and commitment vis-à-vis their children and siblings. Acquisition of ancestry-based citizenship was never a straightforward purchase of the kind offered by citizenship-by-investment programs. Instead, it was a complex act of appropriation that does not conform to any one category of exchange. An application might be initiated for economic motives, but it proceeds as a legal claim for restitution and is justified on the basis of family history.

Family Dynamics

The decision to apply for EU citizenship always involves a whole circle of relatives: not just the immigrant parent or grandparent (if they are alive), but also the children of citizenship applicants, their siblings, and often their spouses. The opportunities provided by EU citizenship are mainly relevant to the younger generation. And, indeed, it is often young people in their twenties and thirties who typically initiate applications after learning about that possibility from their friends or from the media. In other cases, second-generation parents initiate the application in order to improve their children's life prospects. Citizenship lawyers report that an average application "produces" three to five citizens from two or three generations. Applying for a European passport is a family project governed—at least in part—by family logic.

Before going further, I will briefly clarify the generational structure of the Ashkenazi family in Israel, as it was understood by respondents and broader society. Israelis typically refer to a trigenerational family structure. The "first generation" includes individuals who were born in Europe around the years 1910–1930 and immigrated between the 1920s and 1960s. The "second generation," or the parent generation, were born between 1940 and 1960, most of them in Israel and some in Europe. The Ashkenazi "third generation" were born in Israel between 1970 and 1990. At first sight, these terms appear similar to those used in other immigration countries (as in "second-generation immigrants"). In fact, the generational count does not refer to immigration to Israel; instead, the "zero hour" they refer to is the Holocaust. It appears that this entire generational structure is extrapolated from the expression "second generation to the Holocaust," (*Dor Sheni LaShoah*) which originated in the psychotherapeutic discourse about the transmission of trauma.[35]

Most applications followed a typical generational division of labor: first-generation immigrant grandparents provide the basis for eligibility, but (being dead or very old) take no part in the application; and third-generation grandchildren often initiate the procedure, but do not actively contribute to it. The parent generation, in their fifties and sixties, are the ones who carry out the application and provide the necessary labor and expenses. This bureaucratic journey is often undertaken in collaboration with siblings, who also split the costs between them.

In spite of the work they put into obtaining citizenship, second-generation dual citizens typically do not derive any personal benefit from it. Most of them never even use their European passports for international travel. Thus, the primary motive of second-generation parents to apply for citizenship is the feeling that it is "good for the family." For example, fifty-eight-year old Shoshana said: "I only [obtained Hungarian citizenship] so that my children will have a passport. I have no intention of using it. Actually, I am ashamed to have a Hungarian passport. [I am ashamed] because my mother would turn in her grave if she knew. . . . She left Hungary at eighteen and never wanted to talk or visit or hear from them again."

While not all second-generation dual citizens held such negative views of their countries of citizenship, the sentiment of shame expressed by Shoshana is highly typical of that generation. The phenomenon whereby people take the citizenship of countries that they abhor often leads to ironic situations. Consider Haim, a fifty-five-year-old engineer whose German-born father left Germany in 1939 as a boy and was the sole survivor from his large family. Haim boycotted German products his entire life and has never set foot in Germany. However, when his daughters asked him to obtain citizenship for them, he complied. Now he is a German citizen with a German passport who continues to boycott Germany and everything German, including his own passport.

The intergenerational interaction within the Ashkenazi family around citizenship application demonstrates the way emotional and economic elements intertwine with family relations, as pointed out by sociologists, including Pierre Bourdieu and Viviana Zelizer.[36] Second-generation parents are reluctant to become dual citizens but do not hesitate to obtain citizenship for the sake of their children. They view this as an act of good parenthood that strengthens the family through a performance of love and unity. The cooperation between second-generation siblings, which was reported by almost all respondents, sets an example of coordinated family action to the younger generation. And the passport is bestowed upon the third generation as a gift.

The European passport is highly suitable to serve as a gift within the family: it is created through cooperation inspired by fraternal love and given as an act of parental love. Furthermore, it is impossible to quantify and calculate the costs and the benefits of citizenship. This makes the passport suitable as a "gift of love" that serves as an intergenerational transfer of wealth while at the same time reinforcing the noncalculating symbolic basis on which the family rests.

These features make the family dynamic in Israel very similar to those that were found in the Mexican case. This similarity is not self-evident, given the difference between drawing on preexisting ancestral ties and creating a new tie through strategic birth.

The quest for the European passport reinforces the cohesion of the family in an additional manner: it leads family members to engage with old documents like marriage certificates and passports, family photos, and stories—both painful and quotidian—about the lives of former generations. Stories and personalities from past generations come to life, becoming present and relevant. Conversations about them act out the continuity of the family and expand the world of meaning shared by the second and third generations. In some cases, the application process also requires visits to the origin country; such visits often become joint family trips in search of traces of the immigrant generation's past lives and strengthen the sense of a shared family history.

This collective act of weaving a continuous family story carries special meaning because most Israelis understand their family's immigration to Israel (*Aliyah*) not just as a geographical move but as an existential revolution: from the humiliated and miserable life in the diaspora to proud and independent life in Israel. This fundamental aspect of Zionist ideology—the rejection of the Exile (*Shlilat HaGalut*)—played out dramatically in the lives of second-generation Israelis. Growing up in the 1950s and 1960s, they sought to embrace Israeli identity in the most complete way possible, including refusing to understand Yiddish and origin-country languages, Hebraicizing their family names, and rejecting any nostalgia for or interest in their origin country. The total embrace of Israeli identity entailed a feeling of estrangement from, and even shame about, their *Galuti* (diasporic) parents and their past lives. This rupture with the origin country was facilitated by the fact that there were typically no relatives left behind and no possibility of visiting communist dictatorships. Therefore, the application for citizenship provides the second generation with an opportunity to rediscover and reconnect with their family roots together with their children.

At the same time, the acquisition of dual citizenship also reconnects Ashkenazi Israelis with family attitudes and strategies that have developed over the course of Jewish history as an ethnic minority that led a mobile, precarious existence. While demand for citizenship increased in relation to concrete security events, it was linked to a more general existential anxiety. When discussing their motivation to seek EU citizenship, many respondents—especially second-generation parents—brought up Israel's uncertain future, the lessons of Jewish history, and their families' experiences in the Holocaust. This suggests that Israeli parents who acquire EU citizenship for their children are partly inspired by dispositions that form part of a *diasporic habitus*.

The connection between dual citizenship and diasporic family habitus was explored by the anthropologist Aihwa Ong in her research on Chinese diaspora elites in Southeast Asia. Ethnic Chinese in countries like Indonesia and Malaysia have a long history as a mobile ethnic caste of traders and middlemen.[37] The Chinese diaspora flourished under the diverse and segmented arrangement of European colonial rule; under nationalist regimes, they suffered from discrimination and persecution. More recently, thanks to the new opportunities provided by globalization, many overseas Chinese formed business connections across Asia, Europe, and North America. Such families go to great lengths to obtain citizenship in Western countries and relate to it in an instrumental approach that Ong terms "flexible citizenship."

This strategic, nonsentimental approach to national membership is part of the practical, cognitive, and normative dispositions that overseas Chinese families perfected during the course of their history as a mobile, mercantile diaspora in an uncertain environment. The analogy to the Jewish case is obvious: like overseas Chinese, diaspora Jews were a highly mobile and often persecuted ethnic caste that specialized in trade and finance.[38] Such conditions can be expected to lead to the formation of long-term behavioral dispositions—a diasporic habitus—that consist of suspicion toward host states, strong adherence to the family, and an attempt to secure mobility and economic opportunities.[39]

European citizenship acquires value within the family that goes far beyond the right to work or study in Europe. From the perspective of the diasporically conditioned second generation, the offer of citizenship restitution is an attractive opportunity to improve the family's prospects by securing a valuable global resource. In a global context, it is an act of upward social mobility; in the intra-Israeli context, it is an intergenerational transfer of wealth. Moreover, the application procedure itself provides applicants with the opportunity to perform a number of roles within the family: dedicated parents, cooperative siblings, and dutiful sons and daughters who remember and pass on their parents' life stories.

Putting EU Citizenship to Use

OPPORTUNITIES

The most common answer that respondents provided when asked about their motivation to apply was that EU citizenship opened up economic opportunities. This pragmatic approach also dominated media discussions of the phenomenon; several news outlets have even published "consumer guides" that instruct Israelis on how to obtain a second citizenship.[40] EU citizenship does in fact carry potential economic benefits, including eligibility for residence and work in European countries on the basis of EU freedom of movement for workers, and reduced university tuition in some countries. In addition, dual citizens gain the right to purchase real estate in countries where this right is or was restricted to citizens (such as Romania and the Czech Republic), and citizenship may facilitate their claims for restitution of family property in the countries of citizenship.[41]

On the other hand, the statistics that were presented above show that the proliferation of EU dual citizenship did not increase emigration from Israel. This is explained by Israel's high level of economic development, which makes emigration to Europe relatively unattractive: average wages are on par with countries like Spain or Italy, and unemployment is low. Nevertheless, there has been a modest increase in the number of Israelis moving to Europe, and especially to Germany.

An interesting new destination is the German capital Berlin. A recent study by Dani Kranz estimated the number of Israelis in Berlin at around 11,000. About 2,200 of them have German dual citizenship, and many others most likely hold citizenship from other EU countries.[42] This immigration has received attention because of its provocative symbolism: the grandchildren of Holocaust survivors returning to the capital of the Third Reich. It also provides an example of the new modalities of migration and forms of transnationalism that EU dual citizenship has made possible.

Israelis who move to Berlin are not looking for high-paying jobs, which are not that city's strong point. Instead, the German capital has become a mecca for young Israeli artists, musicians and students, who enjoy the city's vibrant and cosmopolitan atmosphere and its low living costs. Many of them divide their time between Tel-Aviv and Berlin. This migration is partly a response to the meteoric rise in real estate prices in Israel after 2008, which in turn has to do with the growing number of Jews from outside Israel (above all, from France) who bought real estate in Israel as an "insurance policy." At the same time that Israelis use EU citizenship as insurance, some European and American Jews view ownership of property in Israel as insurance against risks in their own countries.[43]

Only a small minority of EU-Israeli dual citizens use their citizenship to emigrate to Europe, however. The vast majority continue to live in Israel. Most people who seek EU citizenship are inspired by a rather vague concept of its economic usefulness and not by a concrete plan of action. This attitude can be illustrated through a quotation from Shoshana, a fifty-eight-year-old travel agent from Tel-Aviv who obtained Hungarian passports for herself and her three sons: "Around 2000, that's when [my sister and I] started handling the application [for Hungarian citizenship]. It was then that people started talking about the European Union. And we thought it's a good idea: if we have a European passport, then the kids can study, work, whatever they want. We'll open up new horizons for them." This statement is typical: dual citizens explained that a passport was "practical" because it created opportunities for employment and education in EU countries. Around the year 2000, in Shoshana's words, "people started talking about the European Union." This interest grew in the period leading up to the introduction of the unified Euro currency in 2002 and the accession of ten new members to the EU (including Hungary and Poland) in 2004. Note the broad and nonspecific view of the perceived usefulness of the passport, which she describes as "European" rather than Hungarian. It is useful for the younger generation to do "whatever they want" and will open "new horizons" for them.

This nonspecific attitude toward EU citizenship—epitomized in the typical expression *tov she'yesh* ("it's good to have")—can be contrasted with the highly specific plans that Serbian applicants had for their Hungarian citizenship (e.g., study for a master's degree in the Netherlands, join a cousin who lives and works in Sweden). The Israeli attitude was much closer to that of Mexican upper-middle-class parents, who had a general conception of US citizenship as potentially useful for their children, but could not anticipate more specific scenarios.

There was, however, a key difference that set Israeli citizenship applicants apart from Mexicans who practice strategic birth. Elite *norteños* are often intimately connected to the United States: they speak English, are familiar with American culture, and sometimes have relatives living there. Shopping, studying, and taking vacations in the United States are key practices that define the identity of the elite in northern Mexico. In contrast, Israelis do not see anything particularly exclusive about visiting Europe as tourists (it is the most common go-to destination, and people of all social classes visit there). An education from a European university is not considered as a mark of high status in Israel.[44] There is no folk knowledge about the practical uses of the EU passports, and respondents had little knowledge of tuition rates, wage levels, or potential job opportunities in Europe.[45] This explains the vague expressions cited above: "new horizons," "opening doors," and "whatever they want to do."

SECURITY

In Israel, more than in the other cases in this study, compensatory citizenship is prized as a source of security. Many Israelis referred to their second passport as *Te'udat bituah* (insurance policy) against a range of apocalyptic scenarios. For example, as fifty-six-year-old Sarah, who obtained a Romanian passport for the sake of her daughter, explained her motivation: "With a European passport, she will be able to work and study in Europe, it opens up more options. And besides, it's good to have another passport. We live in a very volatile country. Who knows what will happen here in ten years? Maybe [the Arabs] will throw us to the sea?" This explanation, which was typical, suggests that demand for citizenship is associated not only with immediate security concerns—of the kind that is responsible for the short-term spikes in demand that were portrayed above—but also with longer-term doubts about the very existence of Israel.

While existential anxiety has long characterized Israelis, the specific threats to Israel's survival varied over time. For example, until the 1979 peace treaty with Egypt, fears focused on the Egyptian and Syrian militaries and the promises of these countries' leaders to "throw the Jews into the sea" (Sarah's words above echo the terminology of those years). In the past decade, the most prevalent existential fear had to do with Iran's nuclear program, and its leaders' threats to "wipe Israel off the map".[46] Some respondents referred to other disastrous scenarios: a drastic escalation in the conflict with the Palestinians or a takeover of Israel by Jewish religious extremists.[47]

The respondents who were most interested in the protective capacity of the EU passport were second-generation applicants in their fifties and sixties. Beside the collective diasporic habitus that was discussed above, second-generation Ashkenazim typically had a direct personal reason that made them receptive to the concept of a life-saving document: their own parents' experiences in the Holocaust as victims and refugees. For example, this is how Aviva, the fifty-four-year-old daughter of Holocaust survivors from Poland and Germany, explained why she applied for her passport: "I applied for the German passport to secure a safe place for the children, and also for myself. . . . This is part of being second generation. In my parents' generation, if you had the right papers you were saved, and if you didn't, you were doomed. So I, as their child, internalized this message. You must always have some place that you can escape to." This message that Aviva, a classic "second generation to the Holocaust," internalized through the memories and traumas of her parents is the horror of statelessness. Persons without citizenship are deprived of "the right to have rights" (in Arendt's terms) and do not enjoy the protection of any sovereign.[48] In times of crisis, having the right documents meant having a right to live, and being without papers spelled a death sentence.[49]

This principle was made explicit as in the case of European Jews in the 1930s and 1940s. In the areas under Nazi control, Jews' passports were marked with the letter J to single them out and signal that they did not enjoy the protection of the state. During the Holocaust, Jews without papers were the first to be rounded up and deported. For example, Vichy France quickly handed over Jewish refugees from Germany and Poland to the Nazi regime; Jews with French citizenship were deported at a later stage and had a much higher chance of survival. In Romania, authorities spared most of the country's longstanding Jewish communities (with the exception of the 1941 Iasi pogrom) while exterminating Jews in the Soviet territories that it annexed. Bulgaria carefully protected its Jewish citizens from the Germans but did not object when the Germans deported the Jews of Macedonia to Auschwitz. Even in Germany, deportation to death camps was usually preceded by stripping the victim's citizenship.[50] Meanwhile, many Jews who managed to obtain passports or visas from countries that were not under German occupation—including Spain, Japan, Sweden, or even Paraguay—have used them to escape to safety.[51]

Many survivors owed their rescue to whatever state documents they managed to obtain, including visas, immigration certificates and foreign passports. These events, even if they were not a direct part of the immigrant parent's personal biography, left a strong impression and contributed to the perception that (the right) papers can save one from death. It is partly this lesson, combined with a preexisting diasporic habitus of flexible citizenship that conditions second-generation parents to seek out the protective capacity of the European passport.

The idea of an insurance policy was not limited to the older generation, but also came up in many interviews with younger respondents. Eli, a thirty-four-year-old government employee with German dual citizenship, said: "It's hard for me to say this because I work for the government of Israel . . . [but] as a Jew and as third generation to the Holocaust, I feel that I must always have an insurance policy and backup. Even if the chance I will need it is tiny—and I believe it is—I still want to have it." He added that "[the catastrophe] might be economic or demographic or security-related or political. We live in a world where [catastrophes] happen and I wouldn't attribute it specifically to Israel. I would feel the same in any country that I lived in."

This prevalent view of dual citizenship as the most rational response to insecurity stands in contradiction to classic Zionist thinking, which condemns the search for "insurance policies" and "escape routes" as the mark of the diasporic Jew living in Exile (*Galut*). In classic Zionist thinking, the State of Israel was supposed to provide the ultimate "insurance policy" that guarantees the survival of Jews, the one place where they do not need to secure a "route of escape." The fact that Israelis seek out additional insurance suggests that some elements of the Jewish diasporic habitus have withstood the revaluation of values that Zionism aimed to achieve.[52]

TRAVEL FREEDOM

Travel freedom was another major benefit that Israelis expected to gain from EU citizenship. The most direct gain in the global mobility of dual citizens relative to other Israelis has to do with visa-free access to the United States through electronic preregistration (ESTA). This program is available to citizens of most EU countries, including Germany and Hungary but not Poland, Romania, or Bulgaria (as of 2019). Israelis who have visa-exempt passports and use them to travel to the United States usually spoke about it with great satisfaction. An official at the Polish embassy reported that the most common question that new citizens asked her upon receiving their Polish passport was whether it allowed visa-free travel to the United States (they are disappointed when they find out it doesn't). This reflects Israelis' much stronger cultural and practical orientation toward the United States and their limited interest in Europe.

The second domain where dual citizens may exercise their travel freedom is the EU itself. Israeli citizens are not required to obtain a visa before visiting Schengen-area countries and they are not subjected to strict controls at the border. Nonetheless, many dual citizens felt that the EU passport allowed them to enter Europe more freely. While only a small fraction of the Israeli dual citizen population actually used their new passports to emigrate, there was another, far more common, way for dual citizens to experience a boost in their mobility: presenting their EU passports when crossing borders in Europe.

As in Serbia, Israeli dual citizens were often excited about using their EU passports to enter European countries. The kind of emotions that Israeli respondents reported, however, was very different from Serbians'. Serbians with Hungarian passports felt liberated; their point of reference was their former selves who would wait for hours outside embassies in Belgrade, hoping to get a visa. With a Hungarian passport, they were at last equal to other Europeans. Israelis did not feel a sense of liberation when using their EU passports because the Israeli passport already allows visa-free and hassle-free movement around Europe. Instead, the most commonly cited sentiment was pleasure at being admitted to the EU-nationals line at European airports. Respondents' answers suggested that they viewed the EU-nationals line as a kind of "VIP line." Obviously, this sense of exclusive privilege and superiority does not arise out of the comparison to Europeans. It is aimed at other Israelis who must use the non-nationals line. In the next subsection, I will return to the topic of using the EU passport and discuss how it interacts with the structure of status in Israeli society.

The third category of destinations where the EU passport boosted Israelis' mobility can be described as "the rest of the world." When listing the potential destinations that they might visit thanks to their second passport, Israeli respondents were much more likely to mention countries outside Western Europe and North America. Many respondents said—half-jokingly—that they wished to visit Muslim-majority countries that did not admit Israeli citizens, including Indonesia, Malaysia, Pakistan, Iran, and (less often) Middle Eastern destinations like Dubai.

While very few dual citizens are likely to ever actually visit any of those countries, their recurrent mention says two things. First, it highlights the Western self-understanding, income levels, and travel patterns of Israelis. Like travelers from Western Europe and North America, Israeli respondents were attracted to exotic destinations; in contrast, Mexican and Serbian travelers were interested in classic and "beautiful" destinations like Las Vegas, New York, or Paris. Second, the semifacetious desire to visit Arab and Muslim-majority countries reflects a reaction by Israelis to the sense of siege and exclusion that comes from being surrounded by hostile countries that they may only dream of visiting. This feeling is expressed in the quotation of Nadav (vignette 2), who fantasized about using an EU passport to drive freely around the Middle East.

The EU passport may enhance global travel freedom in other ways besides allowing access to Muslim-majority countries. Even when traveling in countries that do admit Israeli citizens, some Israelis prefer to use their second passport to avoid attracting attention and criticism. Moreover, several respondents said that traveling with a European passport made them safer from terrorists, who often deliberately target Israelis and Jews.[53] Some dual citizens said that their German or Polish passports might allow them to hide their identity and save themselves if they found themselves in the midst of a terrorist attack. Hiding one's Jewish identity to save one's life is of course a familiar idea for the children of Holocaust survivors. Ironically, the German passport now appeared as a potential lifesaver.

There was a recurrent phrase that seemed to express this sense of security in anonymity provided by dual citizenship: "With a European passport, you are a citizen of the world." This is a surprising way of thinking about dual citizenship that would not occur to Mexican or Serbian respondents, who saw dual citizenship as a way of becoming US or European citizens. Why would Israelis with European passports describe themselves as "citizens of the world"?

On one level, the view of the passport as providing global rather than European citizenship simply reflects the fact that Israelis are more disposed to think in global rather than regional terms. Being suspended between Europe and the Middle East while not really belonging in either—they were not really part of any region. This led them to automatically think of European passports as something that could also be useful in the United States or Asia.

On a deeper level, we can view the expression "citizen of the world" as revealing something about the way that Israelis conceive of their own Israeli citizenship. The word "citizen" here is not used in the ordinary sense, as "a full member who enjoys full rights"; instead, "citizen" should be understood as "someone who is accepted and tolerated." Israeli citizens do not see themselves as "citizens of the world" qua Israelis. Not only are there many countries that they are barred from entering, but even visits to friendly countries are fraught with anxiety about being attacked or criticized for their nationality (the Israeli media, by intensively covering such incidents, play a major role in stoking this sense of siege). In this context, the second passport allows Israelis to be received abroad with benevolent indifference. As one respondent put it, "I want the Romanian passport so I can be free from the burden of being Israeli when I'm abroad."

Dual Citizenship as Social Closure: Reclaiming Ashkenazi Privilege

Third-generation dual citizens receive their European passports as gifts from their parents. Nevertheless, they tend to see their passports as pieces of individual property to be used for their personal advancement. As I showed above, most third-generation dual citizens do not take advantage of the opportunity to work or study in Europe. Nevertheless, they are convinced that European passports are a good thing to have, and they speak about them with pride. Many felt that possession of a European passport was an exclusive privilege that signaled social distinction.

The perception of an EU passport as status symbol is rooted in the Israeli system of class and ethnic stratification. Ashkenazi Jews of CEE origin are considered to be the most privileged group in Israel, while Israelis of other origins—Mizrahi Jews of Middle Eastern descent, Russian-speaking Jews, and Arabs—are relatively underprivileged.

Until the late 1970s, Ashkenazim enjoyed undisputed political and cultural dominance in Israel.[54] Historically, two discourses were used to justify Ashkenazi dominance: one was an ideology of republican virtue, which stratified societal groups according to their contribution to the Israeli collective. This view placed the predominantly-Ashkenazi "serving elite" of settlers and fighters (epitomized in the *kibbutz*) at the top of the prestige hierarchy. The second source of legitimation was a modernizing, Eurocentric discourse that constructed Ashkenazi Jews as modern and "European" in opposition to Middle Eastern (Mizrahi) Jews, who were seen as "oriental" and less developed.[55] Since the 1980s, secular Ashkenazim no longer enjoy a monopolistic political hegemony, as multiple groups compete over the state's resources and the power to determine its cultural orientation.[56] Nevertheless, Ashkenazim remain the most privileged sector in terms of income and education.[57]

This shift—from hegemonic group to elite—has shaped the divergent perspectives of the second and third generations on Israeli society. Second-generation Ashkenazim grew up in the 1950s and 1960s as members of the group that defined the Israeli mainstream. In contrast, their third-generation children, who grew up in the 1980s and 1990s, lived through the historic change whereby their ethno-class group was transformed from hegemonic majority into elite minority.[58] The sociologist Orna Sasson-Levy argues that this change in social position went hand in hand with a change in self-understanding. Older Ashkenazi Jews saw themselves as "simply Israeli" while casting all other groups as "minority sects." Younger Israelis of Ashkenazi origin perceive themselves as one sector among several. Status stratification on the basis of republican virtue and service to the nation has declined in importance, while the Eurocentric-modernizing discourse has gained more resonance. Many young secular

Ashkenazim identify themselves as Western while looking down on other sectors (Mizrahim, Russian speakers, religious Jews, and Arabs) that are viewed as less modern and developed.

This pattern was evident in the interviews with third-generation respondents.[59] Their claim to social prestige drew on privileged access to Europe and the West and was often coupled with a desire to distance themselves from the Israeli mainstream. Many young respondents characterized themselves as individualistic, liberal, and open-minded, while contrasting these values with most other Israelis, who they described as nationalistic and primitive. The European passport came up during the interviews as a rhetorical prop that reinforces this self-presentation.

Shlomit, a thirty-year-old German dual citizen, said that she was happy to have a German passport because it made her into "an Israeli with an alternative, someone who has the option of leaving." Yariv, another third-generation respondent, said, "My [Hungarian] passport is a provocation against this thing they keep telling us, that we have no other country." Most respondents preferred not to address directly the gap between Ashkenazim and Mizrahim. A few of them, however, did make explicit references to this topic. Dror, a twenty-eight-year-old Hungarian-Israeli, said: "In some sense [the passport] does feel like a membership in an exclusive club. What would you prefer to belong to—the European Union or the Arab League?"

Younger Israelis were eager to discuss their EU citizenship and enjoyed laying out their family histories and their views on the topic. This was markedly different from Serbia and Mexico, where most respondents did not find the phenomenon interesting and were not eager to talk about it. Moreover, many young respondents referred to EU citizenship as "*magniv.*" This is a slang word that roughly correlates with "cool": something that is *magniv* is good because it expresses its owner's uniqueness and character (it is also used by Nadav in vignette 2).

For young Israelis, speaking about their EU passports displays high status in three ways: 1) it demonstrates that they belong to the high-status Ashkenazi group, 2) allows them to put rhetorical distance between themselves and other Israelis ("I have an alternative"), and 3) suggests some degree of uniqueness and sophistication. The European passport, then, is a performative device, part of an array of Ashkenazi strategies of social distinction.[60] One of the main things that Israelis do with European citizenship is to talk about it. In the coming years, as increasing numbers of Sepharadic Jews acquire Spanish and Portuguese passports, EU passports are expected to lose their unique association with Ashkenazim—although not necessarily their association with high social status.

Interestingly, the distance that respondents put between themselves and "mainstream Israel" did not make them identify themselves as less Israeli. On the contrary, the recurring response to interview questions about their identity was that they felt "100 percent Israeli." Moreover, third-generation respondents spoke of their connection to the nation in surprisingly visceral and deterministic terms. Yariv said, "I carry this genetic disease of being Israeli, my mental structure is in Hebrew and I could never leave Tel Aviv completely, even if I tried to live abroad." Sivan, a thirty-year-old German-Israeli dual citizen, said: "When I spent a summer in Germany, I realized how Israeli I was. I couldn't identify with [the Germans]. I sit like an Israeli, gesticulate like an Israeli, talk like an Israeli, I think differently from them."

In those quotations, being Israeli is an embodied, indelible characteristic that is inscribed in one's mental structure, language, and even bodily posture. Respondents framed the differences between Israelis and non-Israelis in ethnocultural terms, not in spiritual or racial terms: none of them said that Israelis had different souls or different bodies. Nevertheless, they saw these differences as solid enough to make assimilation into any other culture impossible. This essentialist, unconditional manner of understanding their own Israeli identity is an important element in the generational value shift away from a traditional Zionist view that conditions Israeli national identity on residence and exclusive allegiance.

Precisely because third-generation respondents saw their belonging to Israel an indelible part of their minds and bodies, they refused to accept that any action on their part—including the acceptance of another citizenship or leaving Israel—would make them less Israeli. This confidence in being "100 percent Israeli" is the basis for the gap between them and their parents: whereas second-generation parents were ashamed to be dual citizens, their third-generation children were proud to have a second passport. It is an attitude that echoes the approach of young ethnic Hungarians in Serbia (chapter 2), who claimed that there was no connection between their Hungarian identity and whether or not they held citizenship from Hungary.

Alongside everyday conversations, there was another social site where European citizenship could be converted into an experience of social distinction: passport controls at European airports. For example, twenty-eight-year-old Omer explained that one of the main reasons he obtained his Czech passport was because "it allows me easy access to European countries—you don't need to stamp it and all that, just show it and go through." This was typical of third-generation respondents. Although the amount of time that EU citizens save rarely exceeds ten minutes, the experience of taking the EU-nationals line came up in many interviews, and numerous respondents rhapsodized about the "pleasures" of taking it.

If the preoccupation with lines and stamps seems petty, it must be remembered that situations like the passport-control line, where people are hierarchically arranged in space, are a prominent site for the display of status differences. For many young Ashkenazim, this is essentially what the European passport is about: not having to stand in the same line with other Israelis. This is illustrated by the story told by Yariv, a twenty-nine-year-old from Tel-Aviv. Using his Hungarian passport to gain access to the EU-nationals line, he said, is "one of my greatest pleasures when I visit Europe." He continued: "On my last flight to Europe, I arrived in Spain on a plane full of charter-flight passengers who at best could get a Moroccan passport. And of course they all tried to get into the shorter EU-nationals line, but the local gendarmes drove them back. I went right through, while the other Israelis stayed there for another ten minutes. Now that was fun."

In this account, the European passport appears as a global status symbol that reaffirms Israeli class boundaries along the familiar lines of ethnicity ("Moroccan passport," alluding to the Middle Eastern origin of the other Israeli passengers), patterns of consumption ("charter flights" are all-included deals popular with lower-class Israelis), and "civilized" behavior ("they" are barbarically trying to push themselves into the line where they do not belong). The European law enforcer, by deciding who to let through and who to push away, provides objective, state-sanctioned validation to the distinction between those Israelis who are "European" and worthy, and those who are "non-European" and of lesser worth. As the interviews made clear, many dual citizens think of the EU-nationals line as a VIP line: what makes it prestigious is the fact that other Israelis are not allowed to use it. The European passport serves as a portable status symbol that allows dual citizens to reproduce Israeli ethno-class hierarchy abroad and experience it in terms of an objectively justified global order.

Conclusions

Since the year 2000, over 85,000 Israelis have acquired citizenship from CEE countries. Applicants had no interest in becoming German or Polish and saw their second citizenship as having no bearing on their national identity. Their primary motivation was to gain a "European passport" that will give them access to opportunities in the EU and global freedom of movement. The analysis of trends in citizenship applications suggests another reason: Israelis seek EU citizenship in the context of geopolitical insecurity and demand surges in response to wars and terrorist attacks. Migration statistics, however, reveal that few Israeli dual citizens actually use their passports to move to Europe, whether for security or economic reasons.

This highlights the importance of noneconomic, nonpractical motivations in shaping Israeli demand for EU citizenship. These motivations vary between the two generations involved in the phenomenon. Second-generation parents appropriate the passport for the service of the family; for them, an additional passport is an "insurance policy," a view conditioned by Jewish life in the diaspora and reinforced by the grandparent generation's experiences in the Holocaust. In addition, EU citizenship serves as an intergenerational transfer of wealth and a gift that reinforces the cohesion of the family. For the younger generation, the passport is a useful piece of private property that broadens their opportunities in the global market of labor and education. It also operates as a status symbol: the European passport is talked about and displayed in a way that demonstrates its bearer's Ashkenazi origin and personal sophistication.

Within the context of this comparative framework, EU-Israeli dual citizenship represents a case of compensatory citizenship that was acquired on the basis of ancestry. It has several features that set it apart from the Serbian and Mexican cases; most of them would also supposedly be found in other cases of ancestry-based dual citizenship—for example, in Brazil or Argentina.

Unlike in Serbia and Mexico, in Israel the second citizenship is not acquired from a neighboring country and is detached from a context of ongoing migration. This entails a much greater cultural distance from the granting country. Moreover, the procedure of acquiring citizenship on the basis of ancestry does little to bridge that distance. Whereas strategic applicants in Serbia and Mexico must undertake a difficult (and sometimes risky) personal journey in order to obtain citizenship—studying a new language, giving birth in a foreign country—in Israel, seekers of citizenship do not have to modify any part of their identity or lifestyle.[61] They must only secure bureaucratic recognition of their family's preexisting legal status and kinship ties. Most applicants do not even handle the procedure themselves: they only locate whatever documents they have and pay a lawyer to do the rest.

In the experience of those applicants, then, acquiring EU citizenship is an almost naked exchange of money for passports. This attitude is reinforced by the highly commercialized nature of the industry around EU citizenship. The relative affordability of EU citizenship makes it into a casual middle-class consumption article. These factors explain the highly instrumental and economic relation of Israelis to their EU citizenship. German or Romanian citizenship is not experienced as an identity-relevant legal status that binds them to a certain collective, but rather as a piece of private property, which is obtained through a process of restitution that costs money (but no special effort) and bears the form of a concrete physical object—the European passport—that is only loosely national.

Conclusion

THE RISE OF THE SOVEREIGN INDIVIDUAL

Citizenship sorts individuals into unequal positions within a stratified global society. Until recently, changing one's place in the "birthright lottery" of citizenship was an extremely difficult endeavor. It involved immigrating to another country and living there for years, adopting a foreign language and culture, and being ready to give up one's original nationality. Today, following the widespread toleration of dual citizenship, it has become much easier to acquire another citizenship. People may acquire a second citizenship through a simple bureaucratic procedure without having to leave their home country or embrace another culture, and without jeopardizing their original nationality. These legal changes contribute to a transformation in the meaning of citizenship: from a rigid category that is determined at birth and cannot be changed into a flexible resource that one may pick and choose—or even strategize to maximize utility and compete with other actors. Citizenship is changing from an ascribed to an achieved status.

As individuals around the world gain greater autonomy to determine their own citizenship status, a new, openly instrumental attitude toward citizenship comes to the fore. As this book shows, dual citizenship is often used as a practical resource. Specific uses vary: respondents in Israel and Mexico mainly sought dual citizenship as an insurance policy and a key to opportunities in the United States or the EU (in Israel, social status also played a role), whereas in Serbia applicants were concerned with travel freedom and a potential for labor migration, and many also used citizenship to express their ethnic identity. These differences reveal variations in the kinds of citizenship deficits that individuals in those middle-tier countries experienced: geopolitical risk in Israel, crime-related insecurity in Mexico, and restricted economic opportunities and travel freedom in Serbia.

Citizenship is open ended and flexible in its potential uses. It is a relatively secure asset that, once acquired, may be held in the family for many years. Respondents often said that they could not predict all the uses that they or their children might find for their citizenship. The phenomenon of compensatory citizenship demonstrates how individuals on the ground decouple citizenship from its association with a specific national identity and reframe it as a piece of private (or, more precisely, family) property that provides practical advantages on a global scale.

In this concluding chapter, I discuss the theoretical implications of the findings that were presented in this book. I make four arguments that pertain to each of the four dimensions of citizenship that were brought up in the introduction: status, rights, identity, and global sorting. Regarding citizenship as status, I argue that the emergence of local citizenship industries around the world plays a central role in the commodification of citizenship. With regard to citizenship as rights, the book's findings highlight the key importance of territorial rights, including the right to enter a territory, as well as global travel freedom. Concerning citizenship as identity, I find that the legal acceptance of dual citizenship encourages an instrumental attitude toward citizenship and legitimizes the pursuit and maximization of personal utility. Finally, regarding citizenship as global sorting, I argue that dual citizenship challenges the traditional construction of nations as self-contained, unitary, and equal political communities.

Status: Citizenship Industries and Inevitable Opportunism

Citizenship is an object of closure, a crucial stake in a multisided political contestation over the boundaries of the nation. Scholars who studied classificatory struggles over citizenship have mostly examined law and policy, focusing on the actions of political elites.[1] In this book, I examined another, mostly overlooked arena of contestation: that which occurs between individuals seeking external dual citizenship and the granting state's bureaucratic apparatus. This approach aligns closely with the work of Jaeeun Kim on members of the Korean diaspora and their interactions with the South Korean state. It highlights applicants' bottom-up strategies and officials' responses to those strategies, exposing unintended consequences of policy that top-down analyses often overlook.[2] Two of my findings are relevant to the study of citizenship as a contested status: the emergence of citizenship industries, and the inevitability of opportunism.

Citizenship industries have emerged in all three cases that were examined in this book. They consist of specialized professionals who facilitate the acquisition of compensatory citizenship. The nature of the services varies depending on the granting country's evidentiary regime. In Israel, the industry of ancestry-based EU citizenship involves lawyers and translators who locate documents and handle bureaucratic procedures; in Serbia, it consists of persons who teach the Hungarian language on a small scale, often as a part-time job; meanwhile, the world-spanning interest by well-off parents who wish to give birth in the United States creates a profitable business for private birth clinics.

The cost and affordability of compensatory citizenship varied widely between cases. The typical expenditure involved in obtaining EU citizenship in Israel is about $1,500 per person. In terms of the average salary in Israel, this is equal to about two weeks' pay. In northern Mexico, the cost of giving birth in the U.S. starts at $7,000 to $10,000, about a year of average income, and also involves the risk of losing one's visa. This makes EU citizenship in Israel twenty-five times more affordable than strategic US citizenship for Mexicans. In Serbia, ethnic Hungarians obtain citizenship with practically no monetary expenditure; strategic applicants who study Hungarian have to spend about three hundred euros, a month's income in average Serbian salaries, apart from the effort of studying a difficult foreign language.

These cost differences translate into large gaps in citizenship uptake. In Serbia, where application is easiest, about two-thirds of ethnic Hungarians have acquired dual citizenship. In Israel, 8 to 10 percent of individuals who are eligible for citizenship from CEE countries have acquired it. In contrast, only 1.6 percent of Mexican *norteños* were born in the United States, and only a minority among them were born there by parents' strategic decision.[3]

Another potential dimension of comparison besides cost would be the degree of organization of different citizenship industries. The citizenship industry in Israel, moreover, is much more competitive and organized. Whereas in Serbia and Mexico, applicants locate specialists through informal networks, citizenship experts in Israel create attractive websites and invest in online and newspaper advertising.

Citizenship industries vary in their degree of institutionalization as well as in the socioeconomic status of their potential clients. Mexican strategic birth is essentially an elite phenomenon, whereas European passports are widely available to Israel's middle class; in Serbia, Serbs who study Hungarian belong to the educated urban middle classes, while ethnic Hungarians of any socioeconomic class may easily acquire citizenship.[4]

While these local citizenship industries differ in size and structure, they are small in comparison to the high-profile global industry that provides citizenship by investment. Small Caribbean island nations have been offering "citizenship for sale" schemes since the 1980s; after 2008, similar programs were launched by numerous other nations, including EU members Malta and Cyprus. The costs of investment citizenship range from $200,000 to $250,000 in Saint Kitts, Antigua, or Grenada, to over 1.2 million euros for Maltese citizenship and 2.5 million euros for a Cypriot passport.[5]

Other, less direct, options for changing cash into legal status include investor immigrant visas offered by the United States, Britain, or Canada, and the offer of resident status in Spain or Portugal for foreigners who buy expensive real estate.[6] The industry of investment citizenship and residence is a big global business worth billions of dollars; the market mostly consists of millionaires from Russia, China, and the Middle East.[7] To attract well-heeled investors, citizenship firms organize glitzy events and produce copious amounts of high-quality marketing material. The approach is explicitly economic. Chris Kälin, the chairman of Henley & Partners, one of the leading firms in the market, said in an interview to CBS News: "You probably have more than one credit card, I would assume. And, you know, if Visa doesn't work, MasterCard will do. So I think any wealthy person nowadays should have more than one credit card. And likewise, you'd have more than one passport."[8]

While it is marked by higher public visibility, the global industry of citizenship by investment actually creates very small numbers of citizens compared to the millions who have acquired citizenship on the basis of ancestry or ethnicity. Globally, there is an extremely diverse array of citizenship industries and brokers: from global firms like Henley & Partners or Arton, to retired schoolteachers in Vojvodina who instruct their neighbors in the Hungarian language. The potential market includes millions of people in middle- and third-tier countries who occupy a vast range of social positions: unemployed persons in Serbia, Ukraine, or Macedonia; upper-middle-class Israelis, Taiwanese, Turks, and Mexicans; and multimillionaires from Russia, China, and the Middle East. There is no strict set of conditions that must be fulfilled for a citizenship industry to emerge; they appear wherever there is a legal opening, independent of whether the citizenship-granting countries encourage it or not.

This suggests that the growth of citizenship industries is a direct consequence of the legitimization of dual citizenship. Citizenship specialists—whether Hungarian language instructors in Serbia, Israeli citizenship lawyers, or executives in global citizenship-by-investment firms—promote dual citizenship as an asset that can and should be acquired strategically for personal gain. Applicants often pay specialists to handle their interactions with the state, bringing the acquisition procedure closer to a naked exchange of money for citizenship. Therefore, these different citizenship industries play a role in the refashioning of citizenship as a market commodity.

This leads to another finding: the proliferation of an opportunistic attitude to citizenship among individuals. The word opportunism is not used here in a normative sense; it refers to the manipulation of relevant characteristics in order to secure technical compliance with an administrative requirement.

The book surveyed a range of opportunistic strategies. Thousands of Serbs study Hungarian in order to fulfill a language criterion that was inserted in order to exclude them. Tens of thousands of parents from Mexico, Turkey, China, and elsewhere travel to the United States to give birth, benefiting from an evidentiary regime that was designed to include the children of residents and immigrants, not tourists. In other cases, applicants manipulated their ethnic identity, such as Macedonians, who declare that they feel Bulgarian in order to qualify for EU citizenship from Bulgaria.[9] Others choose their marriage partners with an eye to securing citizenship: a study of CEE immigrants in Italy found that immigrants' levels of intermarriage with Italians dropped significantly following the year when their origin countries joined the EU—in other words, when they no longer had a need for Italian citizenship.[10]

These opportunistic strategies constitute an unintended, bottom-up response to states' citizenship policies. Given the strong worldwide demand for first-tier citizenship, such opportunism is bound to arise in response to any system of citizenship allocation. The inevitability of opportunism can be seen when we compare the citizenship policies of Hungary and the United States.

Hungary actively promotes nonresident dual citizenship for cross-border Hungarians and even set a target for the number of new citizens it sought to create. Moreover, it is actually willing to accept strategic applicants. This is reflected in the receptive attitude of consular officials, who invite applicants who fail the interview to study more Hungarian and try again. The United States, in contrast, does not encourage external citizenship. Native-born children are granted citizenship based on the expectation that they would continue to live in the country. Moreover, the borders of the United States are closely guarded, and the country has one of the world's most restrictive visa admissions systems.[11] Furthermore, American citizens are required to report their income and pay taxes regardless of their place of residence. Nevertheless, external dual citizenship has emerged in both cases.

In the Israeli case, the acquisition of citizenship on the basis of ancestry does not easily lend itself to strategic manipulation (that would require falsifying documents). Therefore, EU-Israeli dual citizens do not employ opportunistic strategies like strategic birth or studying a new language. In the cases where European countries' external citizenship policy is predicated on the idea of restitution (as they are in Germany, and to some degree in Poland), Israeli applicants are indeed their intended recipients. On the other hand, to the extent that such policies aim to reconstitute a disrupted ethnonational community (and this is the situation in most other CEE countries), then Israelis should be considered as opportunistic applicants. They are accidental beneficiaries of policies aimed at the ethnic diaspora. In either case, Israeli applicants display an opportunistic attitude toward their second, EU citizenship, in the sense that they do not feel any belonging with the country in which they become citizens.

The analysis demonstrates that very different citizenship and evidentiary regimes lead to similar dynamics of opportunism, including the rise of citizenship industries. This is an example of equifinality: different starting positions lead to similar outcomes. Opportunism seems to follow as a natural consequence of the legitimization of dual citizenship. Once individuals are given the option to hold more than one citizenship, it becomes a good that may be acquired and accumulated.

Citizenship brokers and specialists emerge who encourage individuals to seek dual citizenship, highlighting its practical usefulness and helping to frame the acquisition of citizenship as a monetized market transaction. Dual citizenship is recast as a commodity that can be bought for money, and it also becomes a subject of competition. Individuals may now distinguish themselves in the quantity and quality of their nationalities: citizenship as a competitive achievement. In the tension between two classic models of citizenship—the Greek one, which is based on civic virtue, and the Roman model, which is based on property—dual citizenship clearly pushes in the direction of the latter.[12]

Rights: The Centrality of Territorial Rights

Thomas Marshall's classic model of citizenship rights, which was formulated in the mid-twentieth century, is premised on a concept of exclusive and territorial citizenship. Marshall takes the citizen's presence in the territory for granted and therefore leaves it out of his theory. In a similar vein, most of the social science literature on citizenship focuses on immigrants in Western countries and assumes that they intend to remain in those countries. As a consequence, scholars have tended to overlook the crucial role that territorial rights play in citizenship: the right to enter and remain in the territory of the citizenship-granting country (right of abode), as well as the right to use that country's passport to visit other countries (travel freedom). My findings highlight the key importance of territorial rights as a component of citizenship.

The right of abode provides the basis for most of the economic uses of compensatory citizenship, including employment and education. Freedom of employment is a civil right, but it cannot be exercised without presence in the territory. Moreover, the importance of territorial rights for seekers of compensatory citizenship extends far beyond the purely economic. The wish to gain an unrestricted right to enter the United States or the EU, and to obtain a premium passport, played a major role in motivating applications.

For many Israelis and Mexicans, the right to enter another territory was a source of security. Israelis viewed it an insurance policy in case Israel were destroyed and they became refugees, as their grandparents had been. A second passport guaranteed that there would be another country that would be ready to accept them. Mexicans used American citizenship as an escape route to protect themselves against criminal violence and lawlessnes. In both cases, citizenship provides security by guaranteeing the right to access the safer territory of the United States or the EU. Other researchers reported comparable framings of dual citizenship as security in Lebanon (citizenship as an escape route in case of war), Argentina (insurance against economic crisis), and Turkey (insurance against authoritarian repression).[13]

Another crucial territorial right that applicants sought to secure through dual citizenship is travel freedom. For many respondents, particularly in Israel and Serbia, having dual citizenship was mainly about carrying a second passport. In Serbia, strategic applicants' leading motive was to ensure easy access to EU countries: when the EU threatened to impose visa requirements on Serbian citizens, applications for Hungarian citizenship shot up. While Israelis did not need a visa to enter EU countries, they were nonetheless fascinated with the idea of having a "European passport" and using the EU-nationals line at European airports. Travel freedom is closely connected to social status. While mobility restrictions are basically impersonal—they target categories rather than individuals—travelers often experience border control in a very personal way that might include a range of intense emotions, including shame, pride, liberation, and entrapment.[14]

This finding is consistent with arguments made by scholars of globalization like Zygmunt Baumann, Stephen Castles, and Ronen Shamir, who pointed out that the ability to cross borders has become a key aspect of stratification in the contemporary world.[15] Over the past decades, the selective growth of visa waiver agreements has contributed to the growth of a "mobility divide" between the citizens of rich and poor countries.[16]

The EU has been a key contributor to the consolidation of global mobility hierarchies. As EU countries harmonized their visa policies to create the Schengen zone of free movement, the territorial rights of each member nationality expanded while the position of all nonmember nationalities was weakened. In the regions that border the EU—Eastern Europe, Western Asia, and North Africa—the question of which nationalities had visa-free access to Schengen became crucial.[17] In countries that do not enjoy visa-free access to Schengen (such as Turkey or Russia) or were denied such access until recently (such as Serbia, Bosnia, or Ukraine), EU passports are valued primarily as a means to access EU territory. Even in Israel, subtle distinctions have emerged between those who use the EU-nationals line and the rest. The same logic can be seen in the surge in the growing demand for EU passports in Britain ahead of Brexit.

Even though it is extremely unlikely that Schengen countries will require visas from British citizens, many people are eager to make sure that they have the highest and most secure degree of access to the EU.[18]

These cases demonstrate that territorial access and travel freedom play a key role in the power of a second citizenship to provide security, opportunities and status. To some extent, these findings are also relevant to immigrants who acquire a second citizenship through naturalization. Recent research in the United States has found that the wish to secure the right to enter and stay in the country is a key motivation that drives immigrants to naturalize.[19] The everyday civil and social rights enjoyed by legal permanent residents and citizens do not differ significantly, but citizens are territorially secure whereas permanent residents may have their status terminated.[20]

In contrast to the strong preoccupation of applicants with territorial rights, civil and social rights play a relatively modest role in motivating applications for compensatory citizenship. The low interest in civil rights can partly be explained by the fact that the cases I studied here involved populations that are either part of the majority or constitute a tolerated minority. One could imagine that individuals in authoritarian countries or those who belong to threatened minorities might be much more interested in securing protection from a Western power (naturally, such dual citizenship would also be more politically controversial). The limited interest in social rights has another reason: welfare regimes are typically premised on residence, and social rights are not usually available for people who live outside the national territory, especially if they have never worked there.[21]

Finally, what is the role of political rights in external dual citizenship? This dimension has received a great deal of attention in the literature. Emigrant and coethnic diasporas are often politically engaged, with emigrant organizations lobbying their origin country to permit dual citizenship and absentee voting and playing a role in shaping political outcomes. Diaspora political involvement, which Benedict Anderson called "long-distance nationalism," has played an important role in the politics of diverse countries across different continents and levels of development.[22]

The findings of this study suggest that citizen diasporas produced through long-distance strategic acquisition do not usually share this passion for homeland politics. Interest in political rights in the granting country played no role in motivating applications. The typical person with compensatory citizenship had no interest in engaging with the politics of the long-distance citizenship country and did not vote there.[23] Most American-Mexican or German-Israeli dual citizens would not even know the procedure needed to vote in the United States or Germany.

The one instance where the political dimension of citizenship finds strong resonance is the Hungarian-Serbian case. In this case, the citizenship-granting government aggressively promotes nonresident voting among its cross-border citizens. About one-third of Hungarian-Serbian dual citizens in Serbia voted in Hungary's 2014 elections, and the turnout in 2018 seems to have been similar if not higher.[24] The rate of support by cross-border Hungarians for Prime Minister Viktor Orbán—about 95 percent—reminds one of election results in Middle Eastern dictatorships. Cross-border voters often did not deliberate who to support in the elections but simply voted for Orbán as a show of gratitude to the leader who granted them EU citizenship. Voting was experienced more as an obligation than a right. In any case, the desire to vote in Hungarian elections was not a major motivation for citizenship applicants.

One can imagine that a diaspora of citizens created on the basis of long-distance acquisition might organize as a community to promote its interests vis-à-vis the external homeland. In fact, scholars have identified such dynamics among Italian dual citizens in Argentina and Bulgarian dual citizens in Turkey.[25] Nonetheless, it is not likely that political rights will become a central component of compensatory dual citizenship, for two main reasons. First, the location of external dual citizens outside the state's territory limits the scope of benefits that they can expect from it. And, second, governments can easily limit the impact of nonresident voting, either by procedural means (e.g., limiting the number of consulates where nonresidents may vote) or by changing the law. While diasporas may exert a big influence on home countries through financial or ideological means, we are unlikely to find massive voting by nonresident citizens who do not pay taxes or fulfil civic obligations. Even in the age of "long-distance" or "post-territorial" nationalism, the territorial foundation of the nation-state as a political model remains too strong to legitimize direct diaspora interference of this kind.[26]

Identity: The Rise of the Sovereign Individual

Citizenship was traditionally understood as a sacred status that is intimately tied to national identity.[27] Decisions about citizenship status—whether to give up one's citizenship or take up another passport—were not left to the individual. He or she had to take account of social norms and preserve the honor of the nation, and failure to do so would attract social censure and even ostracism. Alongside the sacred aspect of allegiance to a state, citizenship also carries the affective aspect of belonging to a nation. Passports are decorated with national symbols (e.g., the national eagles of the United States or Mexico; the seven-branched menorah of Israel) to which citizens are programmed since childhood to respond with emotion. New entrants into a country's citizenry must make solemn oaths and are welcomed through dramatic ceremonies.[28]

Against this background, the interviews in Serbia, Mexico, and Israel demonstrate the proliferation of instrumental and individualist attitudes toward nationality. In each case, the citizenship dyad in question would have been unthinkable two or three decades previously. When Yugoslavia took over Vojvodina after World War I, residents of the region had to relinquish their Hungarian citizenship and become Yugoslav or leave; in Mexico, there was historically widespread condemnation of emigrants who "betrayed" the nation by taking up US citizenship; and for several decades following the Holocaust, the vast majority of Israelis would be horrified by the thought of requesting German citizenship.[29]

The present legitimacy of dual citizenship in these cases provides evidence of a normative shift toward greater individual autonomy and maximization of personal utility. Strategic citizenship seekers were aware of the traditional objections to dual citizenship—Serbian fear of Hungarian irredentism, Mexican resentment at American dominance, the memory of the Holocaust in Israel—but brushed them aside with no great difficulty. They dismissed critics as conservative, closed-minded, or hypocritical persons.

While they shared the basic sense of freedom to strategize citizenship, respondents differed in the discourses that they used to legitimize strategic behavior and justify their right to a second citizenship. I will first compare Israel and Mexico, where seekers of strategic dual citizenship felt at ease employing the discourse of the sovereign individual, and then discuss the Serbian case, where instrumentalism gained lesser acceptance.

In Mexico, upper-class individuals who engaged in or benefited from birth strategies saw themselves as members of a global capitalist class. They pointed to this cosmopolitan identity, defined primarily by their high economic status, when justifying their instrumental bid for US citizenship. Respondents argued that their spending in the United States as tourists and shoppers gave them a right to citizenship. At the same time, they also stressed that they were attached to Mexico and did not feel American or Mexican American.

When articulating their connection to Mexico, upper-class Mexican respondents did not emphasize primordial characteristics such as the Spanish language, the Catholic religion, or mestizo origin. Instead, they said that they preferred Mexico over the United States because of superior business opportunities, comfort, and luxury. They did not rule out moving to the United States in the future. Thus, they exhibited a form of capitalist cosmopolitanism that treated both citizenships in an instrumental manner.[30] This attitude can be compared to the approach that Aihwa Ong calls flexible citizenship, which she found among Chinese elites who strategically acquire citizenship in Western countries through residence programs.[31]

In Israel, respondents exhibited an instrumental-individualistic relation to their EU citizenship and used an economic argument to justify their right to it. Their specific economic claim on citizenship and their understanding of the nation were markedly different from those of Mexicans, however. Israelis saw their origin-country citizenship as a piece of inherited property that was unjustly taken from their families. Whereas upper-class Mexicans claimed US citizenship as consumers, Israelis claimed EU citizenship as heirs seeking restitution. The basic position of Mexican elite respondents was that, by strategically obtaining US citizenship, they came to owe something to the United States that they expected to repay with their spending. In contrast, Israeli applicants felt that European countries already owed them citizenship; they did not bother to justify their right to citizenship with any argument beside the legal one.

Discourses of national identity also varied: while Mexicans and Israelis were in agreement that their secondary citizenship did not come with any strong obligations or an identity commitment, Israelis were much more likely to stress their attachment to their Israeli citizenship and their distance from their secondary EU citizenship.[32] The rhetoric they used was different from the instrumental, lifestyle- and opportunity-oriented discourse used by upper-class Mexicans. Israelis articulated their Israeli identity in explicitly ethnic, visceral terms. They argued that their Israeli upbringing and the Hebrew language intimately shaped their mentality and demeanor, making them unassimilable in Europe. Respondents had a strong sense of partaking in a Jewish destiny that they could not escape—in the words of one respondent, "I will never be anything but a Jew from the Land of Israel." EU-Israeli dual citizens are instrumental and individualistic about their EU citizenship but sentimental and collectivistic about their Israeli citizenship. They can be described as "rooted cosmopolitans."[33]

In Serbia, the penetration of individualistic, commodified attitudes to citizenship has been slower than in Israel and Mexico—not a surprise, given the country's very recent communist past. Serbian respondents did not typically use property metaphors when discussing citizenship. While their motivation to apply was very openly economic, they did not justify their right to citizenship in economic terms, but referred instead to ethnic identity or cultural affinity. Furthermore, Serbian respondents were far less confident in claiming a right to take citizenship decisions according to their own best interests. They did not see citizenship as completely detached from national allegiance. Some felt that their bid for Hungarian citizenship was a kind of "fraud" because, in the words of one respondent, "I am not really Hungarian."

Another, related sentiment was shame. Ethnic Serbs who sought Hungarian citizenship could be seen as betraying their Serbian roots while also potentially exposing the region of Vojvodina to Hungarian irredentist designs. The uneasy relation to the instrumentalization of citizenship was also expressed in the tendency of respondents to criticize Serbia when justifying their interest in dual citizenship. Respondents felt that by seeking another citizenship, they were in some way breaking a contract between themselves and their country. They sought to show that it was Serbia that broke the citizenship contract first, by failing to provide "a normal life." In spite of these dilemmas, the practical value of the EU passport has led many Serbians—of Hungarian as well as Serbian ethnic origins—to try and acquire Hungarian citizenship through behavior that they themselves often perceived as opportunistic.

This discussion suggests that the diffusion of compensatory dual citizenship is associated with a growth in the legitimacy of instrumental, even opportunistic behavior in the domain of citizenship. At the moment, the post-exclusive turn in citizenship directly affects only a small minority of the world's population: about 2 percent of the population in the sample analyzed in chapter 1 holds dual citizenship. In the foreseeable future, most people will continue to live their entire lives with the same citizenship with which they were born. Nonetheless, the presence of millions of individuals with dual nationality—many of them strategic long-distance citizens—contributes to a change in the meaning of citizenship.

The essence of sacredness consists in the taboo on instrumental, profane relation to the sacred object. The rise of acquisitive, instrumental behavior and the possibility of exchanging citizenship for money constitute a profanation of citizenship that works against its sacred dimension. In the same vein, the presence of citizens with weak ties to the nation might work to dilute the association between citizenship and national identity.[34]

Dual citizenship is at the forefront of the shift from the construction of citizenship as a high-stakes, high-commitment, sacred status to what Christian Joppke has called "citizenship light." Joppke describes this lightening as a paradox: even as the objective value of citizenship increases, its subjective value decreases.[35] The findings of this book align with Joppke's argument and extend it by specifying some of the mechanisms of lightening. The interviews demonstrate that citizenship becomes lighter—less sacred and less national—as a consequence of commodification.

The commodification of citizenship means that individuals have a new kind of freedom vis-à-vis states: the freedom to choose their citizenship(s) to match their interests and convenience. It reflects a new conception of "the sovereign individual" in the sense that personal interests have become a legitimate basis for individuals' decisions on citizenship. This term builds on Patrick Weil's concept of "the sovereign citizen," which he coined to describe a new legal doctrine formulated by the US Supreme Court in the 1950s and 1960s.[36] The essence of that doctrine was that, since the source of all government authority lay in the citizens, it was unlawful to strip Americans of their nationality against their will. Supreme Court Justice Hugo Black wrote in the 1967 Afroyim vs. Rusk case decision: "In our country the people are sovereign and the Government cannot sever its relationship to the people by taking away their citizenship."[37] In the United States, Weil argues, the acceptance of dual nationality is based on the doctrine of "the sovereign citizen" that puts individual liberties above the interests of the government.

The concept of the sovereign individual is the bottom-up, actor's point of view, counterpart of the legal doctrine that Patrick Weil has articulated. Once the legitimization of dual citizenship broadened the scope of personal choice in the field of citizenship, individuals on the ground experienced this new freedom as a right to which they are naturally entitled. The ideology of the sovereign individual goes hand in hand with the commodification of citizenship; it represents individualistic, instrumental appropriation of a status that developed as a sacred collective good.

Sorting: Citizenship as Global Class Position

For a long time, social scientists have studied citizenship as a dyadic relation between a state and an individual. The perspective that views citizenship as a mechanism of hierarchical global sorting is a more recent development.[38] Most of the scholars who adopted that perspective took a macrolevel approach and analyzed global inequality on the basis of economic statistics or legal structures. Key questions about the subjective dimension of the citizenship hierarchy are yet to be explored. Is this global structure transparent or opaque to the people living in it? How do the global positions in which they find themselves shape their strategies for personal advancement?

My findings show that citizenship is increasingly understood by social actors on the ground through its sorting function and experienced as global class position. Moreover, citizenship is seen as a flexible position that an individual may improve or upgrade over his or her lifetime. This new relation to citizenship entails a cognitive component—the possession of a mental map of different countries' relative citizenship value—as well as a behavioral component: specifically, value orientations and practical dispositions that make it possible to strategically manipulate citizenship status.

The statistical data presented in chapter 1 established the cognitive component. Individuals around the world have a sense of the relative position of their citizenship with the global hierarchy of citizenship value. When making decisions on whether to acquire dual citizenship, they compare the value of the citizenship that they already have with the one that they stand to gain. This is why demand for ancestry-based citizenship is so much higher in less developed countries. Regarding the behavioral-normative component, the ideology of the sovereign individual—citizenship as an achieved, freely chosen status— legitimizes strategic behavior to improve one's global position. Compensatory citizenship is a strategy of upward mobility that is premised on a new understanding of citizenship as global class position.

The growing tendency of individuals to focus on the sorting aspect of citizenship, which is a precondition for the rise of compensatory citizenship, contributes in yet another way to the dilution of the sacred character of national membership. It does so by deepening inequalities within nations in a way that casts doubt on the ideal of an equal citizenry.

Modern citizenship, Rogers Brubaker has argued, is premised on the concept of the nation as a uniform space of political equality.[39] In premodern states, it was acceptable for different population categories to have different legal rights (e.g., the estate society in early modern Europe) and for groups to maintain strong political ties with external powers (e.g., the clergy and Rome in medieval Europe, capitulations in the Ottoman empire). National citizenship eliminated such inequalities, providing the institutional basis for national unity. Modern citizenship disaggregates economic and political inequality, which, historically, usually went hand in hand, in two different systems. In the national space that is delimited by citizenship, economic inequality is tolerated but political inequality is not.[40]

The rise of dual citizenship challenges this (idealized) model by creating new ways in which within-nation and between-nation inequalities interpenetrate.[41] This becomes particularly conspicuous when dual citizenship is accorded to categories of people rather than to specific individuals (as is often the case with coethnic and ancestry-based dual citizenship).

The cases presented in this book underline this complexity. Before the advent of dual citizenship, Ashkenazim in Israel, middle- and upper-class *norteños*, and Serbians from Vojvodina enjoyed some local advantages over their conationals (very modest advantages in the case of Vojvodinians) but had the same status and rights vis-à-vis the outside world. The diffusion of compensatory citizenship means that domestic advantages of origin, wealth, location, and ethnicity can now be converted into global advantages in the form of Western or EU citizenship. Privileges that had an informal, local, and noninstitutionalized nature have turned into a formal status that is institutionalized in the form of a passport and recognized by all of the world's countries.

Differential access to compensatory citizenship brings to the surface internal axes of heterogeneity that processes of nation-building in those countries sought to do away with: in Mexico, the gap between European-origin, globally connected elites and the less privileged mestizo masses; in Serbia, the historical split between a Habsburg-dominated, Central European region north of the Danube and an Ottoman-controlled, Balkan country to the south; and, in Israel, disparities between Jews of European and Middle Eastern origin.[42] Evidence from additional cases—including US dual citizenship in Turkey and Taiwan and EU dual citizenship in Latin America—reinforces the observation that in middle-tier countries, dual citizenship mostly accrues to sectors that are already privileged economically and symbolically.[43] Pablo Mateos has argued that the acquisition of EU citizenship by Mexicans with recent European ancestry revives colonial-era racial hierarchies and challenges Mexico's self-image as a unitary mestizo nation, which was crafted in the wake of the Mexican Revolution.[44] The proliferation of compensatory citizenship among one sector of the population (typically, one that is already privileged) has the potential to undermine conceptions of a unified and equal nation.

In the West as well, dual citizenship creates a potential disruption to national cohesion. It mostly goes in the opposite direction, however. Instead of being an additional resource for elites, dual citizenship is often the mark of suspect immigrant minorities. In the context of the fight against Islamic terrorism, several countries (including Britain, Canada, and Australia) have begun to strip dual national terrorists of their nationality; several additional countries (including France, Germany, and Switzerland) have considered such moves.[45] While citizenship stripping policies may be effective as security measures (by denying terrorists access to the national territory) they also raise formidable constitutional and political problems. One of the problematic aspects of this practice is the fact that it designates dual citizens—who, in the West, are mostly immigrants and their children—as "conditional citizens."[46]

Thus, citizenship stripping may contribute to the creation of a two-tier system that defines naturalized citizens as constitutionally inferior. Such an internal hierarchy in political rights would contradict the ideal of civic equality that Western countries present as central to their politics.[47] There is, then, a global divergence in the meaning of dual citizenship: in middle-tier countries, privileged individuals obtain dual citizenship to gain additional security and social prestige; meanwhile, in the West, dual citizenship (especially from the "wrong" country) increasingly marks its bearer as a suspect and a potential candidate for denationalization.

Concluding Thoughts: The Precarious Future of Dual Citizenship

This book analyzed a growing global phenomenon: the strategic acquisition of a second nationality from EU countries or the United States by citizens of middle-tier countries in Latin America, Eastern Europe, Asia, and the Middle East. This trend is an unintended consequence of the permissive shift in states' relation to dual citizenship, and it represents an overlooked dimension of globalization. Compensatory dual citizenship currently plays an important role in reconfiguring inequalities within and between nations, forming identities and shaping patterns of mobility for the millions of persons. What does the future hold for this controversial model of national belonging? I will conclude with two reflections on the future of dual citizenship and its connection with the rise of populism.

First, is the acceptance of dual citizenship a permanent new norm, or is it a passing trend? In the introduction, I presented statistics on the dramatic shift toward acceptance of dual citizenship after 1990. The permissive trend is not over. New countries continue to join the ranks of those who permit dual citizenship. For example, in 2010 South Korea voted to allow a qualified form of dual citizenship; Denmark joined the trend in 2014.[48]

On the other hand, some countries resist the spread of dual citizenship. The world's largest countries, China and India, remain adamant in their refusal to permit dual citizenship, even as they engage in diaspora outreach. Some countries that experimented with dual citizenship have decided to prohibit it. Ukraine, which informally permitted dual citizenship since the 1990s, made it illegal again after the Russian-supported uprising. Proposals now circulate to criminalize dual citizenship and make it punishable by a prison sentence.[49] Other countries have shown growing strictness in imposing legal restrictions on dual citizens. Finland is considering barring dual citizens—especially Russian-Finnish—from its military.[50] In Australia, more than ten politicians have lost their posts after it was revealed that they held dual citizenship, which is prohibited to holders of office.[51] Austria, which never permitted dual citizenship, stepped up its enforcement of the ban in late 2018, threatening to denationalize hundreds of Austrian citizens who allegedly voted in elections in Turkey.[52]

Dual citizenship tends to become more controversial in a context of geopolitical tensions and anti-immigrant attitudes. With such tensions on the rise across the globe, the political atmosphere is likely to become more suspicious toward dual citizenship. Policymakers will likely pay special attention to countries that are seen as using dual citizenship in an aggressive manner, such as Russia and Turkey. The future of dual citizenship will doubtless be tied to developments in the field of international security and immigration.[53]

This leads to a second question, which concerns the connection between instrumental dual citizenship and the rising tide of populism and nativism. Across Europe and North America, a new style of politics has been gaining ground. Leaders such as US President Donald Trump, Italy's Matteo Salvini and Hungary's Viktor Orbán have gained popular support by proclaiming their opposition to globalization and immigration, and promising to fortify the nation's physical and symbolic boundaries. The 2016 British vote to leave the EU, and the growth of populist nationalism in many countries in Europe, Asia and the Americas, are also part of this global trend.

In an effort to make sense of contemporary populist movements, Rogers Brubaker has argued that they accord central importance to the idea of a pure and virtuous "people," whose voice is the only legitimate source of authority in national politics. The populists' people is defined in opposition to two groups: elites with a cosmopolitan bent, and outsiders, who consist of immigrants or racial minorities.[54] From this angle, elites and outsiders are a threat, or even an enemy. Populist leaders often promise to stop alleged abuses of the political and economic system by these groups, and "restore" the "real" people to its rightful dominant position.

It is telling that the two sectors that are targeted by populist rhetoric are those that are most likely to hold dual citizenship: global-leaning elites, and immigrants and their children. A cursory examination of populist rhetoric suggests that dual citizenship policies, and the instrumental behavior that they make possible, provide rhetorical fodder for populists who condemn them as unfair, dangerous or sacrilegious.

In the US, perceived abuses of birthright citizenship, including "anchor babies" born to undocumented immigrants, and "birth tourism" by wealthy foreigners, were invoked by Republicans during and after the 2016 election campaign. In November 2018, President Trump took up the topic again, saying: "[Birthright citizenship] has even created an entire industry. It's called birth tourism, where pregnant mothers from all over the world travel to America to make their children instant lifelong citizens with guaranteed everything. [. . .] Hundreds of thousands of children born to illegal immigrants are made automatic citizens of the United States every year because of this crazy, lunatic policy."[55]

In Britain, opposition to unregulated immigration by EU citizens from Eastern Europe (including dual citizens from countries outside the EU) played a key role in voters' decision to leave the EU. In many European countries, concerns about the integration of Muslim-origin immigrants crystalize around questions of citizenship. Populist anti-immigrant parties in Germany, France, and elsewhere have called for restricting dual citizenship, arguing that allowing it keeps immigrants from integrating.[56] European governments without explicit populist leanings likewise hardened their position on citizenship matters, as reflected in the growing use of naturalization tests to ensure immigrants' conformity to liberal principles, and the adoption of citizenship stripping as a tool against terrorism.[57]

The objections to instrumental citizenship are driven by practical considerations drawn from the domains of economics and national security. At the same time, they also reflect a more principled opposition to the individualistic spirit that underlies instrumentalism. Christian Joppke has argued that the lightening of citizenship is part of a broader ideological shift, which consists in "the demystification of states and empowerment of individuals."[58] Indeed, the legal toleration of dual citizenship has led to the emergence of citizenship strategies and industries, and a growing sense of individual liberty vis-à-vis states. Citizenship is becoming increasingly open to commodification, and is treated in an irreverent, utility-seeking manner. For many, such attitudes are experienced as a provocative profanation of a sacred status. With the simultaneous growth in instrumentalism and nationalist populism, the coming years will see increased contention between the growing realities of desacralized, individualized citizenship, and the push to reestablish citizenship—and the nation—as sacred collective objects.

ACKNOWLEDGMENTS

This book is the culmination of a long intellectual and personal journey that began almost fifteen years ago. At the time, I was just making my first steps as a student of sociology, while my family was in the process of applying for a Romanian passport. I found myself reflecting more and more on this move and the questions that it raised. Why would Romania offer citizenship to a third-generation Israeli who cannot speak a word of Romanian? Why would I want to acquire citizenship from a country of which I knew very little, and toward which my family harbored no nostalgia? What does this interest on my part— and that of tens of thousands of other Israelis—reveal about our belonging to Israel? More broadly, how can one person belong to two countries and what does this say about identities and boundaries in today's world? The initial spark of curiosity developed into a multiyear research project that took me across three continents and filled up countless hours of discussions, reading, and thinking. I feel privileged to have had the opportunity to pursue these interests so freely and fully.

This book owes its existence to conversations and exchanges with many colleagues and friends. I am deeply grateful to the members of my dissertation committee at Princeton University: Andreas Wimmer, Doug Massey, Paul DiMaggio, Miguel Centeno, and Paul Starr. A special thanks goes to Andreas Wimmer, a great teacher and a source of inspiration, who always came up with the most challenging questions, which turned out to be the most rewarding ones. I had valuable discussions with and received critical feedback from Yinon Cohen, Kim Scheppele, Patricia Fernandez-Kelly, Alejandro Portes, Christian Joppke, David FitzGerald, Adriana Kemp, Yehouda Shenhav, Ronen Shamir, Pablo Mateos, Jaeeun Kim, Szabolcs Pogonyi, David Cook-Martin, Biljana Djordjevic, Krisztina Racz, Eleanor Knott, Alf Garcia, Rene Flores, Maria Abascal, Carla Vazquez, Isaac Sasson, Dimitry Kochenov, and Ben Herzog.

I conducted most of the research for the book while at the Department of Sociology at Princeton University, and I did most of the writing at the Department of Sociology and Anthropology at Tel-Aviv University. I am grateful to both departments for the institutional support and intellectual stimulation. I received valuable feedback on parts of the book at colloquia at Princeton University, Columbia University, Tel-Aviv University, Haifa University, Ben Gurion

University, Central European University, NYU-Abu Dhabi, CIESAS-Noreste in Monterrey, and the Institute for Philosophy and Social Theory in Belgrade. I presented some of my findings at the annual meetings of the American Sociological Association (ASA); the Eastern Sociological Society (ESS); the Association for the Study of Nationalities (ASN); Metropolis; the International Immigration, Integration and Social Cohesion (IMISCOE) network; and others. I thank the participants in those events for their feedback. A special thanks goes to the colleagues who attended the "Strategic Citizenship: Negotiating Membership in the Age of Dual Nationality" conference, and especially to Pablo Mateos, with whom I had the pleasure of co-organizing the conference.

Parts of chapter 1 were published in the *Journal of Ethnic and Migration Studies* in 2019 (vol. 45, no. 6), under the title "Compensatory Citizenship: Dual Nationality as a Strategy of Global Upward Mobility." An earlier version of chapter 4 was published in the *International Migration Review* (vol. 47, no. 1), under the title "Rooted Cosmopolitans: Israelis with a European Passport—History, Property, Identity."

I am extremely grateful to my respondents in Mexico, Serbia, Israel, and the United States, whose generous and patient cooperation made this book possible.

I also thank the excellent team at Princeton University Press, especially Meagan Levinson and Emily Shelton, as well as the two anonymous reviewers.

My deepest thanks go to my family—above all, to my parents Pazi and Maya—for their love and support.

METHODOLOGICAL APPENDIX

Chapter 1

Sources for Table 1.1:
Germany: Göroğlu (2014); data received upon request from Bundesamt für Migration und Flüchtlinge. Data for 2011.
France: calculation based on Simon (2012), INSEE (2012). Data for 2008.
Netherlands: Statistics Netherlands (2012). Data for 2011.
Canada: Statistics Canada (2011). Data for 2011.
Spain: INE (2015), Shachter (2015). Data for 2014.
Switzerland: OFS (2015). Pertains only to population over fifteen years of age. Data for 2012.
Portugal: Shachter 2015. Data for 2011.
Ireland: EMN 2017. Data for 2016.
Finland: Statistikcentralen 2017. Data for 2016.
Brazil: author's calculation based on the number of dual citizens with Spanish, French, Italian, Swiss, and Portuguese citizenship. I used consular statistics from those five countries, which list the number of nonresident citizens registered in their consulates and whether they are dual citizens (for France, Italy, and Switzerland) or whether they were in the granting country (for Spain and Portugal). I assumed that Spanish and Portuguese citizens who were born outside Spain and Portugal, respectively, were dual citizens, since Latin American countries grant automatic citizenship at birth. This minimum estimate only includes dual citizens from these five countries who registered at the consulates. The omission of other countries should not significantly bias the results, because the number of immigrant naturalizations in Brazil and other South American countries is low—between 1,000 and 4,000 a year on average, based on Acosta 2013; Courtis and Penchaszadeh 2015. *Sources:* AIRE (2012), Assemblée des Français (2013), EDA (2013), Ministero dell'Interno (2013), PERE (2014), Observatório da Emigração (2014). Data for 2012.
Israel: author's calculation based on the figure of 380,000 EU and Swiss dual citizens in addition to estimates of 230,000 American-Israeli dual citizens, 160,000 Russian dual citizens, and an estimated 70,000 from Turkey, Canada, Australia, and Latin American countries. These are minimum estimates and the

full figures may be higher. *Sources*: EU citizens: see chapter 4. USA: 79,082 US-born in Israel (UN 2015) in addition to 150,000 passports issued to persons born in Israel or Jerusalem (Paraszczuk 2011). While some Israeli-born Americans may have returned to the United States, there are also Israelis who have naturalized there and then returned to Israel. Therefore, 230,000 is a safe minimum estimate. This figure is roughly consistent with estimates from Democrats Abroad and Republicans Overseas, two organizations that encourage voting by Americans living abroad. Russia: MPC 2013. Other countries: extrapolations based on Toktas 2006, countries' consular reports, and Israeli migration statistics. Due to the diversity of sources, it is impossible to pinpoint a year for the data, but most statistics were from the period 2010–15.

Bosnia-Herzegovina: Štiks 2010. Data for 2010.

Argentina: see Brazil.

Mexico: author's calculation based on estimates of US dual citizens and EU dual citizens. US dual citizens were calculated on the basis of the US-born population in Mexico from which I deducted the number of US citizens with visas (Chávez and Cobo 2012). This is a minimum estimate. See chapter 3, note 32. The number of EU dual citizens was calculated in the same way as in Brazil. Data for 2012.

Venezuela: see Brazil, in addition to figures on Colombian dual citizenship from Schwarz (2014) and Galeano David (2015). Data for 2012.

Romania: census data from Shachter (2015) in addition to post-2011 Hungarian citizens from Bálint (2014). Data for 2014.

Serbia: data received upon request from Serbian Bureau of Statistics in addition to Bálint (2014). Data for 2014.

Poland: GUS 2013. In addition to 327,500 persons who declared dual citizenship in the national census, the report notes that there were an additional 1.93 million for whom it is not known whether they hold another citizenship. Data for 2011.

Moldova: minimum estimate based on at least 300,000 Romanian citizenships granted to Moldovans in 1992–2016 (Dumbrava 2019) as well as 26,000 Bulgarian citizenships in 2000–11 (Harpaz 2015a). The full figure may be higher. Data for 2016.

Greece: data received upon request from Greek National Statistical Bureau; Stjepanovic 2015. Data for 2011.

Hungary: Shachter 2015. Data for 2011.

Croatia: Shachter 2015. Data for 2011.

Russia: data received upon request from Russian Federal Statistics Service. These are the official census data; actual figures may be higher. Data for 2010.

Czech Republic: data received upon request from Czech Statistical Office. Data for 2011.

Lithuania: data received upon request from Statistics Lithuania. Data for 2011.

Slovakia, Bulgaria, Albania, Armenia, Montenegro: Shachter 2015. Data for 2011.

* The percentage of foreign-born in the population of each country (column 7 in the table) was calculated for 2010, based on United Nations (2015).

* I used country reports from GLOBALCIT as a source of information about citizenship law, citizenship policy and migration trends in European countries. See www.globalcit.eu.

CHAPTERS 2-4

The principal methodology in these chapters consisted of interviews, most of which were carried out in 2014–15. I have been conducting fieldwork and interviews in Serbia since 2012 and conducted the majority of the research between June and October 2014. I carried out the bulk of fieldwork and interviews in Mexico between November 2014 and March 2015. I have been collecting data in Israel since 2008 and conducted most of the interviews between April and August 2015. In each study case, I conducted about fifty interviews with dual citizens and applicants and about ten interviews with bureaucrats, consular officials, and experts who offer services related to citizenship. I also collected citizenship and immigration statistics from various official and unofficial sources. In addition, I carried out ethnographic observation in relevant border crossings, embassies and consulates.

Interviews were 75 to 150 minutes in duration. They were conducted in Serbian, Spanish, Hebrew, or English, according to respondents' preference. Interviews included questions about three topics: 1) how respondents obtained, or tried to obtain, dual citizenship; 2) what motivated them to apply, including the way that they used it or envisioned themselves or others using it; and 3) how they evaluated the phenomenon from a normative perspective. I also noted respondents' life histories in brief. I coded and analyzed the interviews based on predefined themes (e.g., actual and projected uses of second nationality) as well as themes that emerged inductively from the material (e.g., perceptions of migrants in Mexico).

CHAPTER 2

The material primarily consists of forty-eight in-depth interviews with Hungarian-Serbian dual citizens and applicants. The sample is nonrandom, since random sampling would be technically impossible (there is no list of dual citizens). The primary method of selection was strategic sampling: I defined a population of interest and overrepresented it in the sample. This population of interest includes strategic dual citizens—that is, individuals who do not ethnically identify as Hungarian but acquire Hungarian citizenship. While ethnic Hungarians form an estimated 85 to 90 percent of citizenship recipients and strategic applicants only 10 to 15 percent (according to Hungarian consular officials), in the sample these two subgroups were given equal representation.

I conducted most of the interviews between June and October 2014. During that time, I resided in Belgrade and made frequent trips around Vojvodina. I conducted nineteen interviews in Belgrade and twenty-seven in Vojvodina (fifteen in and around Subotica and twelve in other towns). I also interviewed two dual citizens who had migrated to Western Europe. In terms of ethnicity, twenty-one respondents self-identified as ethnic Hungarians and nineteen as ethnic Serbs. Eight respondents of mixed parentage did not identify themselves as either Hungarian or Serb. These respondents defined themselves as Yugoslav or Vojvodinian. Some of the people who identified as Serbs also had some Hungarian, Croatian, German, or Slovak ancestry.

I recruited respondents using a snowball sampling method. Respondent recruitment was made possible thanks to help from personal acquaintances, local academics, and Hungarian language instructors. It was not difficult to locate respondents through these channels, because people were eager to help "friends of friends" and curious about foreigners, especially those who spoke Serbian. Interviews were conducted in Serbian or in English, according to respondents' preference.

The fact that I cannot speak Hungarian affected the selection of ethnic Hungarian respondents, because I only had access to people who spoke Serbian or English and had social ties with Serbs. This meant that almost all my Hungarian interviewees were urban and educated. Moreover, the fact that interviews were conducted in Serbian most likely influenced respondents' self-presentation. Most other studies of Hungarian-Serbian dual citizens were conducted in the Hungarian language, by scholars including Szabolcs Pogonyi, Attila Papp, Tamás Kiss, and Agnes Vass (in English, see Pogonyi 2017, 2019; Danero Iglesias, Sata and Vass 2016).

In addition to interviews with dual citizens, I also conducted interviews with officials at the Hungarian consulate in Subotica and the embassy in Belgrade. During those visits to the consulate and the embassy, I also observed the application procedure and carried out informal conversations with applicants. I visited four language schools in Belgrade and Subotica that offered classes in Hungarian and interviewed directors and teachers there. I attended a Hungarian language course in Belgrade for Serbs who wish to apply for citizenship and observed the dynamics in class.

CHAPTER 3

The analysis draws on forty-six in-depth interviews with dual nationals and with Mexicans who were involved in strategic birth in the United States. They included thirty-six respondents who were born in the United States and ten parents who strategically gave birth in the United States. The bulk of the interviews were conducted between November 2014 and April 2015. During those months, I resided in Monterrey, the largest city in northeastern Mexico. About half of the interviews (twenty-one) were carried out in Monterrey, and fifteen others were conducted in cross-border cities: Reynosa-McAllen, Nuevo Laredo-Laredo, and Tijuana-San Diego. Ten other interviews were conducted with dual nationals who were living in Mexico City, in Colima, or in the United States.

I recruited respondents using a snowball sampling method, as random sampling was impossible. I employed strategic subsampling, meaning that sufficient numbers of respondents were recruited to represent each relevant subpopulation: Monterrey parents who practiced strategic birth and dual nationals, border-town birth strategizers and dual nationals, and US-born return migrants. Interviews were conducted in Spanish, except when respondents preferred English.

I recruited the initial respondents with the help of personal acquaintances and local academics in Monterrey. The recruitment of respondents was significantly more challenging than in the other cases. Most potential respondents did not find the topic of dual nationality interesting, and exhibited a suspicious and uncooperative attitude, which made it difficult to secure interviews. This suspicious attitude might be connected to the controversial nature of cross-border births, and to the fact that the research was conducted for an American university.

I communicated with respondents in Spanish, highlighted the fact that I was Israeli, and occasionally shared my own experiences with immigration authorities as an international student in the United States. Nonetheless, it is likely that my affiliation with Princeton University made respondents view me as a connected to the United States, making them evasive at times. In particular, a Mexican interviewer might have gotten less defensive responses to questions like "Why don't you use your citizenship to move to the US?" (the responses discussed under "opportunities" in chapter 3) and "How would you respond to criticisms by Americans saying that you or your child should not get citizenship?" (discussed under "dual citizenship as social closure").

The sample is representative of middle- and upper-class individuals in Monterrey and the Texas-Tamaulipas border. This region is similar to other border regions—El Paso-Ciudad Juarez and San Diego-Tijuana—in two features: the tight interconnection between both sides of the border, and the extreme levels of insecurity on the Mexican side. On the other hand, Monterrey is significantly richer than other border cities: in 2012, the city's GDP per capita ($17,661) was 75 to 85 percent higher than in Tijuana or Ciudad Juarez. This difference in economic terms should be kept in mind when drawing more general conclusions from the findings.

In addition to the interviews with dual nationals and birth tourists, I conducted interviews with Mexican and American consular staff at the Mexican consulates in McAllen, Texas and San Diego, California, and the US consulate in Monterrey. I also interviewed providers of medical insurance that cover the costs of births in the United States.

CHAPTER 4

The chapter uses material from fifty in-depth interviews with EU-Israeli dual citizens and applicants. The sample is nonrandom, since random sampling would be technically impossible, and respondents were recruited using a snowball technique. I conducted the interviews in two waves: twenty-two interviews in 2008–9 and twenty-eight interviews in 2015. In addition to the new interviews in 2015, I also conducted follow-up interviews with six of the first-wave respondents.

Interviewees held dual citizenship from Germany (fifteen respondents), Romania (ten), France (nine), Poland (five), or Hungary (four). There were one to two respondents who had sought citizenship from each of the following countries: Britain, the Czech Republic, Bulgaria, Greece, and Italy. Forty interviewees were between twenty and thirty-five years old ("third generation") and ten were between fifty and seventy years old ("second generation").

I conducted all of the interviews in Hebrew. One factor that was likely to have had an effect was the fact that I am myself part of the studied population. I am a third-generation Israeli of Romanian origin and, since 2007, a dual citizen of Israel and Romania. Having the same background as my respondents and partaking in the same phenomenon made it easy to build rapport, which helped them to open up quickly. My close familiarity with Israeli society and culture also allowed me to identify various nuances in their discourse.

In addition to interviews with dual citizens, I also conducted interviews with officials at the German, Romanian, Polish, and French embassies in Tel-Aviv. I also carried out several sessions of ethnographic observation at those embassies. In addition, I interviewed lawyers who specialize in citizenship applications.

NOTES

Introduction

1. Spiro 1997; Sejersen 2008; Blätter et al. 2009; Harpaz and Mateos 2019.
2. See Brubaker 1996; Ong 1999; Joppke 2003; Mazzolari 2009; Pogonyi et al. 2010; Tintori 2011; Cook-Martin 2013; Harpaz 2013; Mateos 2015; and Bauböck 1994, 2003, 2010b.
3. Throughout this book, I will use the term "the West" to refer to the countries of Western Europe as well as the United States, Canada, Australia and New Zealand.
4. The names of respondents were changed to protect their privacy. A more detailed account of these cases is given in the relevant chapters.
5. In this book, I focus on citizenship as a formal status, in a sense that largely overlaps with the term "nationality." I will mostly use "citizenship" for the European and Israeli cases (where the involved countries do not make a distinction between citizenship and nationality) while mostly using "nationality" for the American-Mexican case. Mexico makes a distinction between nationals and citizens—the former term simply denotes state membership; the latter denotes full political rights. Dual nationality is allowed but dual citizenship is not. See FitzGerald 2005, 178; Hoyo 2015a,b. On the distinction between nationals and citizens in the United States, see Spiro 1997, 1417n20.
6. See Brubaker 1992a, chapter 1, for a discussion of the reasons behind this neglect.
7. On immigration to the West, see Bauböck 1994, 2003; Yang 1994; Jones-Correa 2001; Staton, Jackson, and Canache 2007; Bloemraad 2004, 2006; Mazzolari 2007; Joppke 2010a; Vink and de Groot 2010; and Vink et al. 2013. On nationalism in Central and Eastern Europe, see Brubaker 1992b, 1996, 1998; Pogonyi 2015, 2017; Ragazzi and Balalosvka 2011; Štiks 2010; Bauböck 2010b; Knott 2015; and Dumbrava 2015.
8. On inclusion and exclusion, see Shafir and Peled 1998; Alba 2005; Simon 2012; and Bloemraad 2018. On citizenship and global inequality, see Shachar 2009; Milanovic 2010; Tanasoca 2014; Boatcă 2015; and Harpaz 2015a, 2019.
9. Joppke 2007. See also Bloemraad 2018. Another key dimension of citizenship that was identified in the literature is citizenship as practice and as civic participation. The discussion of these components is given here under rights and identity.
10. Brubaker 1992a.
11. Brubaker 1992a, 1996. See also Hayden 1992; Liebich 2000; and Joppke 2005.
12. See Brubaker 1992a; Joppke 2005; Gerstle 2015; Spiro 2015; and Bloemraad and Sheares 2017.
13. Shachar 1998; Dumbrava 2014b, 2015; Tsuda 2010; see also Brubaker and Kim 2011; and Kim 2016.
14. Weil 2001; Brubaker 1999.
15. Weil 2001; Hansen and Weil 2001; Joppke 2019.
16. Martin 2002; Howard 2008; Naujoks 2009; Joppke 2010.
17. Howard 2005.

154 NOTES TO INTRODUCTION

18. See Ong 1999; Joppke 2005; Vink and de Groot 2010; Vink and Bauböck 2013; and Dumbrava 2014b.

19. Marshall 1950.

20. John Torpey has famously argued that the modern state monopolizes the means of legitimate movement. Torpey 2000.

21. See Morris 2012.

22. Joppke 2007.

23. According to the *Economist* Democracy Index, just under half of the world's countries (49.3%) are democratic. The Polity IV index published by the Center for Systemic Peace uses slightly different measures and categorizes 58% of the world's countries as democracies. See Desilver 2017; and Democracy Index 2016.

24. Brubaker 1990, 1992a.

25. Kochenov 2019. See also Weber 1961; Heather 2004; Sassen 2006; and FitzGerald and Cook-Martin 2014.

26. Yang 1994; Bloemraad 2006; see Bloemraad 2018.

27. Bloemraad 2013; Hakimzadeh and Cohn 2007; Bloemraad and Sheares 2017; Simonsen 2017; Warikoo and Bloemraad 2017.

28. Alba and Foner 2014.

29. Light, Massoglia and King 2014; Pietrantuono 2016. See Bloemraad and Sheares 2017.

30. Weil 2001; Shachar 1999; Gerstle 2015; Spiro 2015.

31. Brubaker 1990. See also Weil 2012, 4.

32. See discussion in chapters 2, 3, and 4 of this book. Also see Cohen 2007; FitzGerald 2009; and Harpaz 2013.

33. Joppke 2019:14. See also Joppke 2010.

34. Ong 1999; FitzGerald 2012; Harpaz 2013; Harpaz and Mateos 2019.

35. Brubaker 2017a; see also Joppke 2014, 2016; and Fargues 2017.

36. Brubaker 1996.

37. Brubaker 1992a, 31. See also Hindess 1998.

38. Bauböck 2019.

39. Arendt 1951; Darling 2009.

40. Malkki 1992.

41. Spiro 1997; Shuck 2002; Harpaz and Mateos 2019.

42. In this text, I refer to global hierarchy in the sense of a stratified global structure. This usage should be distinguished from hierarchy in the sense of a structure of authority, as used by David Lake (2007).

43. Macklin 2007.

44. Shachar 2009. See also Macklin 2007; and Shachar and Hirschl 2007, 2013, 2014.

45. Mau et al. 2015.

46. Spiro 1997, 2019; Koslowski 2000; Shuck 2002; Weil 2011; Harpaz and Mateos 2019.

47. Naturalization is far from being the only pathway to dual citizenship. More people acquire this status at birth because one or both their parents is an immigrant. Nonetheless, naturalization law provides a good indicator of countries' relation to dual citizenship because it is a site where access to citizenship is relatively easy to control (compared to transmission at birth) and such legislative changes are relatively easy for scholars to identify.

In figure I.1, the Western Europe category includes EU15 countries as well as Switzerland, Norway, and Iceland (eighteen countries). Latin American countries include all South and Central American countries as well as the Dominican Republic, Cuba, and Haiti (twenty-one countries). CEE countries include the post-communist members of the EU as well as Russia, Belarus,

NOTES TO INTRODUCTION 155

Moldova, Ukraine, Georgia, Azerbaijan, Armenia, Turkey, and Malta (ten countries in 1990, twenty-five in 2016). Asian countries include Bangladesh, Bhutan, Cambodia, China, East Timor (which did not exist in 1990), India, Indonesia, Japan, Laos, Malaysia, Myanmar, Nepal, Pakistan, the Philippines, Singapore, South Korea, Sri Lanka, Taiwan, Thailand, and Vietnam. More data on dual citizenship are found at the MACIMIDE Global Dual Citizenship Database compiled by Maarten Peter Vink, Gerard-Rene de Groot, and Chun Luk. A recent paper that used that database to analyze trends in dual citizenship permission (Vink et al. 2016) came up with similar results to the ones presented here. See https://macimide.maastrichtuniversity.nl/dual-cit-database.

48. Weil 2011.
49. Ellis et al. 2007; Escobar 2007; Lafleur 2011; Collyer 2014.
50. Spiro 1997; Howard 2005; Faist and Gerdes 2008; Sejersen 2008; Weil 2011.
51. See, for example, Ragazzi and Balalovska 2011; and Vink and Bauböck 2013.
52. Weil 2012, 2017; Spiro 2015.
53. GLOBALCIT country reports: Bernitz 2010; Fagerlund and Brander 2013. See Howard 2005; Vink and de Groot 2010; Vink and Bauböck 2013; and Vonk 2012.
54. GLOBALCIT country reports: Kadirbeyoglu 2012; Hoyo 2015a. See FitzGerald 2005; Escobar 2007; Vonk 2014; and Leblang 2017.
55. Iordachi 2004; Ragazzi and Balalovska 2011; Štiks 2010; Pogonyi 2017; Rava 2013; Dumbrava 2019. See Brubaker 1996; Bauböck 2003; and Pogonyi et al. 2010.
56. Vink et al. 2013; Simon 2012; Tintori 2011; Izquierdo and Chao 2015; Mateos 2019.
57. See, however, Harpaz 2015a, 2019; and Shachter 2015. Some of data used in those publications, in addition to new statistics, are reanalyzed in chapter 1.
58. For example, Brubaker 1992a, 1996; Bauböck 1994, 2003; Bloemraad 2006; and Joppke 2010.
59. Tintori 2011; Cook-Martin 2013; Harpaz 2013, 2015; Izquierdo and Chao 2015; Mateos 2016, 2019.
60. EU dual citizenship in Latin America has already received significant scholarly attention (see previous note).
61. Iordachi 2004; Neofotistos 2009; Harpaz 2015a; Knott 2015; Dumbrava 2019; Pogonyi 2019. Japan and Korea also offer some access to coethnics abroad which in some cases might be used to obtain citizenship and then emigrate onward. See Tsuda 2010; and Kim 2016.
62. Lien 2006; Balta and Altan-Olcay 2016; Feere 2015; Grant 2015.
63. The focus on strategic births by Mexicans rather than by Chinese or Russian allows me to explore this phenomenon in the broader context of immigration and cross-border interaction.
64. Paul 2011; Harder and Zhyznomirska 2012; Mateos 2013.
65. Curiel 2004; Balistreri et al. 2017; Azzolini and Guetto 2017.
66. Dzankic 2012; Shachar and Bauböck 2014; Shachar 2017; Joppke 2019.
67. Israel's GDP per capita (PPP) in 2017 was $38,261, equal to 93% of EU average. Mexico's GDP per capita (PPP) at $18,273 and Serbia's at $15,428 represent 44% and 37% of EU average, respectively (World Bank statistics). In 2010–11, the number of Serbian-born persons living in OECD countries equaled 9% of the Serbian population, in Serbia reflecting a relatively high emigration rate. Emigration from Mexico is even higher, with 12.1% of Mexican-born living abroad. The equivalent figure for Israel is 4.1% (OECD 2015). About 80% of Mexico's exports go to the United States and about 65% of Serbia's exports go to the EU. Israel's exports are more evenly distributed, with 30% going to the United States, 35% to the EU, and 35% to the rest of the world.
68. The US government cannot deport US citizens. However, when Mexican immigrant parents are deported, their underage children typically leave with them. See Mateos 2014, 2016, 2019; and chapter 3 of this book.

Chapter 1: Dual Citizenship as a Strategy of Global Upward Mobility

1. Bloemraad 2004, 2006; Simon 2012; Vink et al. 2012; Jones-Correa 2001; Mazzolari 2009; Staton, Jackson, and Canache 2007; Portes, Escobar, and Arana 2008.
2. FitzGerald 2012.
3. Portes, Guarnizo, and Haller 2002. See also Amit 2014.
4. Some citizens of Western countries have a practical interest in dual citizenship as a means of evading tax authorities or law enforcement. Such dual citizenship is neither sentimental nor compensatory. This is a relatively small minority mainly composed of globally mobile professionals, millionaires, and criminals.
5. See Bloemraad 2004; and Morawska 2004. I do not argue that immigrants in the West completely lose interest in their original citizenship. The persistence of such interest is proven by the fact that immigrants from countries that permit dual citizenship are more likely to naturalize (Vink et al. 2013). However, as the literature shows, the actual usefulness of such citizenship is usually quite limited.
6. In Germany, only 14% of first-generation immigrants and 9% of second-generation immigrants are dual nationals (Statistiches Bundesamt 2012). In the United States, out of 40 million descendants of Mexican and Italian immigrants who are potentially eligible for dual citizenship, only about 110,000 (or 0.3% of the total) have applied for descent-based dual citizenship. Source: MPI Data Hub, "Estimates of the Top 20 Diaspora Groups in the United States, 2011"; Tintori 2012; Escobar 2015. When calculating demand in the United States, I deducted foreign-born Mexicans and Italians in order to include only US-born descendants. In Canada, only 190,100 out of 5.7 million second-generation Canadians (i.e., Canadian-born citizens who have at least one foreign-born parent) had dual citizenship—about 3.3 % (Canada Statistics 2011, 2015). Even though data are incomplete, the pattern in Germany, the United States, and Canada seems to reflect the general trend in rich Western countries. One outlier seems to be France, where 23% of second-generation immigrants were dual citizens (Simon 2012). In France, children of North African and Turkish immigrants had much higher rates of dual citizenship than descendants of Italians or Spaniards. This has to do with Turkish and Moroccan laws that make citizenship transmission *jure sanguinis* automatic, but likely also reflects an identity element.
7. On ethnic citizenship in Eastern Europe, see Brubaker 1992b, 1998, 2000; Bauböck 2003; and Dumbrava 2014b, 2019. On ancestry- and ethnicity-based citizenship acquisition in general, see Dumbrava 2014a,b; and Harpaz 2015a,b. On Spanish and Italian citizenship in Latin America, see Tintori 2011; Cook-Martin 2013; Izquierdo and Chao 2015; and Mateos 2013, 2019. On dual citizenship in Israel, see Harpaz 2013. On Malaysian citizenship: Ong 1999. Bulgarian citizenship: Maeva 2005; Neofotistos 2009. On Romanian citizenship: Knott 2015, 2019; Hungarian citizenship: Pogonyi 2017, 2019. On residence and birth strategies, see Ong 1999; Mateos and Durand 2012; Mateos 2013; Grant 2015; Yan 2015; and Balta and Altan-Olcay 2016.
8. Hindess 1998:68. Cf. Brubaker 1992a.
9. See Castles 2005; Shachar 2009; and Harpaz 2019. On the application of global inequality to explain immigration and naturalization, see Massey et al. 1993; and Vink et al. 2013. On its role within discussions of distributive justice, see Macklin 2007; Shachar and Hirschl 2007; and Tanasoca 2014.
10. Milanovic 2010.
11. Milanovic 2010, 2012.
12. Piketty 2014; Lakner and Milanovic 2013. See also Korzeniewicz and Moran 2009.
13. Gaps in literacy: World Bank 2016a. Child mortality: UNDP 2013; see Shachar and Hirschl 2007. Crime: UNODC 2014.
14. Wang 2004; Shamir 2005; Mau et al. 2015.
15. Czaika and de Haas 2014.

NOTES TO CHAPTER 1   157

16. Shachar 2009.

17. Macklin 2007.

18. This is not to deny, of course, that many citizens in Western countries suffer from poverty and exclusion.

19. An alternative index that ranks countries by citizenship value was created in 2016 by Chris Kälin (founder of the consulting company Henley & Partners) and Dimitry Kochenov (see https://nationalityindex.com). The Kälin and Kochenov index determines countries' rank order while updating it annually to take into account economic and political changes; thus, its main aim is descriptive. In contrast, the aim of the model I outline here is analytical: it identifies enduring structures of global citizenship inequality and serves as the basis for a theory that explains variations in the acquisition and use of dual citizenship around the world. One key difference is that in the Kälin and Kochenov index, 30% of the value of a country's citizenship is based on citizens' right to reside and work in other countries. I do not treat this factor as a component in the value of citizenship, because of its derivative and transient character. See also Harpaz, forthcoming.

20. Meyer et al. 1997; Wimmer and Feinstein 2010.

21. As a robustness test, I repeated the modeling with Polity IV regime type data. Country positions did not change significantly.

22. I use country rankings and not scores because all these indices are relative, meaning that scores have no meaning in themselves. The CQI was calculated by taking a geometric mean of a country's rankings in the three indices mentioned above (HDI, State Fragility Index, and Democracy Index). The geometric mean is used in order to standardize the rankings. Countries' ranks in different indicators were highly correlated with each other. Rank order correlations (Spearman's rank correlation coefficients, which assesses the degree to which they follow the same order, from 0 [no similarity] to 1 [identical]) were between 0.65 and 0.89, at $p<0.001$.

23. The hierarchy of passports may be expressed not only in terms of quantity—how many countries one may enter—but also in terms of quality, or the attractiveness of the countries to which one may enter. Citizens of most Asian and African nations are not allowed into EU countries without a visa; the United States is even more selective and also requires visas from Latin American and Eastern European citizens who have visa-free access to the EU. Here, for the sake of simplicity, I use Henley & Partners' simple count of the number of countries one may enter. See however Henley & Partners and Kochenov's new index, which also takes into account the "weight" of the countries to which one is allowed entry. Source: Henley & Partners Visa Restrictions Index 2016.

24. The division into three tiers also echoes well-established ways of discussing class structure, with a structure of upper, middle, and lower/working classes. It is more useful than the dichotomous division to global "north" and "south" because of the huge gaps in citizenship value between different countries outside the West (e.g., GDP per capita in Mexico or Turkey is ten to twenty times higher than in poor African or Asian countries). See Wallerstein 1974; and Clark and Beckfield 2009; Harpaz, forthcoming.

25. Japan and South Korea enjoy first-tier citizenship, but they will not be discussed in this book because they do not offer many possibilities for dual citizenship, let alone long-distance citizenship. Therefore, they do not play a major role in the phenomenon of compensatory citizenship. See the work of Takeyuki Tsuda (2010) and Jaeeun Kim (2011, 2016, 2018, 2019) on return migration to Japan and South Korea by descendants of emigrants.

26. Countries were classified as first-tier citizenship countries if they were in the top 15% of the Citizenship Quality Index and the top 10% of the Passport Index. The Passport Index is distributed more densely because it allows "ties"—that is, two or more countries may have the same ranking, whereas the CQI does not.

27. Countries were classified as middle-tier if they were ranked between the 50th and the 85th to 90th percentiles in both indices. I also classified some countries as having middle-tier citizenship if they were ranked well above the median in one measure and almost at it on the other.

This led to the inclusion of Russia, Jamaica, the United Arab Emirates, Kuwait and Ukraine in the middle tier.

28. Note that long-distance citizenship acquisition includes two forms of eligibility that have been created through very different historical processes. Eligibility for ancestry-based acquisition is the result of historical voluntary emigration, whereas coethnic citizenship is usually offered to stranded minorities that have seen borders move "over" them, usually against their will. These differences are discussed in depth in chapters 2 and 4.

29. See Surak 2016; and Shachar 2017.

30. I presented and analyzed some of these data in a recent paper (Harpaz 2019). That paper included analyses of part of the dataset on prevalence that is presented here (13 countries); here I analyze the full dataset, which includes 30 countries. Jason Shachter (2015) presents census data on dual citizenship in 18 countries, but does not analyze the causes for differences in prevalence.

31. Source: United Nations 2015.

32. Hundreds of thousands of Colombian immigrants naturalized in Venezuela in the 2000s. The data are for 2012; given the crisis that Venezuela is currently suffering from, it is likely that many persons with dual citizenships have emigrated out of the country. In Mexico, dual citizenship with the United States is mostly produced in one of three pathways: voluntary return migration of migrants with US-born children, forced deportation of parents to such children, and deliberate "birth tourism" by nonmigrant parents (see chapter 3). Long-distance acquisition was an additional major pathway to dual citizenship in Mexico, Israel, and Venezuela. In each of the former two countries, over 100,000 have acquired ancestry-based EU citizenship, whereas in Venezuela the number exceeds 300,000. See Mateos 2019; Harpaz 2013, 2015; and Schwartz 2014. The high number of foreign-born in Croatia and Serbia consists mostly of coethnics who arrived from other former Yugoslav republics during the wars of the 1990s (e.g., ethnic Serbs who left Croatia and Bosnia-Herzegovina to resettle in Serbia).

33. Harpaz 2015a.

34. For Hungary, I use statistics from Bálint 2014 that pertain to the period January 2011–August 2014. I do not use here more up-to-date acquisition statistics published in Pogonyi 2017 because they do not include specific acquisition data for countries outside the CEE region. In chapter 2, I use the most up-to-date data available that pertains to citizenship acquisition from Serbia, Romania, Ukraine, and Slovakia.

35. Sartori 2011. The average annual naturalization figure was calculated for 1998–2009.

36. Sartori 2011; Eurostat 2015.

37. The Other category includes Israel (1.5% of the total sample) and unspecified countries (3%), at least half of which can be assumed to be middle tier. Therefore, we can safely say that 90% of the long-distance acquisition in the sample were made by citizens of middle-tier countries.

38. Note, also, the absence of third-tier countries (except Cuba), as few European descendants or coethnics live in those countries. This corroborates the theory's prediction regarding the low availability of Western dual citizenship in third-tier countries.

39. I used statistics that pertain to the years 2011–14 because they also include details on acquisition by citizens of non-European countries (data for later years, which will be used in chapter 2, only pertain to countries from Central and Eastern Europe).

40. In Eastern European countries, the number of people who identified as Hungarian speakers was nearly identical to the number of people who declared their ethnic identity to be Hungarian, reflecting the overlap between language and ethnicity in the region (see chapter 2). The United States, Canada, and Australia do not collect data on the ethnic identity of whites, only on ancestry and language use. The number of people who reported Hungarian ancestry in each of those countries was much higher than those who spoke Hungarian. For example, in the United States, 1.5 million people reported Hungarian ancestry but only 93,102 spoke it at home (US Census 2012;

ACS 2013). I used the figure on Hungarian speakers in order to capture people who would not need to learn Hungarian especially for that purpose and to make the populations comparable.

41. Romanian National Institute of Statistics 2013; Bálint 2014.

42. The figure represents just 0.1% out of the 1.5 million Americans who reported having Hungarian ancestry (US Census 2012; ACS 2013).

43. Romanian citizens were limited in terms of their EU free movement rights until 2014 and were prohibited from working in countries such as Germany and Austria. The EU citizenship of Croatians is still limited as of 2018.

44. The acquisition data are based on Tintori 2012. The migration data were calculated on the basis of AltreItalie 2014. I calculated the number of Italians who settled in each country by deducting the number of return migrants from those who left for the country. The data on return migration is likely to be imperfect; it only lists returnees since 1900, whereas emigration data begin in 1860. When ignoring the statistics on return and counting only emigrants, the results stayed the same.

45. Italy also offers dual citizenship to Italian speakers in territories that it had lost to Yugoslavia, but they are not included in the statistics presented here.

46. There are many factors that affect the size of the eligible population beside original population size (see Hout and Goldstein 1994). One of the most crucial in this case is the timing of migration. Italian emigration to the United States, Argentina, and Brazil peaked between 1890 and 1920, whereas emigration to Canada, Australia, and Western Europe mostly took place in the 1950s and 1960s. In this analysis, I will disregard these differences and the potential bias they might produce.

47. In the 2009 US census, 18 million people reported having Italian ancestry. Latin American and European countries do not collect this kind of information. Source: US Census 2012.

48. Harpaz 2015a.

Chapter 2: Serbia: Becoming Hungarian, Returning to Europe

1. Weiler 1997; Kochenov 2014.

2. Dumbrava 2014b.

3. Pogonyi et al. 2010; Dumbrava 2019; Harpaz 2015a. The integration of Macedonia was a major Bulgarian objective in the First and Second Balkan Wars and the First and Second World Wars. Other EU countries that offer citizenship to coethnics in "lost" territories include Greece, Croatia, Germany, and Italy.

4. Simon 2017.

5. Subotica.com 2018.

6. Pogonyi 2017. On coethnic citizenship, see Brubaker 1996, 2000, 2006; Iordachi 2004; Pogonyi et al. 2010; and Kovacs and Tóth 2013. On former Yugoslavia, see Jansen 2008; Štiks 2010; Ragazzi and Balalovska 2011; Vasilijević 2014; and Krasniqi and Stjepanović 2015.

7. The common usage of "nation" in Central and Eastern Europe is different from its usage in the English-speaking world: in the West, "nation" roughly correlates with "country," whereas in Central and Eastern Europe it is usually synonymous with "ethnic group." See Verdery 1998. Similarly, "nationality" in Central and Eastern Europe is synonymous with "ethnic identity" and not, as in the West, with "citizenship." For example, the question in the Serbian census about citizens' "national belonging" (*nacionalna pripadnost*) is translated in the English version of the census as "ethnicity."

8. I am not aware of this distinction being widely used in English. I introduce it here for the sake of clarity (inspired by the distinction in Russian between *русский* (pertaining to Russian ethnicity) and *российский* (pertaining to the Russian state). Most Serbians would refer to Serbian Hungarians as *Mađari iz Srbije*—Hungarians from Serbia—and this is how this population usually

refers to itself. The underlying assumption is that only ethnicity is strong and "essential" enough to be represented with a noun.

9. In 1918, the Kingdom of Serbia (which existed officially since 1882) expanded at the expense of the late Austria-Hungary and united with Montenegro. It became the Kingdom of Serbs, Croats, and Slovenes, renamed Yugoslavia in 1929. The name Yugoslavia survived until 2004, by which point it included only the republics of Serbia and Montenegro. It was succeeded by the State Union of Serbia and Montenegro, which existed until 2006. In that year, Montenegro seceded and Serbia became a separate country once again.

10. Vojvodina actually comprises three geographical subregions: Bačka, Banat, and Srem. Historically, only Bačka (the largest and most populous subregion) had a strong Hungarian presence. During World War II, only Bačka was under Hungarian occupation, whereas Banat and Srem were under German or Croatian control. For the sake of simplicity and clarity, I will ignore intraregional differences and refer to Vojvodina, which includes the entire area that Hungary lost to Yugoslavia after World War I and remains a distinct administrative unit within Serbia.

11. There were a number of massacres and deportations of Serbs by Hungarians and of Hungarians by partisans. Nonetheless, the situation in Vojvodina during World War II was very different from the genocidal ethnic conflict that claimed hundreds of thousands of lives in Croatia and Bosnia-Herzegovina, with Serbs suffering the heaviest casualties. After the war, about 500,000 ethnic Germans were expelled from Vojvodina. See Ludanyi 1979; Boarov 2001; Bieber and Wintergarten 2006; and Laszak 2010.

12. Bieber and Wintergarten 2006.

13. Boarov 2001; Manic 2011; Sobyak 2012.

14. We can track this decline with relative accuracy because CEE countries include questions about ethnic identity and mother tongue in their national censuses. See Serbia Census 2012; and Ilić 2010.

15. The demographic weight of minorities in Vojvodina was diluted through massive resettlements of Serbs from Bosnia-Herzegovina and Croatia in the 1940s and then again in the 1990s. See Boarov 2001.

16. In 2005, Hungarian voters rejected in a referendum a proposal to offer dual citizenship to cross-border Hungarians. The reluctance to offer dual citizenship presumably had to do with a wish to avoid conflict with neighboring countries (above all Slovakia) and a reluctance to share the country's scant resources with new citizens from poorer countries. Moreover, the socialist party, which was in power for most of the early 2000s, suspected that the new citizens might lean to the right politically (which they did). See Sütő 2012; and Kovács and Tóth 2013.

17. This reluctance to use ethnic categories also sets Hungary's citizenship law apart from "classic" laws of ethnic repatriation like those of Israel (the 1950 Law of Return) or Germany (the 1949 Basic Law), which do not shy away from using the terms "Jew" or "German." See Joppke 2005; and Harpaz and Herzog 2018. See also FitzGerald et al. 2018 about the avoidance of explicit racial and ethnic categories in the policies of European countries.

18. Furthermore, if the law were defined as reacquisition of the citizenship that were lost by applicants' parents or grandparents, Hungary would potentially be in violation of the Treaty of Trianon, which mandated that individuals should choose just one citizenship.

19. Starr 1992; Dumbrava 2014b; Joppke 2005.

20. Pogonyi 2017, chapter 3.

21. *Daily Mail* 2010.

22. CSI 2018. For criticisms that were leveled against the citizenship policies of EU entrants, see BBC 2009; Bauböck 2010; and EUDO 2010.

23. Küpper 2006; Bauböck 2010; Dumbrava 2014b; Pogonyi 2017.

24. A clear expression of this ideology—Hungary as the protector of all Hungarians—can be seen in the deliberate policy of including ethnic Hungarians from Vojvodina and western Ukraine among Hungary's delegates to the European Parliament. This is meant to demonstrate to cross-border Hungarians outside the EU that, thanks to Orbán, they are members of the EU not just as individual passport holders but also as a political community.

25. Kovács and Tóth 2013; Scheppele 2014a. This hypothesis is further reinforced by the Hungarian government's aggressively promoting nonresident voting among transborder "new Hungarians" while at the same time making voting difficult for Hungarian emigrants in Western Europe.

26. Voter turnout among cross-border Hungarians—in Serbia, about 35% according to Hungarian consular officials—was lower than among Hungary's resident citizens, but is high when compared to other nonresident citizen populations. Scheppele 2014b.

27. In 2018, there were 225,025 valid votes by mail in the 2018 elections (mostly representing the cross-border diaspora) and 96% of them went to Fidesz. Source: http://www.valasztas.hu/dyn/pv18/szavossz/hu/levjkv.html.

28. As far back as the eighteenth century, the German philosopher J. G. Herder predicted the extinction of the Hungarian language and the assimilation of Hungarians into the so-called sea of Germanics and Slavs that surrounds them. See Verdery 1979; and Abulof 2009.

29. Hungary Today 2018.

30. *Economist* 2019.

31. Bauböck 2010.

32. Brubaker 1992b, 1998, 2000.

33. Štiks 2010.

34. Figures are for 2011. Source: data received upon request from Serbian census.

35. Vasilijević 2012; Rava 2013; Waterbury 2014. In a manner consistent with the compensatory citizenship hypothesis, the number of ethnic Serbs from Bosnia, Croatia, and Montenegro who have taken up Serbian citizenship is not high.

36. This term was coined in Ragazzi and Balalovska 2011; see also Žilović 2012.

37. Pogonyi 2017.

38. There are also small Hungarian minorities in the remaining two countries that border Hungary—Croatia and Austria.

39. There were five countries where between 1,000 and 3,000 people applied for citizenship: Croatia, Russia, Israel, Australia, and the United States. See Bálint 2014. Croatia borders Hungary and actually has a small Hungarian community of 15,000. By August 2014, eleven percent of them gained Hungarian citizenship. Croatia is excluded from the following analysis because data for it were not available for 2016.

40. Compare to Pogonyi 2017, 170–71, and Pogonyi 2019. In the figure, ethnic Hungarians are those who identified in the national census as being of Hungarian ethnicity. There are also non-Hungarians who obtain Hungarian citizenship, and they will be discussed them in the next section.

41. Pogonyi 2017.

42. Danero Iglesias et al. 2016.

43. I received the data from the Hungarian consulate in Subotica, which is responsible for 93% of citizenship acquisition in Serbia. Note, however, that a full third of successful citizenship applications by Serbians were not filed in Serbia, but were submitted either on Hungarian territory or in Hungarian consulates in other countries (such as Austria). This was calculated in the following manner: 118,936 Serbian citizens acquired Hungarian citizenship from January 2011 to August 2014. Of this total, about 80,000 acquired their citizenship in Subotica and 5,839 at the embassy in Belgrade (personal communication with officials at the embassy on August 28, 2014).

162 NOTES TO CHAPTER 2

The remaining 32,000 new dual citizens can be assumed to have filed their application in Hungary or elsewhere. The April 2013 data show that more than 200,000 citizenship applications were filed in the territory of Hungary.

44. B92 2013; *Economist* 2013.

45. These two trends—a growth in Serbian emigration and growing discrepancy between Serbian-born and Serbian citizens—were observed in some of these datasets. I do not provide precise numbers because the different data sources provide different figures and are sometimes incomplete. On recent emigration from Serbia, see also Grečić 2016. Eurostat: "Population on 1 January by Five-Year Age Group, Sex, and Country of Birth"; "Population on 1 January by Five-Year Age Group, Sex, and Citizenship." http://ec.europa.eu/eurostat/web/population-demography-migration-projections/population-data/database. United Nations Population Division (UNPD): "International Migrant Stock 2015, by Destination and Origin." http://www.un.org/en/development/desa/population/migration/data/estimates2/estimates15.shtml. OECD: OECD International Migration Database. https://stats.oecd.org/Index.aspx?DataSetCode=MIG.

46. In the Israeli and Mexican cases, security was an independent motive that received a great deal of attention ("the passport as insurance policy"); this concern played a much smaller role in the Serbian case and therefore I do not assign it a subsection of its own.

47. The names of all respondents were changed to protect their privacy.

48. *Bunjevci* (plural of *Bunjevac*) are a small ethnic group (about 20,000 persons) found almost exclusively in Vojvodina. Bunjevci are Catholic and speak Serbo-Croatian, and until 1991 most of them identified as Croatian. In 1991, Serbia introduced a Bunjevac ethnic category in the census. Source: Serbia Census 2011. Most people who identify as Bunjevac in Serbia today would say *Bunjevci* are distinct from Croats and some even argue that *Bunjevci* are Catholic Serbs. Croatia, for its part, recognizes them as Croatian and offers them citizenship. Cf. Stjepanovic 2015.

49. There are about 1.3 million ethnic Serbs in Vojvodina (out of a total population of 1.9 million). It can be estimated that roughly half of them, or 650,000 people, hail from families with Vojvodinian ancestry. This calculation is based on the fact that immediately after World War II, there were about 580,000 Serbs in Vojvodina. The region has received about 225,000 Serb settlers after World War II and about 300,000 during the 1990s, and the population growth rate is close to zero. Of the population that is neither Serb nor Hungarian—about 350,000 people—between one-third and two-thirds can be assumed to be descended from families who have lived there for a long time (most ethnic Croats, Bunjevci, Slovaks, Czechs, and Romanians date from Austro-Hungarian times, while many Montenegrins and Roma settled in the region after 1920). Source: Ipsos 2011; Boarov 2011.

50. See Tatrai et al. 2017 for a discussion of comparable dynamics in Ukraine.

51. Castles 2004; cf. Cook-Martin 2013; Harpaz 2013.

52. Source: http://www.centarzaedukaciju.com/madjarski.php.

53. Pogonyi 2017; FitzGerald et al. 2018.

54. See Pogonyi 2017

55. Serbs actually have the same belief and are very surprised to meet foreigners who can speak Serbian. Many respondents assumed initially that I could speak the language because I had Serbian or Croatian ancestry.

56. MTI 2014; Simon 2017.

57. Bourdieu 1986, 1987.

58. Lazić 2000; Lazić and Cvejić 2007; Baćević 2014; cf. Eyal, Szelényi and Townsley 1998.

59. The preservation of records has to do with the fact that Hungarian authorities never attempted to exterminate Serbs. In contrast, in the parts of Vojvodina that were under Croatian control in World War II, birth records in many Serbian communities were destroyed.

60. See Pogonyi 2017, 2019 for a further discussion of these points.

NOTES TO CHAPTER 2   163

61. The case of Mladen (vignette 2), whose mother also applied for citizenship, is atypical in this sense. It is significant that they applied in 2011: if they applied in 2013 or later, it would have been more difficult for his mother to obtain citizenship because the required level of proficiency in Hungarian would be higher.
62. InSerbia 2014.
63. See Volčič 2007.
64. Lazić 2003.
65. Eyal et al. 1998.
66. e.g. Mojić 2012
67. Similar results were reported by Judit Molnár, a geographer who has conducted a series of research interviews with Hungarian political elites in Vojvodina (personal communication). Most of her respondents spontaneously brought the subject of emigration. See also Németh 2013.
68. Personal communications, September 2014. A report detailing those trends (in Hungarian) can be found at http://www.mnt.org.rs/22-Kiemelt-kozlemenyek/1043-Beszamolo-az-MNT-4-eves-tevekenysegerol.
69. GradSubotica 2016; Gluscevic 2017.
70. Moreh 2014.
71. Brubaker 2009.
72. Jansen 2009.
73. Tudurić 2008.
74. Jansen 2009.
75. Lazić 2000.
76. The view of visa restrictions as sanctions is inaccurate; the visa requirement was kept even after Milošević was replaced by a pro-European government in 2000, and Western-backed Bosnia-Herzegovina was subject to the same visa regime as Serbia. Interestingly, many Bosnian Muslims also believe that the visa requirement imposed on them until 2010 were motivated by vindictive discrimination (in their case, anti-Muslim).
77. World Bank 2016b. In 2010, Serbia's Gini index was 29.7, similar to Hungary's (29.4) and lower than that of Germany (31.1) or France (33.8). In the same year, the Gini index of the United States was 40.5, of Israel 42.8 and of Mexico 48.1.
78. Lazić 2003; Baćević 2014.
79. Lazić 2003; Ragazzi and Balalovka 2011; see also Wimmer 2002.
80. Bourdieu 1989.
81. Ramet 1996; Lazić 2000.
82. Lazić 2003.
83. On the other hand, emigration was not stigmatized as long as one preserved one's identity.
84. Tatrai et al. 2017; Higgins 2018.
85. Huszka 2007; Manić 2011.
86. Racz 2012.
87. Ilić 2010.
88. Hungarian citizenship policy is currently having a similar effect in Ukraine. See Tatrai et al. 2017. Another example in which a marginalized minority finds that its language has become valuable concerns German speakers in Hungary, who were able to reconnect with Germany and Austria after the fall of communism. See Gal 1993.
89. The same point came up in interviews that Szabolcs Pogonyi conducted among Vojvodina Hungarians. See Pogonyi 2017, 2019.
90. Personal communication, Katinka Beretka, Hungarian National Council.
91. Brubaker 1996; Bauböck 2010a; Štiks 2010; Ragazzi and Balalovska 2011; Stjepanovic 2015; Knott 2015, 2019; Poyongi 2017, 2019; Dumbrava 2019.

Chapter 3: Mexico: Strategic Birth as Elite Investment

1. See Massey and Espinosa 1997; Durand, Massey, and Zenteno 2001; Massey, Durand, and Malone 2002; Smith 2005; Telles and Ortiz 2008; FitzGerald 2009; and Alarcon 2011; Alba and Foner 2014.

2. See, however, Portes and Curtis 1987; FitzGerald 2005, 2009; Fox and Guglielmo 2012; and Mateos 2019. Note that in Mexico, citizenship and nationality are not the same. Nationality means state membership whereas citizenship which entails full political rights. Mexico does not permit dual citizenship, only dual nationality, and severely curtails the political rights of dual nationals. See FitzGerald 2005; and Hoyo 2015a, b.

3. This stands in contrast to Western Europe, where struggles over citizenship continue in the second (sometimes even third) generation of immigrants. These contestations stem from the dominance of *jus sanguinis* citizenship laws and the absence of automatic *jus soli* in most European countries and the origin countries (e.g., Turkey or Morocco). Under these conditions, the citizenship of the second generation becomes the object of dispute between the origin country, the destination country, and the individuals themselves. See Bauböck 2010. Immigration to Western Europe creates a "triadic nexus" of minority, homeland and external homeland that is similar to Brubaker's (1996) argument about coethnic minorities in Eastern Europe.

4. The term "citizenship constellation" is from Bauböck 2010.

5. This represents a break with the pattern of settlement-oriented immigration that dominated since the 1980s and intensified in the 1990s. Alarcon 2011; Massey, Durand, and Pren 2014; Gonzalez-Barrera 2015.

6. Mateos 2019. This estimate includes naturalized Mexican immigrants in the United States and their US-born children. Most of these individuals do not act upon their eligibility for dual nationality.

7. Several studies have begun to explore some aspects of American-Mexican dual nationality, including its political aspects (FitzGerald 2009), demographic proportions (Mateos 2019), and legal codification (Escobar 2015; Hoyo 2015a).

8. See Mateos 2019 for a more extensive discussion of these pathways.

9. Note that strategic birth is distinct from the well-known and pejorative term "anchor babies," which is applied to births by undocumented immigrants. This term is seen by some as dehumanizing because it implies that undocumented immigrants use children as "anchors" to protect themselves against being deported; in fact, having a US-born child does not protect one against deportation. Cf. Lien 2006; Balta and Altan-Olcay 2016; and Grant 2015.

10. Some European countries—for example, Germany or France—apply qualified forms of *jus soli*. Children of foreigners who were born in those countries and grew up there may obtain citizenship relatively easily. Strategic cross-border births, however, may only be practiced in countries with automatic *jus soli*, where any child born in the country receives citizenship automatically and unconditionally. Most Latin American countries have similar clauses and there are reports of strategic birth among them: for example, some Venezuelans and Paraguayans give birth in Brazil, apparently due to better health services as well as a wish to secure citizenship for their children.

11. Lien 2006; Feere 2015; Grant 2015; Yan 2015; Balta and Altan-Olcay 2016.

12. Sarabia 2015.

13. Hansen and Weil 2001.

14. For various reasons, however, the naturalization rate of immigrants in the United States is lower than in Canada and some Western European countries. See Bloemraad 2006; and Spiro 2015.

15. Gerstle 2015.

16. Alba 2005.

17. Weil 2012, 2017. See also Herzog 2010a.

18. Weil 2012, 2017; Spiro 1997, 2015. The "sovereign citizen" approach also contributed to the refusal of the US government to join the secular trend toward reactivating the practice citizenship stripping, unlike other countries such as Britain or Australia (at least as of early 2019). See Spiro 2014; and Joppke 2016.

19. Weil 2012

20. Feere 2015; Yan 2015; Jordan 2019.

21. Hoyo 2015a,b.; FitzGerald 2005.

22. Durand, Massey, and Zenteno 2001; Alarcon 2011.

23. The average naturalization rate for immigrants of all national origins was 61% in 2011. Sources: FitzGerald 2009; Durand, Massey, and Zenteno 2001; Gonzalez-Barrera et al. 2013; Massey, Durand, and Pren 2014.

24. Mateos 2019. The principle of no loss applies only to persons who acquired Mexican nationality at birth. It does not include people who became Mexican by naturalization.

25. Hoyo 2015a; see also FitzGerald 2005; Escobar 2007, 2015; Mateos 2019.

26. Massey, Durand, and Pren 2014; Gonzalez-Barrera 2015; Jensen 2015; Cohen, Passel, and Gonzalez-Barrera 2017; Gonzalez-Barrera and Krogstad 2017.

27. Skeldon 2013. The term "migration hump" was also used by Phillip L. Martin in 1993 to refer to the surge in Mexico-United States immigration that was expected as a result of NAFTA (Martin 1993).

28. Mateos 2019. There are no official data on the total number of Mexican-American dual nationals in the United States, as neither government collects this information. However, the Mexican Foreign Ministry (*Secretaria de Relaciones Exteriores*) published statistics on the number of people who declared Mexican dual nationality in Mexican consulates abroad in 2000-2010. The total number of declarations for these 11 years was 85,316—a small figure relative to the large population of potentially eligible individuals. Retrieved from https://sre.gob.mx/estadisticas-de-los-servicios.

29. Mateos 2014, 2019; Jacobo and Espinosa 2015; Velasco and Coubes 2013.

30. I combine data from two sources because in the years when data exist from both sources (1990, 2000, 2010), the figures are almost identical. For example, in 2010 the Mexican census notes 738,103 US-born in Mexico and UN statistics note 741,918. Immigrants to Mexico from other countries beside the United States numbered only 220,000 in 2010 and experienced a far more modest growth of 130% relative to 1970.

31. Chavez and Cobo 2012.

32. At this point, it was not possible to calculate the total number of US citizens in Mexico. Evidence suggests, however, that it is significantly higher than the number of US-born persons recorded by INEGI. For example, staff at the American consulate in Tijuana provided an informal estimate of about 250,000 US citizens in the Mexican state of Baja California (personal communication, December 2014). This is double the number of US-born reported in INEGI data for that state. In 1999, a State Department document estimated that about one million American citizens were living in Mexico. At the time, INEGI data recorded only 344,000 US-born persons in the country. Source: Shachter 2006. Based on these non-systematic observations, it is safe to assume that the total number of US citizens in Mexico is at least double the number of US-born reported in INEGI statistics.

33. Chavez 2013.

34. Mateos 2019.

35. This is justified for three reasons. First, the figures come from different sources. While the number of US mononationals comes from the administrative records of the *Instituto Nacional de Migracion*, the number of US-born comes from the census. It is likely that the census surveyors

undercounted foreigners because they could not speak Spanish or because they were not present in Mexico when the census was conducted. Second, even if we assume that all 60,000 US mononationals in Mexico were included in the census, this represents only about 8% of the US-born in Mexico. And, third, this percentage is even lower in the northern border states that are our region of interest. There were only 16,000 US mononationals in Mexico's northern border states (author's calculation based on Chavez and Cobo 2012). This represents less than 5% of the 330,000 US-born individuals in those states.

36. Author's calculations based on statistics from Albo and Luiz 2011; CONAPO 2014; Chavez 2013.

37. Ibid. A census of primary and secondary school students carried out by INEGI supports these findings. It shows that Baja California and Chihuahua received only about 4% of return migrants from the United States but hosted 20% of the foreign-born school students. See Jacobo and Espinosa 2015. Some of this effect is produced by deportees who settle in border states with their US-born after being forced across the border from the United States. However, a survey among deportees in Tijuana shows the almost all of them return to their original community in Mexico or their home in the United States, and only 12% wish to stay in the border region. See Velasco y Coubès 2013.

38. For each birth in the NCHS dataset, information is available on the mother's residence status (as well as on many other factors). The mother might be a "resident" (same county), "intrastate resident" (same state, different county), "interstate nonresident" (different state), or "foreign resident" (place of residence outside the United States). The latter category represents births to mother who did not provide a US address and can therefore be assumed to be temporary visitors. I assume that this category is made up of foreign mothers who came to the United States to give birth. I identified Mexicans based on statistics on ethnic origin for 1994–99 and 2003–14; for 2000–2002, I used statistics on place of birth. The use of birthplace and ethnicity interchangeably is justified in this case because the statistics refer to persons with no US address, and therefore most people who report Mexican ethnicity are assumed to be Mexicans, not Mexican-Americans. Source: Vital Statistics Online Data Portal, Birth Data Files. Retrieved from https://www.cdc.gov/nchs/data_access/vitalstatsonline.htm.

39. Statistics from the National Center for Health Studies (NCHS).

40. Statistics received upon request from the Mexican consulate in El Paso, Texas.

41. The correlation between the two variables in 1994–2014 was 0.89 at p<0.00001.

42. Kearney 1991; Martinez 1994; Sandoval 2008; Sarabia 2015.

43. Respondents' names were changed to protect their privacy.

44. Escobar 2015; Hoyo 2015a; Jacobo and Espinosa 2015.

45. Another kind of fraud was in fact directed at the United States: some midwives would work on both sides of the border, and they would register births as having taken place in the United States, even if they took place in Mexico. In recent years, the US government has cracked down on this practice, challenging the citizenship status of persons who were born outside hospitals. See Katz 1995; and Pérez 2018.

46. Mateos 2019.

47. Jacobo and Espinosa 2015; see also Mateos 2014.

48. Ibid.

49. Bernstein 1971; Bourdieu 1986.

50. For Mexicans from border towns the costs are lower and it is a little easier to obtain a visa.

51. Source: http://www.observatoriolaboral.gob.mx/swb/es/ola/Panorama_laboral_por_Estados.

52. Sandoval 2008; Sarabia 2015.

53. Source: https://doctoresparati.com.

54. Source: https://www.deluxechildbirth.com.
55. Source: http://rodi-v-amerike.com.
56. See Durand 2015; Grant 2015; Balta and Altan-Olcay 2016; Oni 2016; Tam 2018.
57. There were some attempts at suppressing Chinese birth tourism in California but it is not clear whether they seriously impacted this practice. See Yan 2015; Shyong 2016; Jordan 2019. I did not find evidence for any systematic policy against Mexican birth strategies.
58. Salter 2006.
59. This threat is less intimidating for undocumented immigrants, since they are "stuck" in the United States anyway. Massey, Durand, and Pren 2015.
60. Chavez 2011; Martinez 2016.
61. Massey 2013, Univision 2014.
62. Zelizer 2005.
63. University of Kent 2015.
64. OECD Society at a Glance 2014. Social Indicators: reports for United States, Mexico. Retrieved from http://www.oecd.org.
65. Bourdieu 1986.
66. The reluctance of elites to move was demonstrated in a recent paper that examined millionaires' responses to changes in states' tax rates. See Young, Varner, and Lurie 2016.
67. ACS 2007, 2010, 2014; Reyes and Estrada 2013.
68. US citizens over the age of 21 may sponsor their immediate family members to come to the United States. After obtaining residency there, the parents would either stay there or return to their original towns in Mexico, secure in the knowledge that they can always come back.
69. Harpaz 2013.
70. The interviews were conducted during Obama's presidency. Respondents would likely have argued this point even more forcefully if they had been conducted during Trump's tenure.
71. Malinche (or Malintzin) was an Aztec princess who married the conquistador Hernan Cortes and was crucial in the Spanish takeover, thanks to her translation and advice. She is at the same time a traitor to Mexico and the mother of the nation: the mixed-race child of Malinche and Cortes is often referred to as "the first Mexican."
72. Note that the tone of these references among middle-class *regio* interviewees was humoristic, even conciliatory: they seemed to view *malinchismo* as a mildly embarrassing feature common to *all* Mexicans, not as some abominable sin.
73. Telles 2014.
74. Telles 2014; Hoyo 2015b.
75. Telles 2014; De la Miyar 2013.
76. In the PERLA survey, 22% of respondents in northern Mexico self-identified as white, compared with only 13% in the country overall. Fair-skinned individuals in the north were far more likely to identify as white than in the rest of Mexico. Sources: Telles 2014; Rene Flores, personal communication.
77. Mateos 2019.
78. FitzGerald 2009.
79. Wilkinson and Ellingwood 2011.
80. Evren Balta and Özlem Altan-Olcay (2016) found a similar hyperpatriotic rhetoric among Turkish parents who strategically gave birth in the United States.
81. Some dual national respondents voted in US elections when they happened to live in the country at a time of elections. In contrast, none of them have voted from Mexico. This marks them as very different from "classic" expatriates, who have a strong American identity and high interest in politics. Croucher 2009; Klekowski von Koppenfels 2014.

82. This distinction seemed to be much less crucial for people from small towns near the border, as seen in the quotation from Carmen's mother (vignette 2): one of the aims of cross-border birth, she openly says, is that her children "will never stay without work."
83. Other studies that have adopted such an approach include Reyes and Estrada 2013; and Sarabia 2015.
84. Shachter 2006; AARO 2016.
85. Croucher 2009; Klekowski von Koppenfels 2014.
86. For example, Grant 2015; Balta and Altan-Olcay 2016; and Mateos 2019.

Chapter 4: Israel: European Passports as Insurance and Restitution

1. Tintori 2011; Cook-Martin 2013; Izquierdo and Chao 2015; Harpaz 2015a.
2. Rivlin 2008; Weiman 2008.
3. *Times of Israel* 2018.
4. Gónzalez 2018; Liphshiz 2018a; d'Oliveira 2015. Additional information obtained through an interview conducted in October 2018 with an Israeli lawyer who deals with the acquisition of Portuguese citizenship.
5. Della Pergolla 2001.
6. Cohen 2002.
7. In a survey by Konrad Adenauer Stiftung and Pardo (2009), 40 percent of respondents said that they were eligible for EU citizenship. This leads to an estimate of 2.5 million potentially eligible individuals. A calculation based on CBS statistics produced a similar figure. The same survey also reported that 4 percent already had EU citizenship. Note that not every Israeli with CEE ancestry is actually eligible for citizenship. This calculation does not take into account Spanish and Portuguese citizenship, which have been available since 2015, and which extend hypothetical eligibility by 3 to 3.5 million persons.
8. Cohen 2002; Shenhav 2006; Cohen, Haberfeld and Kristal 2007.
9. Lendvai 1971; Rothschild 1993; Gross 2001.
10. Tintori 2011; Cook-Martin 2013.
11. Herzog 2010a; Harpaz and Herzog 2018.
12. Weil 2001.
13. Shachar 1999; Kalekin-Fishman 2007; Herzog 2010b; Harpaz and Herzog 2018. In contrast, non-Jewish immigrants who wish to naturalize in Israel must fulfill residence and language requirements and renounce their original citizenship. Dual citizenship never became a politically contentious issue in Israel, and there have been no serious proposals in the parliament to restrict it. There are, however, numerous limitations on dual citizens: they cannot serve as members of parliament or serve in some sensitive security positions.
14. Brubaker 1992, Dumbrava 2014b.
15. Iordachi 2004.
16. Hailbronner 2010. In those years, Germany prohibited dual citizenship but made an exception for German Jews and their descendants: since the Nazi law that stripped them of citizenship was deemed illegal, it was decided that they had an unconditional right to regain it.
17. The emergent discourse of restitution in Poland is focused on those who emigrated and were stripped of citizenship in the context of anti-Semitic persecutions in 1968. Plocker 2008; Gorny and Pudzianowka 2010.
18. Estimate based on statistics that I have obtained from the embassies of European countries in Israel or from government websites. I obtained statistics from the following countries: Austria,

Bulgaria, Czechia, Finland, France, Germany, Hungary, Greece, Italy, Poland, Portugal, Romania, Spain, Switzerland, and Britain. There are large numbers of Israelis who hold a second citizenship from France (at least 75,000) and Britain (at least 70,000). This is a minimum estimate because figures are missing for some countries, and figures for some countries might be higher than reported here.

19. Data received upon request from European consulates in Israel, in addition to Liphshitz 2018b, *Times of Israel* 2017.

20. For a more detailed, comparative analysis of time variation in citizenship acquisitions, see Harpaz 2015.

21. I found no such correlation with economic factors like growth rate or unemployment rates, or with the level of emigration.

22. Porat 2011.

23. Aderet 2015.

24. In 1990–94, the average migration balance of Israelis (the number of Israelis who returned from abroad minus Israelis who left, without counting new immigrants) was -2.6 per 1,000 per year. The same rate was found for the years 2000–2004. In 2010–14, the rate was -0.85 per 1,000 per year. Source: Israeli CBS migration statistics, population totals from http://worldpopulationreview.com.

25. OECD 2015.

26. In 2015, there were about 85,000 Israeli-born persons living in all European countries put together, and they constituted 32% of Israeli-born living abroad. This represents an increase relative to 2000, when only 55,000 Israeli-born lived in Europe, and they constituted 29% of all Israeli emigrants. For the sake of comparison, in 2015 there were 135,000 Israeli-born in the United States (52% of all Israeli emigrants), up from 110,000 in 2000. Source: United Nations Population Division (UNPD): "International Migrant Stock 2000, by Destination and Origin"; "International Migrant Stock 2015, by Destination and Origin." http://www.un.org/en/development/desa/population/migration/data/estimates2/estimates15.shtml.

27. According to the Polish citizenship law that was in force until 1951, Poles who served in a foreign military lost their Polish citizenship.

28. Not everyone whose ancestors immigrated from European countries is eligible for citizenship. Eligibility for citizenship may be created in two ways: either the immigrant parent/grandparent has never lost her citizenship (and then it was transmitted *jure sanguinis* to their descendants in Israel) or they have lost it illegally and may now regain it. If, on the other hand, they lost their citizenship legally, they may not regain it. There is a random element here that depends upon countries' changing citizenship laws. For example, many Jews who left Poland in the 1950s have never lost their citizenship and simply have to reactivate it; those who left in 1968 were stripped of their citizenship in a procedure that Poland's current government considers flawed and may apply for its return. However, Polish citizens who served in the Israeli military between 1948 and 1951 have automatically lost their Polish citizenship and cannot reacquire it. Most German Jews were stripped of citizenship by the Nazis and may now regain it. In Romania, as in Poland, both situations exist. I will set aside this criterion because it is of no sociological interest. It is impossible to determine precisely what proportion of European-origin Israelis are potentially eligible for citizenship but it appears that they are the majority.

29. Some Israelis actually study Hungarian for the sake of citizenship. They remain, however, a small minority among dual citizens. None of the respondents I have interviewed had studied any language or made an ethnic performance for the sake of citizenship.

30. Dumbrava 2014a, b.

31. Such "bureaucratic cleansing" is typical of other cases of genocide and ethnic cleansing. For example, it was practiced by fascist Croatia against some of the Serbs in its territory.

NOTES TO CHAPTER 4

32. See Harpaz 2009.

33. Such sentiments were very common among applicants for Polish, Hungarian or Romanian citizenship, and far less typical of applicants for German citizenship. This resulted from the far greater order and professionalism in the German embassy but also—ironically—with the fact that many German Jewish families had an ambivalent relation to Germany, whereas other Ashkenazim often had an entirely negative view of their origin country.

34. Alongside this view, some respondents also justified their right to citizenship in less economistic terms. Some of them said that they deserved citizenship because their immigrant parent or grandparent was born in the granting country and spoke its language.

35. None of the respondents used these generational terms to refer to their family's duration in Israel. Moreover, Israelis who were born in Europe after 1945 are also referred to as "second generation." Several respondents used the full expression and referred to themselves as "second/third generation to the Holocaust," as a way of explaining various complexes and anxieties.

36. Bourdieu notes that a crucial element in the construction of the family in Western capitalist societies is the separation between the logic of the market, which is based on calculation and interests, and the logic of the family, which is supposedly based on pure love and free from overt calculation and expectation for repayment. Viviana Zelizer, in her work, has shown how this ideology—which she calls "hostile worlds"—masks the tremendous importance of economic transfers and exchanges in any kind of intimate relationship. Bourdieu 1988, Zelizer 2005.

37. Ong 1999; see Weber 1958.

38. Slezkine 2004.

39. The key role of cooperative family strategies in the social and economic advancement of Jewish immigrants was documented in the United States. Silverman 1988.

40. Such guides were published in the popular websites Ynet and Walla as well as the *Achbar Ha'Ir*, which is a local Tel-Aviv culture weekly. See Goldstein and Barzilay 2004; Walla 2005; Halperin 2011.

41. Weinbaum 1999.

42. Kranz 2015.

43. See Kranz 2015.

44. Note, however, that several thousands of Israelis study medical professions in Italy, Hungary, the Czech Republic, or Romania (attending English-language private programs) or pursue advanced degrees in Western European universities.

45. Respondents believed that a "European passport" gave them the right to free university education in any European country. In fact, citizenship has no effect on tuition in France or Germany, and EU citizens who did not live in Europe were not eligible for a reduced fee in Britain. In contrast, Mexican respondents were usually aware of the costs of studying in the United States and the reduced fee for Texas-born students at Texas institutions. Serbians knew about wages in Western Europe and had some idea about what jobs were available there.

46. Nana10 2009.

47. The latter scenario mirrors the concerns about religious extremism that were voiced by members of the secular elite in Turkey who strategically gave birth in the United States. Balta and Altan-Olcay 2016.

48. Arendt 1951; Malkki 1992; Jean 2011.

49. Foucault 1978, 2009; Agamben 1998.

50. Reitlinger 1968; Ancel 2003; Weil 2005; Iordachi 2010.

51. Reitlinger 1968; Yahil 1983; Marrus 1985; *Washington Post* 1982; Green 2013; Stein 2016.

52. Avineri 1981; Conforti 2011; Neumann 2011.

53. Recent examples include the 2008 attack in Mumbai as well as suicide bombings against Israelis in Bulgaria in 2012 and in Istanbul in 2016. Historically, there were incidents when terrorists

would release most hostages and keep only Israelis and Jews; this was done most famously in the Air France flight that was hijacked to Entebbe in 1976.

54. Kimmerling 2001.
55. Shafir and Peled 2002; Khazzoom 2003, 2008; Shenhav 2006.
56. Kimmerling 2001.
57. Cohen, Haberfeld, and Kristal 2007.
58. Sasson-Levy 2008.
59. Obviously, the association between Ashkenazi origin and EU citizenship will weaken in the coming years, as more Sepharadic-origin Israelis acquire EU passports from Spain and Portugal.
60. Cf. Bourdieu 1984.
61. Of course, ethnic Hungarians in Serbia do not have to make any special effort to acquire citizenship.

Conclusion: The Rise of the Sovereign Individual

1. For example, see Brubaker 1992; Howard 2005; Escobar 2007; Vink and de Groot 2010; and Brubaker and Kim 2011.
2. The concept of struggle over classifications draws on the work of Pierre Bourdieu, and especially the insight that the authority to institutionalize categories and sort individual into them, is a key element in the state's power (see Bourdieu 1986, 1989). In applying it to the case of citizenship, I draw on the work of Jaeeun Kim. Kim 2011, 2016, 2018, 2019.
3. The figure for Serbia refers to the total number of citizenship acquisitions as of December 2018 (180,000), from which I deducted 10 percent to account for non-Hungarian applicants, and then divided it by the ethnic Hungarian population of Serbia (250,000).
4. Mexican cross-border birth is more affordable and less exclusive for residents of border towns like Tijuana and Ciudad Juarez compared to residents of Monterrey. There may be a class component in the acquisition of Hungarian citizenship by ethnic Hungarians in Serbia; however, it is not mediated by price but by other mechanisms, such as education or intentions to emigrate.
5. Surak 2016.
6. Shachar 2017; Dzankic 2012; Shachar and Bauböck 2014.
7. Surak 2016; Kroft 2017.
8. Kroft 2017.
9. Neofotistos 2009;
10. Azzolini and Guetto 2017; see also Curiel 2004.
11. The United States allows visa-free access to the citizens of about 40 countries, making it much more selective than the EU Schengen zone, which admits the citizens of almost 100 countries without a visa requirement. Harpaz, forthcoming.
12. Pocock 1998. See also FitzGerald 2006; and Joppke 2019.
13. Statsiulis 2017; Cook-Martin 2013; Balta and Altan-Olcay 2016; see Harpaz 2013, 2015.
14. Jansen 2009; Harpaz 2013.
15. Baumann 1998; Castles 2005; Shamir 2005; Salter 2006; Urry 2012.
16. Mau et al. 2012, 2015.
17. Margiotta and Vonk 2010; Kochenov 2014; Maas 2017.
18. On British demand for EU citizenship, see *New European* 2018.
19. Bloemraad 2018. For arguments about immigrants' use of citizenship to gain secure residence or onward mobility, see Paul 2011; Mateos 2013; and Kim 2016, 2019.
20. Shuck 1989; and Spiro 2008.

21. Pensions are an exception to this rule and are now largely payable across borders. This has to do with the fact that pensions are tied to contributions that the recipient has already made, not to expected future contributions. Child benefits are also paid across borders in some cases—for example, to the foreign-resident children of immigrants in Germany. For a discussion of transnational social rights, see Levitt et al. 2016.

22. Anderson 1998; Bauböck 1994, 2003; Tintori 2011; Portes, Escobar, and Arana 2008; FitzGerald 2009; Ragazzi and Balalovska 2011; Collyer 2014; Pogonyi 2017.

23. Dual citizens were interested in their granting countries' politics from the perspective of their primary citizenship country: Mexican dual nationals in Mexico were disturbed by the anti-Mexican tendencies of US President Trump and Israeli dual citizens complained about EU countries' anti-Israeli bias. But they did not form a perspective on these politics as American or European citizens and did not seek to influence them by voting or lobbying.

24. *Hungarian Free Press* 2018. See chapter 2.

25. Maeva 2005; Tintori 2011.

26. The term "post-territorial nationalism" is used by Ragazzi and Balalovska 2011, which analyzes citizenship politics in the countries of former Yugoslavia.

27. Brubaker 1990. See also Smith 2000.

28. Aptekar 2012.

29. Boarov 2001; FitzGerald 2005.

30. I should qualify this finding by noting that there might be an interviewer effect at work. Some respondents might have been perceived me as representing an American gaze and responded by emphasizing that they are not taking advantage of the United States and that Mexico is equal to the United States. If similar interviews had been conducted by a Mexican, there might have been greater emphasis on Mexican nationalism.

31. Ong 1999.

32. Here, too, there might be some interviewer effect. Israeli avowals of their identity can be compared to the exculpatory declarations of Turkish patriotism that the respondents of Evren Balta and Özlem Altan-Olcay often made when explaining their decision to seek US citizenship for their children. Balta and Altan-Olcay 2016.

33. Harpaz 2013.

34. Joppke 2010b, 2019.

35. Joppke 2010a, b.

36. Cf. Weil 2012.

37. Weil 2012, 173.

38. Hindess 1998; Macklin 2007; Shachar 2009; Milanovic 2010. In addition, since the 1970s world-system theory has developed a Marxian approach to analyze the world as a system of stratification and its insights have been instrumental to the global sorting approach. This theory, however, takes states and societies rather than individual citizens as its unit of analysis. See Wallerstein 1979.

39. Brubaker 1990, 1992a.

40. Marshall 1950.

41. See Spiro 2019.

42. The diffusion of Spanish and Portuguese citizenship among Middle Eastern Jews in Israel may mean that, in the future, dual citizenship will presumsbly no longer draw a boundary between Ashkenazi and Sepharadic Jews. Once most Israeli Jews are eligible for EU citizenship, it will contribute to reinforcing the nation's most fundamental divide, that between Jews and Arabs.

43. Wang 2004; Balta and Altan-Olcay 2016; Cook-Martin 2013; Mateos 2019. The association with privilege does not seem to hold for coethnic citizenship in Eastern Europe.

44. Mateos 2019.

45. Macklin 2014; Spiro 2014; Joppke 2016; Weil 2017.

46. Ibid. See also Stasiulis and Ross 2006, Nyers 2006.
47. Weil 2012; Spiro 2016.
48. Yonhap 2017; Miller 2014.
49. Shevel 2013; UNIAN 2018.
50. Yie 2018.
51. Koziol 2018.
52. Huggler 2018. On tightening citizenship requirements in other cases, see also Patriquin 2006; and Orgad 2010.
53. On the other hand, Spiro 2019 has argued that dual citizenship is by now "intractable" because of the strength in numbers and influence of the persons who hold this status.
54. Brubaker 2017a,b.
55. NDTV 2018.
56. Euronews 2017.
57. Orgad 2010; Spiro 2014. Cf. Joppke 2019.
58. Joppke 2019: 875

REFERENCES

Abulof, Uriel. 2009. "'Small Peoples': The Existential Uncertainty of Ethnonational Communities." *International Studies Quarterly* 53, no. 1: 227–48.

Aderet, Ofer. 2015. "Haza'am hitchalef bechibuk: eich hishtana hayachas lemu'tzarim germani'im be'israel" [The rage was replaced by an embrace: how the relation to German products in Israel changed]. *Haaretz*. Published on June 26, 2015. Retrieved from https://www.haaretz.co.il/news/education/.premium-1.2669206 [Hebrew].

Agamben, Giorgio. 1998. *Homo Sacer: Sovereign Power and Bare Life*. Stanford, CA: Stanford University Press.

Alarcon, Rafael. 2011. "US Immigration Policy and the Migration of Mexicans (1882–2005)." *Migraciones Internacionales* 6, no. 1: 185–218.

Alba, Richard. 2005. "Bright vs. Blurred Boundaries: Second-generation Assimilation and Exclusion in France, Germany, and the United States." *Ethnic and Racial Studies* 28, no. 1: 20–49.

Alba, Richard, and Nancy Foner. 2014. "Comparing Immigrant Integration in North America and Western Europe: How Much Do the Grand Narratives Tell Us?" *International Migration Review* 48, no. S1: S262–90.

Albo, Adolfo, and Juan Luis Ordaz Diaz. 2011. "La Migración Mexicana hacia los Estados Unidos: Una breve radiografía" [Mexican migration to the United States: a short scan]. BBVA Research. Working Paper 11/05, February 2011.

AltreItalie [Other Italies]. 2014. "Espatriati per paese di destinazione—Dati per decennio 1861–1990 (valori assoluti) [Expatriates by country of destination—data by decade 1861–1990 (absolute values)]", "Rimpatriati per paese di provenienza—Dati per decennio 1861–1990 (valori assoluti) [Repatriates by country of origin—data by decade 1861–1990 (absolute values)]." Calculations by Guido Tintori for Altreitalie from Istat data. http://www.altreitalie.it/Risorse/I_Numeri_Delle_Migrazioni/Dati_Italiani/MOVIMENTO_MIGRATORIO_ITALIANO_CON_LESTERO_18611990/Nota_Sulle_Fonti.kl.

American Community Survey (ACS). 2007, 2010, 2014. "Selected Characteristics of the American Community Survey." Retrieved from https://www.census.gov.

American Community Survey (ACS). 2013. "Language Use in the United States: 2011." By Camille Ryan. Issued August 2013. Retrieved from http://www.census.gov/prod/2013pubs/acs-22.pdf.

Amit, Vered. 2014. "Inherited Multiple Citizenships: Opportunities, Happenstances, and Improvisations among Mobile Young Adults." *Social Anthropology* 22, no. 4: 396–409.

Anagrafe Italiani Residenti All'estero (AIRE). 2012. "Popolazione italiana residente all'estero con la sola cittadinanza italiana e con cittadinanza italiana ed altra cittadinanza per sesso, area geografica e paese di residenza al 21 marzo 2003." Ministero degli Affari Esteri e Istat—Archivi delle anagrafi consolari, June 13, 2012. Retrieved from www.istat.it.

Ancel, Jean. 2003. "Seizure of Jewish Property in Romania." In *Confiscation of Jewish Property in Europe, 1933–1945: New Sources and Perspectives, Symposium Proceedings*, 43–56. Washington, DC: Center for Advanced Holocaust Studies, US Holocaust Memorial Museum.

REFERENCES

Anderson, Benedict. 1998. "Long-distance Nationalism." In *The Spectre of Comparisons: Nationalism, Southeast Asia, and the World*, 58–74. London: Verso, 1998.

Aptekar, Sophia. 2012. "Naturalization Ceremonies and the Role of Immigrants in the American Nation." *Citizenship Studies* 16, no. 7: 937–52.

Arendt, Hannah. 1951. *The Origins of Totalitarianism*. New York: Schocken.

Assemblée des Français à l'Étranger. 2013. "Rapport du Directeur des Français à l'étranger et de l'administration consulaire. XVIIe Session de l'Assemblée des Français de l'étranger 3 au 8 septembre 2012." Retrieved from http://www.assemblee-afe.fr/rapport-du-directeur-des-francais,1150.html.

Association of Americans Abroad (AARO). 2015. "Eight Million Americans (Excluding Military) Live in 160-plus Countries." Retrieved from https://www.aaro.org/about-aaro/6m-americans-abroad.

Avineri, Shlomo. 1981. *The Making of Modern Zionism: The Intellectual Origins of the Jewish State*. New York: Basic Books.

Azzolini, Davide, and Raffaele Guetto. 2017. "The Impact of Citizenship on Intermarriage: Quasi-experimental Evidence from Two European Union Eastern Enlargements." *Demographic Research* 36: 1299–336.

B92. 2013. "Reintroduction of Visas 'Great Danger for W. Balkans.'" Published December 20, 2013. Retrieved from http://www.b92.net/eng/news/politics.php?yyyy=2013&mm=12&dd=20&nav_id=88726.

B92. 2015. "Šta Sve Treba za Mađarski Pasoš?" [What's the use of a Hungarian passport?]. Published February 24, 2015. Retrieved from http://www.b92.net/info/vesti/index.php?yyyy=2015&mm=02&dd=24&nav_id=961693.

Baćević, Jana. 2014. *From Class to Identity: The Politics of Education Reform in Former Yugoslavia*. Budapest: Central European University Press.

Bálint, Szalai. 2014. "Ma is jönnek a hamisított magyarok" [Today, too, fake Hungarians came]. Index.hu. Published on on September 17, 2014. Retrieved from http://index.hu/gazdasag/2014/09/17/ma_is_jonnek_a_hamisitott_magyarok/?token=c496e3c4381b0db621263eeaba2803f5.

Balistreri, Kelly Stamper, Kara Joyner, and Grace Kao. 2017. "Trading Youth for Citizenship? The Spousal Age Gap in Cross-Border Marriages." *Population and Development Review* 43, no. 3: 443–66.

Balta, Evren, and Özlem Altan-Olcay. 2016. "Strategic Citizens of America: Transnational Inequalities and Transformation of Citizenship." *Ethnic and Racial Studies* 39, no. 6: 939–57.

Barth, Frederick. 1969. *Ethnic Groups and Boundaries: The Social Organization of Culture Difference*. London: Allen & Unwin.

Bauböck, Rainer. 1994. *Transnational Citizenship: Membership and Rights in International Migration*. Cheltenham, UK: Edward Elgar.

Bauböck, Rainer. 2003. "Towards a Political Theory of Migrant Transnationalism." *International Migration Review* 37, no. 3: 700–23.

Bauböck, Rainer. 2010a. "Studying Citizenship Constellations." *Journal of Ethnic and Migration Studies* 35, no. 5: 847–59.

Bauböck, Rainer, ed. 2010b. "Dual Citizenship for Transborder Minorities? How to Respond to the Hungarian-Slovak Tit-for-Tat." EUI Working Paper RSCAS 2010/75. European University Institute, Robert Schuman Centre for Advanced Studies. European Union Democracy Observatory on Citizenship.

Bauböck, Rainer. 2019. "Genuine Links and Useful Passports: Evaluating Strategic Uses of Citizenship." *Journal of Ethnic and Migration Studies* 45, no. 6: 1015–26.

Baumann, Zygmunt. 1998. *Globalization: The Human Consequences*. New York: Columbia University Press.

BBC. 2009. "Alarm at EU Passports for Moldova." Published May 4, 2009. Retrieved from http:// news.bbc.co.uk/2/mobile/europe/8029849.stm.

Bernitz, Hedvig Lokrantz. 2010. Country Report: Sweden. GLOBALCIT Country Reports. European University Institute, Robert Schuman Centre for Advanced Studies.

Bernstein, Basil. 1971. *Class, Codes, and Control: Theoretical Studies Towards a Sociology of Language.* Vol. 1. New York: Routledge.

Bieber, Florian, and Jenni Wintergarten. 2006. "Ethnic Violence in Vojvodina: Glitch or Harbinger of Conflicts to Come?" European Center for Minority Issues (ECMI) Working Paper #27. Flensburg, Germany.

Blatter, Joachim, Stefanie Erdmann, and Katja Schwanke. 2009. "Acceptance of Dual Citizenship: Empirical Data and Political Contexts." Working Paper Series 02, Glocal Governance and Democracy. Institute of Political Science, University of Lucerne.

Bloemraad, Irene. 2004. "Who Claims Dual Citizenship? The Limits of Postnationalism, the Possibilities of Transnationalism, and the Persistence of Traditional Citizenship." *International Migration Review* 38, no. 2: 389–426.

Bloemraad, Irene. 2006. *Becoming a Citizen: Incorporating Immigrants and Refugees in the United States and Canada.* Berkeley: University of California Press.

Bloemraad, Irene. 2013. "Being American/Becoming American: Birthright Citizenship and Immigrants' Membership in the United States." In Who Belongs? Immigration, Citizenship, and the Constitution of Legality, special issue edited by Austin Sarat. *Studies in Law, Politics and Society* 60: 55–84.

Bloemraad, Irene. 2018. "Theorising the Power of Citizenship as Claims-making." *Journal of Ethnic and Migration Studies* 44, no. 1: 4–26.

Bloemraad, Irene, and Alicia Sheares. 2017. "Understanding Membership in a World of Global Migration: (How) Does Citizenship Matter?" *International Migration Review* 51, no. 4: 823–67.

Boarov, Dimitrije. 2001. "Politička istorija Vojvodine" [Political history of Vojvodina]. Novi Sad: Europanon Consalting.

Boatcă, Manuela. 2015. *Global Inequalities Beyond Occidentalism.* Aldershot, UK: Ashgate.

Bourdieu, Pierre. 1986. "The Forms of Capital." In *Handbook of Theory and Research for the Sociology of Education,* edited by J. G. Richardson, 241–58. Westport, CT: Greenwood.

Bourdieu, Pierre. 1987. *Distinction: A Social Critique of the Judgment of Taste.* Cambridge, MA: Harvard University Press.

Bourdieu, Pierre. 1989. "Social Space and Symbolic Power." *Sociological Theory* 7, no. 1: 14–25.

Bourdieu, Pierre. 1998. *Practical Reason.* Stanford, CA: Stanford University Press.

Braham, R. L. 1994. "Anti-Semitism and the Holocaust in the Politics of East Central Europe." In *Anti-Semitism and the Treatment of the Holocaust in Postcommunist Eastern Europe,* edited by R. L. Braham, 1–30. New York: Columbia University Press.

Brubaker, Rogers. 1990. "Immigration, Citizenship, and the Nation-state in France and Germany: A Comparative Historical Analysis." *International Sociology* 5, no. 4: 379–407.

Brubaker, Rogers. 1992a. *Citizenship and Nationhood in France and Germany.* Cambridge, MA: Harvard University Press.

Brubaker, Rogers. 1992b. "Citizenship Struggles in Soviet Successor States." *International Migration Review* 26, no. 2: 269–91.

Brubaker, Rogers. 1996. *Nationalism Reframed: Nationhood and the National Question in the New Europe.* Cambridge: Cambridge University Press.

Brubaker, Rogers. 1998. "Migrations of Ethnic Unmixing in the 'New Europe.'" *International Migration Review,* 32, no. 4: 1047–65.

Brubaker, Rogers. 1999. "The Manichean Myth: Rethinking the Distinction between 'Civic' and 'Ethnic' Nationalism." In *Nation and National Identity*, edited by Hanspeter Kriesl et al., 55–71. Zürich: Rüegger.

Brubaker, Rogers. 2005. "The 'Diaspora' Diaspora." *Ethnic and Racial Studies* 28, no. 1: 1–19.

Brubaker, Rogers. 2006. *Nationalist Politics and Everyday Ethnicity in a Transylvanian Town*. Princeton, NJ: Princeton University Press.

Brubaker, Rogers. 2009. "National Homogenization and Ethnic Reproduction on the European Periphery." In *La Teoria Sociologica e lo Stato Moderno*, edited by Marzio Barbagli and Harvie Ferguson, 201–21. Bologna: Societa Editrice Il Mulino.

Brubaker, Rogers. 2017a. "Between Nationalism and Civilizationism: The European Populist Moment in Comparative Perspective." *Ethnic and Racial Studies* 40, no. 8: 1191–226.

Brubaker, Rogers. 2017b. "Why Populism?" *Theory and Society* 46, no. 5: 357–85.

Brubaker, Rogers, and Jaeeun Kim. 2011. "Transborder Membership Politics in Germany and Korea." *Archives européennes de sociologie* [European journal of sociology] 52, no. 1: 21–75.

Budapest Beacon. 2013. "Unintended Consequences of Expanding Hungarian Citizenship." Hungarian Spectrum. Published on November 17, 2013. Retrieved from https://hungarianspectrum.wordpress.com/2013/11/17/unintended-consequences-of-expanding-hungarian-citizenship/.

Camarota, Steven A. 2015. "There Are Possibly 36,000 Birth Tourists Annually." Center for Immigration Studies. Published April 28, 2015. Retrieved from http://www.cis.org/camarota/there-are-possibly-36000-birth-tourists-annually.

Castles, Stephen. 2004. "The Factors that Make and Unmake Migration Policies." *International Migration Review* 38, no. 3: 852–84.

Castles, Stephen. 2005. "Nation and Empire: Hierarchies of Citizenship in the New Global Order." *International Politics* 42, no. 2: 203–24.

Castles, Stephen, and Mark J. Miller. 1993. *The Age of Migration*. New York: Guilford.

Centeno, Miguel A., and Joseph N. Cohen. 2010. *Global Capitalism: A Sociological Perspective*. Cambridge: Polity.

Center for Economic Studies. 2007. "Tuition Fees in Europe 2007/2008." CESifo DICE Report 4/2007. Munich: Ifo Institute for Economic Research.

Center for Social Investigation (CSI). 2018. "CSI Brexit 4: People's Stated Reasons for Voting Leave or Remain." Retrieved from http://csi.nuff.ox.ac.uk/?p=1153.

Chávez, Ernesto R. 2010. "Extranjeros en México; continuidades y aproximaciones" [Foreigners in Mexico: continuities and estimates]. Working paper. Mexico City: Centro de Estudios Migratorios, INM, INAH, and DGE editions.

Chávez, Ernesto R. 2013. "Ciudadanía y extranjería en México. La doble ciudadanía como estrategia de vida para los hijos de familias mexicanas" [Citizenship and foreignness in Mexico. Dual citizenship as a life strategy for the children of Mexican families]. Presentation at Seminario Internacional: Ciudadania Multiple y Migracion, October 28–29, 2013. CIESAS Occidente, Guadalajara, Mexico.

Chávez, Ernesto R. and Salvador Cobo. 2012. "Extranjeros Residentes en México: Una aproximación cuantitativa con base en los registros administrativos del INM" [Foreigners living in Mexico: A quantitative estimate on the basis of the administrative registries of the National Institute for Migration]. Mexico City: Centro de Estudios Migratorios, Instituto Nacional de Migración, Secretaria de Gobernación.

Chávez, Sergio. 2011. "Navigating the US-Mexico Border: The Crossing Strategies of Undocumented Workers in Tijuana, Mexico." *Ethnic and Racial Studies* 34, no. 8: 1320–37.

Cohen, Nir. 2007. "From Overt Rejection to Enthusiastic Embracement: Changing State Discourses on Israeli Emigration." *GeoJournal* 68, nos. 2–3: 267–78.

Cohen, Yinon. 1988. "War and Social Integration: The Effects of the Israeli-Arab Conflict on Jewish Emigration from Israel." *American Sociological Review* 53, no. 6: 908–18.

Cohen, Yinon. 2002. "Immigration and the Changing Composition of Israel's Population, 1948–1999: Patterns to Israel." In *Challenging Ethnic Citizenship: German and Israeli Perspectives on Immigration*, edited by D. Levy and Y. Weiss, 36–56. New York: Berghahn.

Cohen, Yinon. 2011. "Israeli-born Emigrants: Size, Destinations, and Selectivity." *International Journal of Comparative Sociology* 52, nos. 1–2: 45–62.

Cohen, Yinon, Yitschak Haberfeld, and Tali Kristal. 2007. "Ethnicity and Mixed Ethnicity: Educational Gaps among Israeli-born Jews." *Ethnic and Racial Studies* 30, no. 5: 896–917.

Collyer, Michael. 2014.. "A Geography of Extra-Territorial Citizenship: Explanations of External Voting." *Migration Studies* 2, no. 1: 55–72.

Commonwealth of Australia. 2014. "The People of Australia: Statistics from the 2011 Census." Department of Immigration and Border Protection. Retrieved from https://www.border.gov.au/ReportsandPublications/Documents/research/people-australia-2013-statistics.pdf.

Conforti, Yitzhak. 2011. "'The New Jew' in the Zionist Movement: Ideology and Historiography." *Australian Journal of Jewish Studies* 25: 87–118.

Consejo Nacional de Poblacion (CONAPO). 2014. "Cuadro V.1.1. Migración mexicana a Estados Unidos por entidad federativa, según migrantes de retorno y migrantes a Estados Unidos durante el quinquenio, 2005–2010" [Table V.1.1: Mexican migration to the United States by federal entity, return migrants and migrants to the United States in 2005–2010]. Retrieved from http://www.portal.conapo.gob.mx.

Cook-Martin, David. 2013. *The Scramble for Citizens: Dual Nationality and State Competition for Immigrants*. Stanford, CA: Stanford University Press.

Croucher, Sheila. 2009. "Migrants of Privilege: The Political Transnationalism of Americans in Mexico." *Identities: Global Studies in Culture and Power* 16. no. 4: 463–91.

Curiel, Enrique Martinez. 2004. "The Green Card as a Matrimonial Strategy: Self-Interest in the Choice of Marital Partners." In *Crossing the Border: Research from the Mexican Migration Project*, edited by Jorge Durand and Douglas S. Massey, 86–109. New York: Russell Sage Foundation.

Czaika, Mathias, and Hein de Haas. 2014. "The Globalization of Migration: Has the World Become More Migratory?" *International Migration Review* 48, no. 2: 283–323.

d'Oliveira, Hans Ulrich Jessurun. 2015. "Iberian Nationality Legislation and Sephardic Jews: 'With due regard to European law'?" *European Constitutional Law Review* 11, no. 1: 13–29.

Daily Mail. 2010. "Passport Giveaway Opens UK Back Door: 2m More Hungarians Will Have Right to Work Here." Published on August 6, 2010. Retrieved from http://www.dailymail.co.uk/news/article-1300676/UK-passport-giveaway-hands-2m-Hungarians-right-work-here.html.

Danero Iglesias, J., R. Sata, and Á Vass. 2016. "Citizenship and Identity: Being Hungarian in Slovakia and Romanian in Serbia and Ukraine." *Minority Studies* 18: 15–32.

Darling, Kate. 2009. "Protection of Stateless Persons in International Asylum and Refugee Law." *International Journal of Refugee Law* 21, no. 4: 742–67.

Dawidowicz, Lucy. 1975. *The War against the Jews: 1933–1945*. New York: Bantam.

De la Miyar, Daniel. 2013. "A Descriptive Analysis of the Representation of Social Status through Spanish Print Media." PhD diss., University of Texas at San Antonio.

DellaPergola, Sergio. 2001. "Some Fundamentals of Jewish Demographic History." In *Papers in Jewish Demography 1997*, edited by Sergio Della Pergola and J. Even, 11–33. Jerusalem: Hebrew University.

Democracy Index. 2016. Compiled by the *Economist* Intelligence Unit. Retrieved from http://www.eiu.com.

Desilver, Drew. 2017. "Despite Concerns about Global Democracy, Nearly Six in Ten Countries Are Now Democratic." Pew Research Center. Retrieved from http://www.pewresearch.org/fact

-tank/2017/12/06/despite-concerns-about-global-democracy-nearly-six-in-ten-countries-are-now-democratic/.

Destatis. 2014. "Bevölkerung und Erwerbstätigkeit: Einbürgerungen 2013" [Population and Employment: Naturalizations 2013]. Statistisches Bundesamt, Wiesbaden, Germany.

Dumbrava, Costica. 2014a. "External Citizenship in EU Countries." *Ethnic and Racial Studies* 37, no. 13: 2340–60.

Dumbrava, Costica. 2014b. *Nationality, Citizenship, and Ethno-cultural Belonging: Preferential Membership Policies in Europe*. New York: Springer.

Dumbrava, Costica. 2019. "The Ethno-Demographic Impact of Co-Ethnic Citizenship in Central and Eastern Europe." *Journal of Ethnic and Migration Studies* 45, no. 6: 958–74.

Durand, Jorge. 2015. "Migración y ciudadanía: El caso norteamericano." In *Ciudadanía múltiple y migración: Perspectivas latinoamericanas*, edited by Pablo Mateos, 217–42. CIESAS: México DF.

Durand, Jorge, Douglas S. Massey, and Rene M. Zenteno. 2001. "Mexican Immigration to the United States: Continuities and Changes." *Latin American Research Review* 36, no. 1: 107–27.

Dzankic, Jelena. 2012. "The Pros and Cons of *ius pecuniae*: Investor Citizenship in Comparative Perspective." EUI Working Paper RSCAS 2012/14. GLOBALCIT. European University Institute, Robert Schuman Centre for Advanced Studies.

Economist. 2013. "Asylum System Abuse." Published on January 5, 2013. Retrieved from http://www.economist.com/news/europe/21569064-will-eu-reimpose-visas-travellers-balkan-countries-asylum-system-abuse.

Economist. 2019. "Viktor Orban's Plans to Boost Hungary's Birth Rate Are Unlikely to Work." Published on February 16, 2019. Retrieved from https://www.economist.com/europe/2019/02/16/viktor-orbans-plans-to-boost-hungarys-birth-rate-are-unlikely-to-work.

Eidgenössisches Departement für auswärtige Angelegenheiten (EDA). 2013. "Auslandschweizerstatistik 2012 nach Wohnländern und Konsularbezirken." Data received upon request from Swiss Department of Foreign Affairs.

Ellis, Andrew, et al. 2007. *Voting from Abroad: The International IDEA Handbook*. International Idea. Retrieved from https://www.idea.int/publications/catalogue/voting-abroad-international-idea-handbook.

Escobar, Agustin. 2015. "Migración de retorno y ciudadanía múltiple en México." In *Ciudadanía múltiple y migración: Perspectivas latinoamericanas*, edited by Pablo Mateos, 243–66. CIESAS: México DF.

Escobar, Cristina. 2007. "Extraterritorial Political Rights and Dual Citizenship in Latin America." *Latin American Research Review* 42, no. 3: 43–75.

Euronews. 2017. "Dual Citizenship for Europeans Only, Le Pen Says." Published February 10, 2017. Retrieved from https://www.euronews.com/2017/02/10/dual-citizenship-for-europeans-only-le-pen-says

European Migration Network (EMN). 2017. "Census 2016 Figures Show the Number of Non-Irish Nationals Living in Ireland Decreased by 1.6 Percent between 2011 and 2016." Published on September 22, 2017. Retrieved from http://www.emn.ie/index.jsp?p=100&n=105&a=2482.

European Union Democracy Observatory on Citizenship (EUDO). 2010. "Bulgaria: Diaspora Minister Responds to the UK Concerns about Central European Ethnic Citizenship Policies." Published on August 16, 2010. Retrieved from http://eudo-citizenship.eu/news/citizenship-news/372-bulgaria-diaspora-minister-responds-to-the-uk-concerns-about-central-european-ethnic-citizenship-policies-.

Eurostat. 2015. "EU Member States Granted Citizenship to Almost 1 Million Persons in 2013." Retrieved from http://ec.europa.eu/eurostat/documents/2995521/6897702/3-01072015-AP-EN.pdf/2bbb6946-d2ba-48e9-be57-4c226cd8f6c9.

Eyal, Gil, Iván Szelényi, and Eleanor R. Townsley. 1998. *Making Capitalism without Capitalists: Class Formation and Elite Struggles in Post-communist Central Europe*. New York: Verso.

Fagerlund, Jessica, and Sampo Brander. 2013. Country Report: Finland. GLOBALCIT Country Reports. European University Institute, Robert Schuman Centre for Advanced Studies.

Faist, Thomas, and Jurgen Gerdes. 2008. "Dual Citizenship in an Age of Mobility." Presented at Delivering Citizenship: The Transatlantic Council on Migration Conference. Washington, DC: Migration Policy Institute.

Fargues, Émilien. 2017. "The Revival of Citizenship Deprivation in France and the UK as an Instance of Citizenship Renationalisation." *Citizenship Studies* 21, no. 8: 984–98.

Favell, Adrian. 2008. "The New Face of East-West Migration in Europe." *Journal of Ethnic and Migration Studies* 34, no. 5: 701–16.

Feere, John. 2015. "Birth Tourists Come from Around the Globe." Center for Immigration Studies. Published on August 26, 2015. Retrieved from http://cis.org/feere/birth-tourists-come-around-globe.

FitzGerald, David. 2005. "Nationality and Migration in Modern Mexico." *Journal of Ethnic and Migration Studies* 31, no. 1: 171–91.

FitzGerald, David. 2006. "Rethinking Emigrant Citizenship." *New York University Law Review* 81, no. 1: 90–116.

FitzGerald, David. 2009. *A Nation of Emigrants: How Mexico Manages its Migration*. Berkeley: University of California Press.

FitzGerald, David. 2012. "Citizenship à la Carte: Emigration and the Strengthening of the Sovereign State." In *Politics from Afar: Transnational Diasporas and Networks*, edited by Peter Mandaville and Terrence Lyons, 197–212. New York: Columbia University Press.

FitzGerald, David, and David Cook-Martin. 2014. *Culling the Masses: The Democratic Origins of Racist Immigration Policy in the Americas*. Cambridge, MA: Harvard University Press.

FitzGerald, David, David Cook-Martín, Angela S. García, and Rawan Arar. 2018. "Can You Become One of Us? A Historical Comparison of Legal Selection of 'Assimilable' Immigrants in Europe and the Americas." *Journal of Ethnic and Migration Studies* 44, no. 1: 27–47.

Fox, Cybelle, and Thomas A. Guglielmo. 2012. "Defining America's Racial Boundaries: Blacks, Mexicans, and European Immigrants, 1890–1945." *American Journal of Sociology* 118, no. 2: 327–79.

Foucault, Michel. 1978. *The History of Sexuality*. Vol. 1. New York: Vintage.

Foucault, Michel. 2009. *Security, Territory, Population: Lectures at the College de France 1977–1978*. Vol. 4. New York: Picador.

Franco, Fernando. 2014. "¿Cuál ciudad en México tiene la mayor riqueza por habitante?" [Which city in Mexico has the biggest wealth per capita?] *El Economista*. Published on April 9, 2014. Retrieved from http://eleconomista.com.mx/inventario/2014/04/09/cual-ciudad-mexico-tiene-mayor-riqueza-habitante.

Gal, Susan. 1993. "Diversity and Contestation in Linguistic Ideologies: German Speakers in Hungary." *Language in Society* 22, no. 3: 337–59.

Gergő, Gabor K. 2013. "Adják-veszik a magyar állampolgárságot Szerbiában" [Buy-and-sell for Hungarian citizenship in Serbia]. Published on September 25, 2013. Retrieved from http://www.delmagyar.hu/szeged_hirek/adjak-veszik_a_magyar_allampolgarsagot_szerbiaban/2350791/.

Gerstle, Gary. 2015. "The Contradictory Character of American Nationality: A Historical Perspective." In *Fear, Anxiety, and National Identity*, edited by Nancy Foner and Patrick Simon, 33–58. New York: Russell Sage Foundation.

Glas Dijaspore. 2015. "Za samo 500 Evra: Srbi se žene Mađaricama i dobijaju papire EU!" [For only 500 Euros: Serbs marry Hungarian women and receive EU papers!] Published on April 28, 2015. Retrieved from http://www.glasdijaspore.at/za-samo-500-evra-srbi-se-zene-madaricama-i-dobijaju-papire-eu/#.

Główny Urząd Statystyczny (GUS). 2013. "Ludność. Stan i Struktura demograficzno-społeczna" [Population: Socio-demographic status and structure]. Table 3.3: "Ludność według kraju pierwszego obywatelstwa w latach 2002 i 2011" [Population according to country of first citizenship in 2002 and 2011]. Warsaw, Poland. Retrieved from http://stat.gov.pl.

Gluscevic, Sladjana. 2017. "Kako nestaje multinacionalna Vojvodina" [How multinational Vojvodina is disappearing]. *Voice*. Published on October 21, 2017. Retrieved from http://voice.org.rs/kako-nestaje-multinacionalna-vojvodina/.

Goldstein, T., and T. Barzilay. 2004 "Darkon Eiropei—Eikh Masigim ve-Lama Ze Kedai" [European passport: How to obtain one and why it's worth it]. *Ynet*. Published on May 2, 2004. Retrieved from http://www.ynet.co.il/articles/1,7340,L-2907849,00.html.

Gonzalez-Barrera, Ana. 2015. "More Mexicans Leaving than Coming to the US Pew Research Center, Hispanic Trends." Pew Hispanic Research Center. Published on November 19, 2015. Retrieved from http://www.pewhispanic.org/2015/11/19/more-mexicans-leaving-than-coming-to-the-u-s/.

Gonzalez-Barrera, Ana, Mark Hugo Lopez, Jeffrey S. Passel, and Paul Taylor. 2013. "The Path Not Taken." Pew Hispanic Research Center. Published on February 4, 2013. Retrieved from http://www.pewhispanic.org/2013/02/04/ii-recent-trends-in-naturalization-2000-2011-2.

Gonzalez, Daniel. 2011. "'Birth Tourism' Is Not a Widespread Practice in US, Data Show." *USA Today*. Published on August 17, 2011. Retrieved from http://usatoday30.usatoday.com/news/nation/2011-08-17-birth-tourism-arizona-border_n.htm.

Gónzalez, Miguel. 2018. "Law Granting Spanish Citizenship to Sephardic Jews Meets with Discreet Success." *El Pais*. Published on November 20, 2018. Retrieved from https://elpais.com/elpais/2018/11/19/inenglish/1542623904_928426.html?fbclid=IwAR1rnryGCLGng6_nmkQjgiFB56Tnkhb9pmVreSLhbznYz1vocVw-bdf_3ME.

Gonzalez, Susana G. 2015. "Violencia, quinta causa de migración estatal en México: Inegi" [INEGI: Violence, fifth cause of inter-state migration in Mexico]. *La Jornada*. Published on July 9, 2015. Retrieved from http://www.jornada.unam.mx/ultimas/2015/07/09/violencia-quinta-causa-de-migracion-estatal-en-mexico-inegi-3458.html.

Gorny, Agata, and Dorota Pudzianowska. 2010. "Country Report: Poland." GLOBALCIT Country Reports. European University Institute, Robert Schuman Centre for Advanced Studies.

Göroğlu, Rana. 2014. "Nur jeder 13. Einwohner ist Ausländer" [Only every 13th resident is a foreigner]. Mediendienst Integration, Zensus 2011. Published on April 10, 2014. Retrieved from http://mediendienst-integration.de/artikel/endgueltige-zahlen-zensus-2011-zu-auslaendern-bevoelkerung-veroeffentlicht.html.

GradSubotica. 2016. "Horti: Svakodnevno se iz Vojvodine iseli 12 Mađara" [Horty: Every day 12 Hungarians emigrate from Vojvodina]. Published on November 16, 2016. Retrieved from http://www.gradsubotica.co.rs/horti-svakodnevno-se-iz-vojvodine-iseli-12-madara/.

Grant, Tyler. 2015. "Made in America: Medical Tourism and Birth Tourism Leading to a Larger Base of Transient Citizenship." *Virginia Journal of Social Policy and the Law* 22, no. 1: 160–78.

Grečić, Vladimir. 2016. "How Can the Serbian Diaspora Contribute Much More to the Development at Home Country?" *Bulletin of the Serbian Geographical Society* 96, no. 2: 65–82.

Green, David B. 2013. "This Day in Jewish History 1992: A Fake Diplomat Who Saved 5,200 Jews Dies." *Haaretz*. Published on August 15, 2013. Retrieved from https://www.haaretz.com/jewish/.premium-1992-fake-diplomat-who-saved-5-200-jews-dies-1.5321175.

Gross, Jan. 2001. *Neighbors: The Destruction of the Jewish Community in Jedwabne, Poland*. Princeton, NJ: Princeton University Press.

Hailbronner, Kai. 2010. "Country Report: Germany." GLOBALCIT Country Reports. European University Institute, Robert Schuman Centre for Advanced Studies.

Hakimzadeh, Shirin, and D'Vera Cohn. 2007. "English Usage among Hispanics in the United States." Pew Hispanic Center. Retrieved from https://www.pewhispanic.org/2007/11/29/english-usage-among-hispanics-in-the-united-states/.

Halperin, N. 2011. "Ezrahei ha-Olam: Eikh le-Hotzi Darkon Zar" [World citizens: How to obtain a foreign passport]. *Achbar Ha'Ir*. Published on June 22, 2011. Retrieved from http://www.mouse.co.il/world/CM.articles_item,1559,209,61543,.aspx.

Hansen, Randall, and Patrick Weil. 2001. "Introduction." In *Towards a European Nationality: Citizenship, Immigration, and Nationality Law in the EU*, edited by Randall Hansen and Patrick Weil, 1–23. New York: Palgrave Macmillan.

Harder, Lois, and Lyubov Zhyznomirska. 2012. "Claims of Belonging: Recent Tales of Trouble in Canadian Citizenship." *Ethnicities* 12, no. 3: 293–316.

Harpaz, Yossi. 2009. "Israelis and the European Passport: Dual Citizenship in an Apocalyptic Immigrant Society." MA thesis, Department of Sociology and Anthropology, Tel-Aviv University.

Harpaz, Yossi. 2013. "Rooted Cosmopolitans: Israelis with a European Passport—History, Property, Identity." *International Migration Review*. 47, no. 1: 166–206.

Harpaz, Yossi. 2015a. "Ancestry into Opportunity: How Global Inequality Drives Demand for Long-distance European Union Citizenship." *Journal of Ethnic and Migration Studies* 31, no. 13: 2081–104.

Harpaz, Yossi. 2015b. "Conclusión: La Doble Nacionalidad como Herramienta Geopolítica, Régimen de Movilidad y Forma de Capital" [Conclusion: Dual nationality as a geopolitical tool, mobility regime, and form of capital]. In *Ciudadanía Múltiple y Migración: Perspectivas Latinoamericanas*, edited by Pablo Mateos, 267–89. Mexico City: CIDE-CIESAS.

Harpaz, Yossi. 2019. "Compensatory Citizenship: Dual Nationality as a Strategy of Global Upward Mobility." *Journal of Ethnic and Migration Studies* 45, no. 6: 897–916.

Harpaz, Yossi. Forthcoming. "North vs. South or Integrated vs. Isolated? Notes on the Global Grouping of Nationalities." In *Quality of Nationality Index*, edited by Dimitry Kochenov and Jan Lindebloom, n.p. London: Bloomsbury.

Harpaz, Yossi, and Ben Herzog. 2018. "Report on Citizenship Law: Israel." GLOBACIT Country Report. European University Institute, Robert Schuman Centre for Advanced Studies.

Harpaz, Yossi, and Pablo Mateos. 2019. "Introduction: Strategic Citizenship: Negotiating Membership in the Age of Dual Nationality." *Journal of Ethnic and Migration Studies* 45, no. 6: 843–57.

Hayden, Robert. 1992. "Constitutional Nationalism in the Formerly Yugoslav Republics." *Slavic Review* 51, no. 4: 654–73.

Heather, Derek. 2004. *A Brief History of Citizenship*. New York: New York University Press.

Henley & Partners. 2016. Index of International Visa Restrictions. Retrieved from https://www.henleyglobal.com.

Herzfeld, Michael. 1997. *Cultural Intimacy*. New York: Routledge.

Herzog, Ben. 2010a. "Dual Citizenship and the Revocation of Citizenship." In *Democratic Paths and Trends*, Research in Political Sociology, vol. 18, edited by Barbara Wejnert, 87–106. Bingley, UK: Emerald.

Herzog, Ben. 2010b. "The Revocation of Citizenship in Israel." *Israel Studies Forum* 25, no. 1: 57–72.

Higgins, Andrew. 2018. "At War with Russia in East, Ukraine Has Worries in the West, Too." *New York Times*. Published on October 5, 2018. Retrieved from https://www.nytimes.com/2018/10/05/world/europe/ukraine-hungary-ethnic-languages.html.

Hindess, Barry. 1998. "Divide and Rule: The International Character of Modern Citizenship." *European Journal of Social Theory* 1, no. 1: 57–70.

Howard, Marc Morjé. 2005. "Variation in Dual Citizenship Policies in the Countries of the EU." *International Migration Review* 39, no. 3: 697–720.

Howard, Marc Morjé. 2008. "The Causes and Consequences of Germany's New Citizenship Law." *German Politics* 17, no. 1: 41–62.

Hoyo, Henio. 2015a. "Report on Citizenship Law: Mexico." GLOBALCIT Country Reports. European University Institute, Robert Schuman Centre for Advanced Studies.

Hoyo, Henio. 2015b. "Apertura externa, exclusión interna: el nacionalismo revolucionario y los derechos de migrantes, mexicanos por naturalización, y dobles nacionales en México" [External openness, internal exclusion: revolutionary nationalism and the rights of immigrants, naturalized Mexicans and dual nationals in Mexico]. desiguALdades.net Working Paper Series, no. 87. Berlin: desiguALdades.net International Research Network on Interdependent Inequalities in Latin America.

Huggler, Justin. 2018. "Dual-Nationality Turks Being Stripped of Citizenship by Far Right in Austria's 'Windrush' Scandal." *Telegraph*. Published on November 24, 2018. Retrieved from https://www.telegraph.co.uk/news/2018/11/24/dual-nationality-turks-stripped-citizenship-far-right-austrias/.

Human Development Index. 2015. Compiled by United Nations Development Programme. Retrieved from http://hdr.undp.org/en/statistics/hdi.

Hungarian Free Press. 2018. "Fidesz Registering Voters Abroad by the Tens of Thousands ahead of April Elections." Published on January 5, 2018. Retrieved from http://hungarianfreepress.com/2018/01/05/fidesz-registering-voters-abroad-by-the-tens-of-thousands-ahead-of-april-elections/.

Hungary Today. 2018. "Hungarian Central Statistical Office: Hungary's Population Could Decline to 6 Million by 2070." Published on November 9, 2018. Retrieved from https://hungarytoday.hu/hungarian-central-statistical-office-hungarys-population-could-decline-to-6-million-by-2070/.

Huszka, Beata. 2007. "Decentralization of Serbia: The Minority Dimension." Center for European Policy Studies (CEPS) Policy Brief. No 137, July 2007. Brussels, Belgium.

Ilić, Andjela V. 2010. "Navigating Two Worlds: The Role of Religious Communities in Preserving the Identity of Hungarians in Vojvodina (Serbia)." *Politics and Religion* 3, no. 2 : 303–26.

INSEE. 2012. "IMG1B—Les immigrés par sexe, âge et pays de naissance" [Immigrants by sex, age, and country of birth]. Retrieved from https://www.ined.fr.

InSerbia. 2014. "Average Household Income in Serbia USD 600." Published on September 15, 2014. Retrieved from http://inserbia.info/today/2014/09/average-household-income-in-serbia-usd-600/.

Instituto Nacional de Estadística (INE), Spain. 2015. "2013: Población por nacionalidad, sexo y grupo de edad." Retrieved from www.ine.es.

Instituto Nacional de Estadística y Geografía (INEGI), Mexico. 2011. "Los nacidos en otro país suman 966,121 personas" [Persons born in another country number 966,121]. May 2011. Informativo oportuno, vol. 1, no. 2. Retrieved from https://www.inegi.org.mx.

Iordachi, Constantin. 2004. "Dual Citizenship in Post-Communist Central and Eastern Europe: Regional Integration and Inter-ethnic Tensions." In *Reconstruction and Interaction of Slavic Eurasia and its Neighboring World*, edited by Osama Ieda and Uyama Tomohiko, 105–39. Sapporo: Slavic Research Center, Hokkaido University.

Iordachi, Constantin. 2010. "Country Report: Romania." GLOBALCIT Country Reports. European University Institute, Robert Schuman Centre for Advanced Studies.

Ipsos Strategic Marketing. 2011. "Report: Nation Building–Serbia." October 2011. Retrieved from https://www.hf.uio.no/ilos/forskning/prosjekter/nation-w-balkan/ . . . /nb_serbia.pdf.

Izquierdo, Antonio, and Luca Chao. 2015. "Ciudadanos españoles producto de la Ley de Memoria Histórica: motivos y movilidades." In *Ciudadanía múltiple y migración: Perspectivas latinoamericanas*, edited by Pablo Mateos, 147–78. CIESAS: México DF.

Jacobo, Monica, and Frida Espinosa. 2015. "Retos al pleno derecho a la educación de la niñez transnacional en contexto de migración en México: el caso de la dispensa de la apostilla del Acta de Nacimiento extranjera" [Challenges to the right to education of transnational youth in the context of migration in Mexico: The case of the apostille of a foreign birth certificate]. Paper presented at V Encuentro Internacional Migración y Niñez Migrante, Sonora, Mexico, May 27–29, 2015.

Janos, Andrew C. 1989. "The Politics of Backwardness in Continental Europe, 1780–1945." *World Politics* 41, no. 3: 325–58.

Jansen, Stef. 2009. "After the Red Passport: Towards an Anthropology of the Everyday Geopolitics of Entrapment in the EU's 'Immediate Outside.'" *Journal of the Royal Anthropological Institute* n.s., 15: 815–32.

Jean, Yaron. 2011. "Constellations of a Catastrophe: Jews and Travel Documents in Europe between The Two World Wars." In *Konstellationen*, edited by Nicolas Berg, Omar Kamil, Markus Kirchhoff and Susanne Zepp, 231–47. Göttingen: Vandenhoeck & Ruprecht.

Jensen, Eric. 2015. "China Replaces Mexico as the Top Sending Country for Immigrants to the United States." US Census Bureau. Published on May 1, 2015. Retrieved from http://researchmatters.blogs.census.gov/2015/05/01/china-replaces-mexico-as-the-top-sending-country-for-immigrants-to-the-united-states/.

Jones-Correa, Michael. 2001. "Under Two Flags: Dual Nationality in Latin America and Its Consequences for Naturalization in the United States." *International Migration Review* 35, no. 4: 997–1029.

Joppke, Christian. 2005. *Selecting by Origin: Ethnic Migration in the Liberal State*. Cambridge, MA: Harvard University Press.

Joppke, Christian. 2010a. *Citizenship and Immigration*. Cambridge: Polity.

Joppke, Christian. 2010b. "The Inevitable Lightening of Citizenship." *European Journal of Sociology* 51, no. 1: 9–32.

Joppke, Christian. 2014. "The Retreat Is Real—But What Is the Alternative? Multiculturalism, Muscular Liberalism, and Islam." *Constellations* 21, no. 2: 286–95.

Joppke, Christian. 2016. "Terror and the Loss of Citizenship." *Citizenship Studies* 20, nos. 6–7: 28–48.

Joppke, Christian. 2019. "The Instrumental Turn of Citizenship." *Journal of Ethnic and Migration Studies* 45, no. 6: 858–78.

Jordan, Miriam. 2019. "3 Arrested in Crackdown on Multimillion-Dollar 'Birth Tourism' Businesses." *New York Times*. Published on January 31, 2019. Retrieved from https://www.nytimes.com/2019/01/31/us/anchor-baby-birth-tourism.html.

Kadirbeyoglu, Zeynep. 2012. "Country Report: Turkey." GLOBALCIT Country Reports. European University Institute, Robert Schuman Centre for Advanced Studies.

Kalekin-Fishman, Devorah. 2007. "Multiple Citizenship: Mark of Dominance and Privilege: the Situation in Israel." In *Multiple Citizenship as a Challenge to European Nation-States*, edited by Devorah Kalekin-Fishman and Pirkko Pitkanen, 239–66. Rotterdam: Sense.

Katz, Jesse. 1995. "Rio Grande Midwives Deliver Citizenship: A Birth Certificate Scam Sheds Light on a Thriving Network of Women Who Help Mexican Mothers Have Babies in Texas. Under Lax Laws, They Can Declare the Newborns Americans." *Los Angeles Times*. Published on June 13, 1995. Retrieved from http://articles.latimes.com/1995-06-13/news/mn-12638_1_rio-grande.

Kearney, Michael. 1991. "Borders and Boundaries of State and Self at the End of Empire." *Journal of Historical Sociology* 4, no. 1: 52–74.

Khazzoom, Aziza. 2003. "The Great Chain of Orientalism: Jewish Identity, Stigma Management, and Ethnic Exclusion in Israel." *American Sociological Review* 68: 481–510.

Khazzoom, Aziza. 2008. *Shifting Ethnic Boundaries and Inequality in Israel: Or, How the Polish Peddler Became a German Intellectual*. Stanford, CA: Stanford University Press.

Kim, Jaeeun. 2011. "Establishing Identity: Documents, Performance, and Biometric Information in Immigration Proceedings." *Law and Social Inquiry* 36, no. 3: 760–86.

Kim, Jaeeun. 2016. *Contested Embrace: Transborder Membership Politics in Twentieth-Century Korea.* Stanford, CA: Stanford University Press.

Kim, Jaeeun. 2018. "Migration-Facilitating Capital: A Bourdieusian Theory of International Migration." *Sociological Theory* 36, no. 3: 262–88.

Kim, Jaeeun. 2019. "'Ethnic Capital' and 'Flexible Citizenship' in Unfavourable Legal Contexts: Stepwise Migration of the Korean Chinese within and Beyond Northeast Asia." *Journal of Ethnic and Migration Studies* 45, no. 6: 939–57.

Kimmerling, Baruch. 2001. *The Invention and Decline of Israeliness: State, Society, and the Military.* Berkeley: University of California Press.

Klekowski von Koppenfels, Amanda. 2014. *Migrants or Expatriates? Americans in Europe.* London: Palgrave Macmillan.

Klekowski von Koppenfels, Amanda, and Joe Costanzo. 2013. "Counting the Uncountable: Overseas Americans." Migration Information Source. Published in May 2013. Retrieved from http://www.migrationinformation.org/Feature/display.cfm?id=951&utm_source=E-mail+Updates&utm_campaign=0103dd6ba3-.

Knott, Eleanor. 2015. "What Does it Mean to Be a Kin Majority? Analyzing Romanian Identity in Moldova and Russian Identity in Crimea from Below." *Social Science Quarterly* 96, no. 3: 830–59.

Knott, Eleanor. 2019. "Strategy, Identity, or Legitimacy? Analysing Engagement with Dual Citizenship from the Bottom-Up." *Journal of Ethnic and Migration Studies* 45, no. 6: 994–1014.

Kochenov, Dimitry. 2014. "EU Citizenship without Duties." *European Law Journal* 20, no. 4: 482–98.

Kochenov, Dimitry. 2019. *Citizenship.* Cambridge, MA: MIT Press.

Konrad Adenauer Stiftung (KAS), and Sharon Pardo. 2009. *Measuring the Attitudes of Israelis Towards the European Union and its Member States.* Jerusalem: Konrad Adenauer Stiftung.

Korzeniewicz, Roberto P., and Timothy P. Moran. 2009. *Unveiling Inequality: A World-historical Perspective.* New York: Russell Sage Foundation.

Koslowski, Rey. 2003. "Challenges of International Cooperation in a World of Increasing Dual Nationality." In *Rights and Duties of Dual Nationals: Evolution and Prospects*, edited by Kay Hailbronner and David Martin, n.p. London: Kluwer Law.

Kovacs, Maria M., and Judith Toth. 2013. "Country Report: Hungary." GLOBALCIT Country Reports. European University Institute, Robert Schuman Centre for Advanced Studies.

Koziol, Michael. 2018. "High Court Rules Labor's Katy Gallagher Ineligible and Sets Up Four Likely Byelections." *Sydney Morning Herald*. Published on May 9, 2018. Retrieved from https://www.smh.com.au/politics/federal/high-court-rules-labor-s-katy-gallagher-ineligible-and-sets-up-four-likely-byelections-20180509-p4ze5f.html.

Kranz, Dani. 2015. "Israelis in Berlin: Wie viele sin des und was zieht sie nach Berlin?" [Israelis in Berlin: how many are there and what pulls them to Berlin?]. Working paper in Deutschlandradio project "Fazination und Befremden—50 Jahre deutsche-israelische Beziehungen." Gütersloh, Germany: Bertelsmann Stiftung.

Krasniqi, Gëzim, and Dejan Stjepanović. 2015. "Uneven Citizenship: Minorities and Migrants in the Post-Yugoslav Space." *Ethnopolitics* 14, no. 2: 113–20.

Kroft, Steve. 2017. "Passports for Sale." CBS News. Published on January 1, 2017. Retrieved from https://www.cbsnews.com/news/60-minutes-citizenship-passport-international-industry/.

Küpper, Herbert. 2006. "From the Status Law 'Dual Citizenship': Aspects of Domestic International Law." In *Beyond Sovereignty: From Status Law to Transnational Citizenship?*, edited by Osamu Ieda, 159–82. Sapporo: Slavic Research Center.

Lafleur, Jean-Michel. 2011. "Why Do States Enfranchise Citizens Abroad? Comparative Insights from Mexico, Italy, and Belgium." *Global Networks* 11, no. 4: 481–501.

Lake, David A. 2007. "Escape from the State of Nature: Authority and Hierarchy in World Politics." *International Security* 32, no. 1: 47–79.

Lakner, Christopher, and Branko Milanovic. 2013. "Global Income Distribution: From the Fall of the Berlin Wall to the Great Recession." Policy Research Working Paper 6719. World Bank, Development Research Group, Poverty and Inequality Team. December 2013.

Laszak, Melinda. 2010. "Critical Discourse Analysis of Post-1989 Hungarian Historiography in Vojvodina." MA thesis, Nationalism Studies Department, Central European University, Budapest, Hungary.

Lazić, Mladen. 2000. "The Adaptive Reconstruction of Elites." In *Elites after State Socialism–Theories and Analysis*, edited by John Higley and Gyorgy Lengyel, 123–42. Oxford: Rowman & Littlefield.

Lazić, Mladen. 2003. "Serbia: A Part of Both the East and the West?" *Sociologija* 45, no. 3: 193–216.

Lazić, Mladen, and Vladimir Vuletić. 2009. "The Nation-state and the EU in the Perceptions of Political and Economic Elites: The Case of Serbia in Comparative Perspective." *Europe-Asia Studies* 61, no. 6: 987–1001.

Lazić, Mladen, and Slobodan Cvejić. 2007. "Class and Values in Postsocialist Transformation in Serbia." *International Journal of Sociology* 37, no. 3: 54–74.

Leblang, David. 2017. "Harnessing the Diaspora: Dual Citizenship, Migrant Return Remittances." *Comparative Political Studies* 50, no. 1: 75–101.

Lendvai, Peter. 1971 *Anti-Semitism without Jews: Communist Eastern Europe*. New York: Doubleday.

Levitt, Peggy, Jocelyn Viterna, Armin Mueller, and Charlotte Lloyd. 2016. "Transnational Social Protection: Setting the Agenda." *Oxford Development Studies* 45, no. 1: 2–19.

Liebich, Andre. 2000. "Plural Citizenship in Post-Communist States." *International Journal of Refugee Law* 12, no. 1: 97–107.

Liebich, Andre. 2009. "Introduction: Altneuländer or the Vicissitudes of Citizenship in the New EU States." In *Citizenship Policies in the New Europe*, edited by R. Bauböck, B. Perching, and W. Sievers, 21–42. Amsterdam: Amsterdam University Press.

Lien, Luyi. 2006. *Obtaining Dual Citizenship for their Babies: The Experience of Taiwanese Women Giving Birth in the United States*. PhD diss., University of Minnesota.

Light, Michael T., Michael Massoglia, and Ryan D. King. 2014. "Citizenship and Punishment: The Salience of National Membership in US Criminal Courts." *American Sociological Review* 79, no. 5: 825–47.

Liphshiz, Cnaan. 2018a. "A Soaring Number of Jews Acquired Portuguese Citizenship in 2017." *Times of Israel*. Published on February 24, 2018. Retrieved from https://www.timesofisrael.com/a-soaring-number-of-jews-acquired-portuguese-citizenship-in-2017/.

Liphshiz, Cnaan. 2018b. "Poland Gives Out Record Number of Passports to Israelis." *Times of Israel*. Published on August 24, 2018. Retrieved from https://www.timesofisrael.com/poland-gives-out-record-numbers-of-passports-to-israelis/.

Ludanyi, Andrew. 1979. "Titoist Integration of Yugoslavia: The Partisan Myth and the Hungarians of the Vojvodina, 1945–1975." *Polity* 12, no. 2: 225–52.

Maas, Wilhelm. 2017. "Multilevel Citizenship." In *The Oxford Handbook of Citizenship*, edited by A. Schachar, R. Bauböck, I. Bloemraad, and M. Vink, 644–68. Oxford: Oxford University Press.

Macklin, Audrey. 2007. "Who Is the Citizen's Other? Considering the Heft of Citizenship." *Theoretical Inquiries in Law* 8, no. 2: 333–66.

Macklin, Audrey. 2014. "Citizenship Revocation, the Privilege to Have Rights, and the Production of the Alien." *Queen's Law Journal* 40, no. 1: 1–54.

Maeva, Maria. 2005. "Bulgarian Turks and the European Union." In *EU Integration Process from EAST to EAST: Civil Society and Ethnic Minorities in a Changing World. Proceedings from a Round Table for Young Social Scientists*, edited by H. Rusu and B. Voicu, 119–26. Sibiu: Psihomedia.

Malkki, Liisa. 1992. "National Geographic: The Rooting of Peoples and the Territorialization of National Identity Among Scholars and Refugees." *Cultural Anthropology* 7, no. 1: 24–44.

Manić, Željka. 2011. "Položaj mađarske nacionalne manjine u vojvodini: sociološko-pravni aspekt" [The position of the Hungarian national minority in Vojvodina: sociological-legal aspect]. *Sociologija* 53, no. 3: 345–66.

Mannheim, Karl. 1936. *Ideology and Utopia*. New York: Harvest.

Margiotta, Costanza, and Olivier Vonk, 2010. "Nationality Law and European Citizenship: The Role of Dual Nationality." EUI-RSCAS Working Papers 66, European University Institute, Robert Schuman Centre of Advanced Studies.

Marrus, M. R. 1985. *The Unwanted: European Refugees in the Twentieth Century*. Oxford: Oxford University Press.

Marshall, Thomas H. 1950. *Citizenship and Social Class*. London: Cambridge University Press.

Martin, Philip L. 1993. *Trade and Migration: NAFTA and Agriculture*. Washington, DC: Institute for International Economics.

Martin, Phillip L. 2002. "Germany: Managing Migration in the Twenty-First Century." Comparative Immigration and Integration Program (CIIP) Working Paper 1.

Martinez, Daniel E. 2016. "Coyote Use in an Era of Heightened Border Enforcement: New Evidence from the Arizona-Sonora Border." *Journal of Ethnic and Migration Studies* 42, no. 1: 103–19.

Martinez, Oscar. 1994. *Border People: Life and Society in the US-Mexico Borderlands*. Tucson: University of Arizona Press.

Massey, D. S., J. Arango, G. Hugo, A. Kouaouci, A. Pellegrino, and J. E. Taylor. 1993. "Theories of International Migration: A Review and Appraisal." *Population and Development Review* 19, no. 3: 431–66.

Massey, Douglas S. 2013. "America's Immigration Policy Fiasco: Learning from Past Mistakes." *Daedalus* 142, no. 3: 5–15.

Massey, Douglas S., and Kristin E. Espinosa. 1997. "What's Driving Mexico-US Migration? A Theoretical, Empirical, and Policy Analysis." *American Journal of Sociology* 102, no. 4: 939–99.

Massey, Douglas S., Jorge Durand, and Nolan J. Malone. 2002. *Beyond Smoke and Mirrors*. New York: Russell Sage Foundation.

Massey, Douglas S., Jorge Durand, and Karen A. Pren. 2014. "Explaining Undocumented Migration to the US." *International Migration Review* 48, no. 4: 1028–61.

Massey, Douglas S., Jorge Durand, and Karen A. Pren. 2015. "Border Enforcement and Return Migration by Documented and Undocumented Mexicans." *Journal of Ethnic and Migration Studies* 41, no. 7: 1015–40.

Mateos, Pablo. 2013. "External and Multiple Citizenship in the European Union. Are 'Extrazenship' Practices Challenging Migrant Integration Policies?" Population Asociation of America Annual Meeting, April 11–13. New Orleans, LA.

Mateos, Pablo. 2014. "Apatridas o doble ciudadanía" [Apatrides or dual citizens]. *La Jornada* Published on January 5, 2014. Retrieved from http://www.jornada.unam.mx/2014/01/05/opinion/011a1pol.

Mateos, Pablo. 2019. "The Mestizo Nation Unbound: Dual Citizenship of Euro-Mexicans and US-Mexicans." *Journal of Ethnic and Migration Studies*. 45 (6): 917–38.

Mau, Steffen, Fabian Gülzau, Lena Laube, and Natascha Zaun. 2015. "The Global Mobility Divide: How Visa Policies Have Evolved over Time." *Journal of Ethnic and Migration Studies* 41, no. 8: 1192–213.

Mau, Steffen, Heike Brabandt, Lena Laube, and Christof Roos. 2012. *Liberal States and the Freedom of Movement*. New York: Palgrave Macmillan.

Mazzolari, Francesca. 2009. "Dual Citizenship Rights: Do They Make More and Richer Citizens?" *Demography* 46, no. 1: 169–91.

McKinley, James C. 2010. "Fleeing Drug Violence, Mexicans Pour into US." *New York Times*. Published on April 17, 2010. Retrieved from http://www.nytimes.com/2010/04/18/us/18border.html?_r=0.

McKinsey's Global Institute (MGI). 2016. "Poorer than their Parents? Flat or Falling Incomes un Advanced Economies." July 2016. Retrieved from https://www.mckinsey.com/featured-insights/employment-and-growth/poorer-than-their-parents-a-new-perspective-on-income-inequality.

Meyer, John W., John Boli, George M. Thomas, and Francisco O. Ramirez. 1997. "World Society and the Nation-State." *American Journal of Sociology* 103, no. 1: 144–81.

Migration Policy Center (MPC). 2013. "Migration Profile–Russia." MPC Team Report. European University Institute, Robert Schuman Center for Advanced Studies.

Migration Policy Institute (MPI). 2013. Tabulation of Data from US Department of Homeland Security, Office of Immigration Statistics, Yearbook of Immigration Statistics (various years). Retrieved from http://www.dhs.gov/files/statistics/publications/yearbook.shtm.

Milanovic, Branko. 2010. *The Haves and the Have-Nots: A Brief and Idiosyncratic History of Global Inequality.* New York: Basic Books.

Milanovic, Branko. 2012. "Global Income Inequality by the Numbers: In History and Now." Policy Research Working Paper 6259. World Bank, Development Research Group, Poverty and Inequality Team. November 2012.

Miller, David S. 2014. "Denmark Passes Dual Citizenship Bill." TheLocalDK. Published on December 18, 2014. Retrieved from https://www.thelocal.dk/20141218/denmark-passes-dual-citizenship-bill.

Ministero dell'Interno. 2013. "Statistiche relative all'elenco aggiornato dei cittadini italiani residenti all'estero (AIRE) alla data del 31 Dicembre 2012" [Statistics on an updated list of Italian citizens residing abroad on December 31, 2012]. Retrieved from http://infoaire.interno.it/.

Mojić, Dušan. 2012. "Means of Getting Ahead in Postsocialist Serbia: Perceptions and Preferences of Young People." *Sociologija* 54, no. 2: 303.

Morawska, Ewa. 2004. "Exploring Diversity in Immigrant Assimilation and Transnationalism: Poles and Russian Jews in Philadelphia." *International Migration Review* 38, no. 4: 1372–412.

Moreh, Chris. 2014. "A Decade of Membership: Hungarian Post-Accession Mobility to the United Kingdom." *Central and Eastern European Migration Review* 3, no. 2: 79–104.

Morris, Christopher W. 2012. "The State." In *Oxford Handbook of the History of Political Philosophy*, edited by George Kolsko, 544–60. Oxford: Oxford University Press.

MTI. 2010. "Hungary to Promote Middle East Peace Process, Says FM." Published on November 9, 2010. Retrieved from www.mti.hu.

MTI. 2014. "New Hungarians through Dual Citizenship Scheme to Number 1 Million by 2018, Says Semjén." Published on December 29, 2014. Retrieved from http://www.politics.hu/20141229/new-hungarians-through-dual-citizenship-scheme-to-number-1-million-by-2018-says-semjen/.

Nana10. 2009. "Seker: 30% meha-Tzibur Yishkelu Laazov Et Israel Im Iran Tasig Garin" [Survey: 30% of the public would consider leaving Israel if Iran gets nuclear weapon]. Published on May 22, 2009. Retrieved from http://news.nana10.co.il/Article/?ArticleID=638480.

Naujoks, Daniel. 2009. "Dual Citizenship: The Discourse on Ethnic and Political Boundary-making in Germany." Focus-Migration Policy Brief No. 14, November 2009.

NDTV. 2018. "Birthright Citizenship Has Created 'Birth Tourism Industry': Donald Trump". Published November 2, 2018. Retrieved from https://www.ndtv.com/world-news/donald-trump-says-birthright-citizenship-has-created-birth-tourism-industry-1941900

Németh, András. 2013. "Wave of Emigration, Aging Reduce Ethnic Hungarian Population in Neighboring Countries." *Budapest Telegraph*. Published on June 29, 2013. Retrieved from http://www.budapesttelegraph.com/news/403/wave_of_emigration__aging_reduce_ethnic_hungarian_population_in_neighboring_countries_.

190 REFERENCES

New European. 2018. "Record Numbers Apply for 'EU Passports' in 2017." Published on January 9, 2018. Retrieved from http://www.theneweuropean.co.uk/demand-for-eu-passports-soar-in-2017-1-5348094.

Neofotistos, Vasiliki. 2009. "Bulgarian Passports, Macedonian Identity." *Anthropology Today* 25 no. 4: 19–22.

Neumann, Boaz. 2011. *Land and Desire in Early Zionism*. Waltham, MA: Brandeis University Press.

Nolan, Daniel. 2014. "Semjén Denies Existence of Passport Mafia in Hungary." Published on September 18, 2014. Retrieved from http://budapestbeacon.com/politics/semjen-denies-existence-of-passport-mafia-in-hungary.

Nyers, Peter. 2006. "The Accidental Citizen: Acts of Sovereignty and (Un)making Citizenship." *Economy and Society* 35, no. 1: 22–41.

Observatório da Emigração. 2014. "Indicadores sobre a população portuguesa emigrada" [Indicators on the Portuguese population that has emigrated]. Published on May 27, 2014. Retrieved from http://www.observatorioemigracao.secomunidades.pt/.

OECD. 2015. *Connecting with Emigrants: A Global Profile of Diasporas 2015*. Paris: OECD.

OECD Stat. 2016. International Migration Database. Retrieved from https://stats.oecd.org.

Office fédéral de la statistique (OFS) Switzerland. 2015. "Double nationalité de la population résidante permanente de 15 ans et plus, en 2012" [Dual nationality of the permanent resident population aged over 15, in 2012]. Data received from RS / Service d'informations du relevé structurel.

Ong, Aihwa. 1999. *Flexible Citizenship: The Cultural Logics of Transnationality*. Durham, NC: Duke University Press.

Oni, Jesusemen. 2016. "Foreigners Seeking US Citizenship for Children Flout Law, Can Endanger Babies." Voice of America. Published on December 6, 2017. Retrieved from https://www.voanews.com/a/foreigners-seeking-american-citizenship-children-flout-law-endanger-babies/3626080.html.

Orgad, Liav. 2010. "Illiberal Liberalism: Cultural Restrictions on Migration and Access to Citizenship in Europe." *American Journal of Comparative Law* 58, no. 1: 53–105.

Padrón de Españoles Residentes en el Extranjero (PERE). 2014. Data on Spanish citizens abroad for 2009, 2013. Instituto Nacional de Estadística. Retrieved from http://www.ine.es/jaxi/menu.do?L=0&type=pcaxis&path=%2Ft20%2Fp85001&file=inebase.

Paraszczuk, Joanna. 2011. "US Olim Want 'Israel' on Passport of their Jerusalem-Born Son." *Jerusalem Post*. Published on August 4, 2011. Retrieved from http://www.jpost.com/Features/In-Thespotlight/US-olim-want-Israel-on-passport-of-their-Jlem-born-son.

Patriquin, Martin. 2006. "Canadians out of Convenience." *Maclean's* 119, no. 46: 42–43.

Paul, Anju Mary. 2011. "Stepwise International Migration: A Multistage Migration Pattern for the Aspiring Migrant." *American Journal of Sociology* 116, no. 6: 1842–86.

Pavasovic Trost, Tamara. 2013. "The Complexity of Ethnic Stereotypes: A Study of Ethnic Distance among Serbian Youth." In *Us and Them: Symbolic Divisions in Western Balkan Societies*, edited by Ivana Spasic and Predrag Cveticanin, 135–64. Belgrade: Institute for Philosophy and Social Theory, University of Belgrade.

Paz, Octavio. 1961. *The Labyrinth of Solitude*. New York: Grove.

Pérez, Miriam Zoila. 2018. "Latinos Born Outside Hospitals Face Scrutiny Over Citizenship—and Lawyers Say Tactics Are Escalating Under Trump." Rewire.News. Published on October 30, 2018. Retrieved from https://rewire.news/article/2018/10/30/latinos-born-outside-hospitals-face-scrutiny-over-citizenship-and-lawyers-say-tactics-are-escalating-under-trump/.

Pietrantuono, G. 2016."The Value of Citizenship: Experimental and Quasi-Experimental Evidence from Germany and Switzerland." PhD diss., University of Mannheim, Germany.

Piketty, Thomas. 2014. *Capital in the Twenty-First Century*. Cambridge, MA: Harvard University Press.
Plocker, Sever. 2008 "Jews Who Fled Poland to Regain Citizenship". Ynet. Published on March 4, 2008. Retrieved from http://www.ynetnews.com/articles/0,7340,L-3514697,00.html.
Pocock, John G.A. 1998. "The Ideal of Citizenship since Classical Time." In *The Citizenship Debates*, edited by Gershon Shafir, 31–41. Minneapolis: University of Minnesota Press.
Pogonyi, Szabolcs. 2015. "Transborder Kin-Minority as Symbolic Resource in Hungary." *Journal on Ethnopolitics & Minority Issues in Europe* 14, no. 3: 73–98.
Pogonyi, Szabolcs. 2017. *Extra-Territorial Ethnic Politics, Discourses, and Identities in Hungary*. London: Palgrave Macmillan.
Pogonyi, Szabolcs. 2019. "The Passport as Means of Identity Management: Making and Unmaking Ethnic Boundaries Through Citizenship." *Journal of Ethnic and Migration Studies* 45, no. 6: 975–93.
Pogonyi, Szabolcs. n.d. "Europeanization of Kin-Citizenship and Its Impact on Minority Mobilization." Unpublished manuscript.
Pogonyi, Szabolcs, Mária Kovács, and Zsolt Körtvélyesi. 2010. "The Politics of External Kin-State Citizenship in East Central Europe." Working paper, GLOBALCIT. European University Institute, Robert Schuman Centre for Advanced Studies.
Porat, Elisha. 2011. "A Night of "Vermin and Abomination.'". *Haaretz*. Published on July 15, 2011. Retrieved from http://www.haaretz.com/weekend/magazine/a-night-of-vermin-and-abomination-1.373395.
Portes, Alejandro, Cristina Escobar, and Renelinda Arana. 2008. "Bridging the Gap: Transnational and Ethnic Organizations in the Political Incorporation of Immigrants in the United States." *Ethnic and Racial Studies* 31, no. 6: 1056–90.
Portes, Alejandro, and John W. Curtis. 1987. "Changing Flags: Naturalization and Its Determinants among Mexican Immigrants." *International Migration Review* 21, no. 2: 352–71.
Portes, Alejandro, L. E. Guarnizo, and W. J. Haller. 2002. "Transnational Entrepreneurs: An Alternative Form of Immigrant Economic Adaptation." *American Sociological Review* 2: 278–98.
Racz, Krisztina. 2012. "By the Rivers of Babylon: Multiculturalism in Vivo in Vojvodina/Vajdaság." *Jezikoslovlje* 13, no. 2: 585–99.
Ragazzi, Francesco, and Kristina Balalovska. 2011. *Diaspora Politics and Post-Territorial Citizenship in Croatia, Serbia, and Macedonia*. CITSEE Working Paper. Edinburgh School of Law, University of Edinburgh.
Ramet, Sabrina P. 1996. "Nationalism and the 'Idiocy' of the Countryside: The Case of Serbia." *Ethnic and Racial Studies* 19, no. 1: 70–87.
Rava, Nenad. 2013. "Country Report: Serbia." GLOBALCIT Country Reports. European University Institute, Robert Schuman Centre for Advanced Studies.
Reitlinger, Gerald. 1968 [1953]. *The Final Solution: The Attempt to Exterminate the Jews of Europe, 1939–1945*. 2nd ed. London: Vallentine, Mitchell.
Reyes, Marie Elena, and Veronia Lopez Estrada. 2013. "The Mexican Transnational Experience in South Texas: College Students of Mexican Origin in an Institution Serving Hispanics." *International Journal of Learning in Higher Education* 19, no. 3: 33–41.
Rivlin, Reuven. 2008. "Darkonim Mesukanim" [Dangerous passports]. *Haaretz*. Published on April 17, 2008. Retrieved from
Romanian National Institute of Statistics. 2013. "Press Release No. 159 on the Final Results of Population and Housing Census 2011." Retrieved from http://www.recensamantromania.ro.
Rothschild, Joseph. 1993. *Return to Diversity: A Political History of East Central Europe since World War II*. Oxford: Oxford University Press.

Salter, Mark B. 2006. "The Global Visa Regime and the Political Technologies of the International self: Borders, Bodies, Biopolitics." *Alternatives: Global, Local, Political* 31, no. 2: 167–89.

Sandoval, Efren. 2008. "Memoria y conformación histórica de un espacio social para el consumo entre el noreste de Mexico y el sur de Texas" [Memory and historical conformation of a social consumption space between northeast Mexico and south Texas]. *Relaciones* 29, no. 114: 235–73.

Sarabia, Heidy. 2015. "Global South Cosmopolitans: The Opening and Closing of the USA–Mexico Border for Mexican Tourists." *Ethnic and Racial Studies* 38, no. 2: 227–42.

Sartori, Fabio. 2011. "Acquisitions of Citizenship on the Rise in 2009." Eurostat, Statistics in Focus, Publication 24. Retrieved from https://publications.europa.eu/en/publication-detail/-/publication/382f26d4-26f1-422b-9694-747d529f2dd1.

Sassen, Saskia. 2006. *Territory, Authority, Rights: From Medieval to Global Assemblages.* Princeton, NJ: Princeton University Press.

Sasson-Levy, Orna. 2008. "Aval Ani Lo Rotze Le-Atzmi Zehut Etnit—Gvulut Hebratiim woo-Mehikatam be-Sihim Achshaviim Shel Ashkenaziut" [But I don't want an ethnic identity': Social boundaries and their erasure in contemporary discourses of Ashkenaziut]. *Teovira u'Vikoret* [Theory and Criticism] 33:101–25.

Scheppele, Kim. 2014a. "Hungary, An Election in Question, Part 4." *New York Times*. Published on February 28, 2014. Retrieved from http://krugman.blogs.nytimes.com/2014/02/28/hungary-an-election-in-question-part-4/.

Scheppele, Kim. 2014b. "Legal But Not Fair (Hungary)." April 13, 2014. *New York Times*. Retrieved from http://krugman.blogs.nytimes.com/2014/04/13/legal-but-not-fair-hungary/?_php=true&_type=blogs&_r=1.

Schnellbach, Christoph. 2014. "Ethnic Identities in East-Central Europe: The Results of the Census 2011 in Comparative Perspective." Paper presented at "Whither Eastern Europe? Changing Political Science Perspectives on the Region" workshop, Gainesville, FL, January 9–11, 2014.

Scott, James C. 1998. *Seeing Like a State: How Certain Schemes to Improve the Human Condition Have Failed*. New Haven: Yale University Press.

Sejersen, Tanya B. 2008. "'I vow to thee my countries': The Expansion of Dual Citizenship in the Twenty-First Century." *International Migration Review* 42, no. 3: 523–49.

Serbia Census. 2012. "Ethnicity: Data by Municipalities and Cities." Retrieved from http://popis2011.stat.rs/.

Shachar, Ayelet. 1999. "Whose Republic: Citizenship and Membership in the Israeli Polity." *Georgetown Immigration Law Journal* 13, no. 2: 233–72.

Shachar, Ayelet. 2009. *The Birthright Lottery: Citizenship and Global Inequality*. Cambridge, MA: Harvard University Press.

Shachar, Ayelet. 2017. "Citizenship for Sale?" In *The Oxford Handbook of Citizenship*, edited by A. Schachar, R. Bauböck, I. Bloemraad, and M. Vink, 644–68. Oxford: Oxford University Press.

Shachar, Ayelet, and Rainer Bauböck. 2014. "Should Citizenship Be for Sale?" Research Paper 1, European University Institute, Robert Schuman Centre for Advanced Studies.

Shachar, Ayelet, and Ran Hirschl. 2007. "Citizenship as Inherited Property." *Political Theory* 35, no. 3: 253–87.

Shachar, Ayelet, and Ran Hirschl. 2013. "Recruiting 'Super Talent': The New World of Selective Migration Regimes." *Indiana Journal of Global Legal Studies* 20, no. 1: 71–107.

Shachar, Ayelet, and Ran Hirschl. 2014. "On Citizenship, States, and Markets."*Journal of Political Philosophy* 22, no. 2: 231–57.

Shachter, Jason P. 2006. "Estimation of Emigration from the United States Using International Data Sources." United Nations Secretariat, Department of Economic and Social Affairs, Statistics Division.

Shachter, Jason P. 2015. "Dual Citizenship Trends and Their Implication for the Collection of Migration Statistics." *Realidad, Datos y Espacio: Revista Internacional de Estadística y Geografía* [Reality, data, and space: international journal of statistics and geography] 6, no. 2: 40–51.

Shafir, Gershon, and Yoav Peled. 2002. *Being Israeli: The Dynamics of Multiple Citizenship*. Cambridge: Cambridge University Press.

Shafir, Gershon, and Yoav Peled. 1998. "Citizenship and Stratification in an Ethnic Democracy." *Ethnic and Racial Studies* 21, no. 3: 408–27.

Shamir, Ronen. 2005. "Without Borders? Notes on Globalization as a Mobility Regime." *Sociological Theory* 23, no. 2: 197–217.

Shenhav, Yehouda. 2006. *The Arab Jews: A Postcolonial Reading of Nationalism Religion and Ethnicity*. Stanford, CA: Stanford University Press.

Shevel, Oxana. 2013. "Country Report: Ukraine." GLOBALCIT Country Reports. European University Institute, Robert Schuman Centre for Advanced Studies.

Shuck, Peter. 1989. "Membership in the Liberal Polity: The Devaluation of American Citizenship." *Georgetown Immigration Law Journal* 3, no. 1: 1–18.

Shuck, Peter. 2002. "Plural Citizenships." In *Dual Nationality, Social Rights, and Federal Citizenship in the US and Europe*, edited by Randall Hansen and Patrick Weil, 61–100. New York: Berghahn.

Shyong, Frank. 2016. "Why Birth Tourism from China Persists Even as US Officials Crack Down." *Los Angeles Times*. Published on December 30, 2016. Retrieved from https://www.latimes.com/local/lanow/la-me-ln-birth-tourism-persists-20161220-story.html.

Silverman, Myrna. 1988. "Family, Kinship, and Ethnicity: Strategies for Upward Mobility." In *Persistence and Flexibility: Anthropological Perspectives on the American Jewish Experience*, edited by Walter Zenner, 165–82. Albany: State University of New York Press.

Simon, Patrick. 2012. "French National Identity and Integration: Who Belongs to The National Community?" Research Report, May 2012. Washington, DC: Migration Policy Institute. Retrieved from https://www.migrationpolicy.org/research/TCM-french-national-identity.

Simon, Zoltan. 2017. "Hungary Citizenship Plan Reaches 1 Million Mark in Boost for Orban." *Bloomberg News*. Published on December 17, 2017. Retrieved from https://www.bloomberg.com/news/articles/2017-12-18/hungary-citizenship-plan-reaches-1-million-mark-in-orban-boost.

Simonsen, Kristina Bakkær. 2017. "Does Citizenship Always Further Immigrants' Feeling of Belonging to the Host Nation? A Study of Policies and Public Attitudes in 14 Western Democracies." *Comparative Migration Studies* 5, no. 3. Retrieved from https://comparativemigrationstudies.springeropen.com/articles/10.1186/s40878-017-0050-6.

Skeldon, Ronald. 2013. "Global Migration: Demographic Aspects and Its Relevance for Development." Technical Paper No. 2013/6. United Nations Population Division.

Slezkine, Yuri. 2004. *The Jewish Century*. Princeton, NJ: Princeton University Press.

Smith, Anthony D. 2000. "The 'Sacred' Dimension of Nationalism." *Millennium: Journal of International Studies* 29, no. 3: 791–814.

Smith, Claire M. 2010. "These Are Our Numbers: Civilian Americans Overseas and Voter Turnout." *Overseas Vote Foundation Research Newsletter* 2, no. 4. Retrieved from https://www.usvotefoundation.org/sites/default/files/counting%20american%20civilians%20abroad.pdf.

Smith, Robert. 2005. *Mexican New York: Transnational Lives of New Immigrants*. Berkeley: University of California Press.

Sobyak, Anita 2012. "Implications of Hungary's National Policy on Relations with Neighboring States." Policy paper no. 32, Polish Institute of International Affairs, Warsaw, Poland. June 2012.

South Cross Group. 2011. "About Voting in Australia While You Live Overseas." Published in January 2011. Retrieved from http://www.southern-cross-group.org/archives/Overseas%20 Voting/2007/Brochure_Expat_Voting_Jan_2011.pdf.

Spiro, Peter. J. 1997. "Dual Nationality and the Meaning of Citizenship." *Emory Law Review* 46, no. 4: 1412–85.

Spiro, Peter J. 2008. *Beyond Citizenship: American Identity after Globalization.* Oxford: Oxford University Press.

Spiro, Peter J. 2014. "Expatriating Terrorists." *Fordham Law Review* 82, no. 5: 2169–87.

Spiro, Peter J. 2015. "Report on Citizenship Law: United States of America." GLOBALCIT Country Reports. European University Institute, Robert Schuman Centre for Advanced Studies.

Spiro, Peter J. 2019. "The Equality Paradox of Dual Citizenship." *Journal of Ethnic and Migration Studies* 45, no. 6: 879–86.

Stanković, Vladimir. 2014. "Srbija u procesu spoljnih migracija" [Serbia in the process of external migrations]. Report published by Serbian Census. Belgrade, Serbia. Retrieved from http://pod2.stat.gov.rs/ObjavljenePublikacije/Popis2011/Inostranstvo.pdf.

Starr, Paul. 1992. "Social Categories and Claims in the Liberal State." *Social Research* 59, no. 2: 263–95.

Stasiulis, Daiva, and Darryl Ross. 2006. "Security, Flexible Sovereignty, and the Perils of Multiple Citizenship." *Citizenship Studies* 10, no. 3: 329–48.

State Fragility Index. 2015. Compiled by Monty G. Marshall and Benjamin R. Cole. Retrieved from http://www.systemicpeace.org.

Statistics Canada. 2011. National Household Survey. "Countries of Citizenship (178), Single and Multiple Responses for Citizenship (3), Immigrant Status (4), and Sex (3) for Total Population Living in Private Households, Canada, Provinces, Territories, Census Metropolitan Areas and Census Agglomerations, 2011 National Household Survey." Retrieved from http://www12.statcan.gc.ca/nhs-enm/2011/as-sa/99-010-x/99-010-x2011003_1-eng.cfm.

Statistics Canada. 2012. Canada (Code 01) and Canada (Code 01) (table). Census Profile. 2011 Census. Statistics Canada Catalogue no. 98-316-XWE. Ottawa. Published on October 24, 2012. Retrieved from http://www12.statcan.gc.ca/census-recensement/2011/dp-pd/prof/index.cfm?Lang=E.

Statistics Canada. 2015. "Generation Status: Canadian-born Children of Immigrants." Retrieved from https://www12.statcan.gc.ca/nhs-enm/2011/as-sa/99-010-x/99-010-x2011003_2-eng.cfm.

Statistics Netherlands. 2012. "1.2 Million Dutch with Dual Nationality." Dutch Central Bureau of Statistics. Published on March 20 2012. Retrieved from http://www.cbs.nl/en-GB/menu/themas/bevolking/publicaties/artikelen/archief/2012/2012-3578-wm.htm.

Statistikcentralen Finland. 2017. "Arabiskan blev den tredje största gruppen med ett främmande språk som modersmål" [Arabic became the third largest group with a foreign language as a native language]. Published on March 29, 2017. Retrieved from http://tilastokeskus.fi/til/vaerak/2016/vaerak_2016_2017-03-29_tie_001_sv.html?ad=notify.

Staton, Jeffrey K., Robert A. Jackson, and Damarys Canache. 2007. "Dual Nationality Among Latinos: What Are the Implications for Political Connectedness?" *Journal of Politics* 69, no. 2 : 470–82.

Stein, Sarah Abrevaya. 2016. *Extraterritorial Dreams: European Citizenship, Sephardi Jews, and the Ottoman Twentieth Century.* Chicago: University of Chicago Press.

Štiks, Igor. 2010. "The Citizenship Conundrum in Post-Communist Europe: The Instructive Case of Croatia." *Europe-Asia Studies* 62, no. 10: 1621–38.

Stjepanović, Dejan. 2015. "Claimed Co-ethnics and Kin-State Citizenship in Southeastern Europe." *Ethnopolitics* 14, no. 2: 140–58.

Subotica.com. 2018. "Državljanstvo Mađarske primilo 180 hiljada Vojvođana" [180,000 Vojvodinians have received Hungarian citizenship]. Published on October 25, 2018. Retrieved from https://www.subotica.com/vesti/drzavljanstvo-madjarske-primilo-180-hiljada-vojvodjana-id33341.html?fbclid=IwAR1YPl5Nwc_rI3IjLquBcLZmlJ8UUsq5Inr6dsUDJgSd92oLBoJvyNoocvE.

Surak, Kristin. 2016. "Global Citizenship 2.0: The Growth of Citizenship by Investment Programs." Investment Migration Working Paper 2016/3.

Sütő, Timea. 2012. "How Many Sides Does a Triangle Have? The Effects of Hungary's Support Policies on the Hungarian Minority in Romania." MA thesis, Eötvös Loránd University, Budapest, Hungary.

Tam, Nicole. 2018. "Maternity Tourism in Hawaii." *Hawaii Business Magazine*. Published on March 4, 2018. Retrieved from https://www.hawaiibusiness.com/maternity-tourism-in-hawaii/.

Tanasoca, Ana. 2014. "Double Taxation, Multiple Citizenship, and Global Inequality." *MOPP* 1, no. 1: 147–69.

Tatrai, Patrik, Ágnes Erőss, and Katalin Kovály. 2017. "Kin-state Politics Stirred by a Geopolitical Conflict: Hungary's Growing Activity in Post-Euromaidan Transcarpathia, Ukraine." *Hungarian Geographical Bulletin* 66, no. 3: 203–18.

Telles, Edward. 2014. *Pigmentocracies: Ethnicity, Race, and Color in Latin America*. Chapel Hill: University of North Carolina Press.

Telles, Edward M., and Vilma Ortiz. 2008. *Generations of Exclusion: Mexican-Americans, Assimilation, and Race*. New York: Russell Sage Foundation.

Times of Israel. 2017. "Over 33,000 Israelis Have Taken German Citizenship since 2000." Published on February 12, 2017. Retrieved from https://www.timesofisrael.com/over-33000-israelis-have-taken-german-citizenship-since-2000/.

Times of Israel. 2018. "Portugal and Spain Give 10,000 Passports to Sephardic New Citizens since 2015." Published on November 23, 2018. Retrieved from https://www.timesofisrael.com/portugal-and-spain-gave-10000-passports-to-sephardic-new-citizens-since-2015/.

Tintori, Guido. 2011. "The Transnational Political Practices of 'Latin American Italians.'" *International Migration* 49, no. 3: 168–88.

Tintori, Guido. 2012. "More Than One Million Individuals Got Italian Citizenship abroad in Twelve Years (1998–2010)." GLOBALCIT (previously EUDO Citizenship Observatory). Published on November 21, 2012. Retrieved from http://eudo-citizenship.eu/news/citizenship-news/748-more-than-one-million-individuals-got-italian-citizenship-abroad-in-the-twelve-years-1998-2010%3E.

Todorova, Maria. 1997 *Imagining the Balkans*. Oxford: Oxford University Press.

Toktas, Sule. 2006. "Turkey's Jews and Their Immigration to Israel." *Middle Eastern Studies* 42, no. 3: 505–19.

Torpey, John. 2000. *The Invention of the Passport: Surveillance, Citizenship, and the State*. Cambridge: Cambridge University Press.

Tóth, Judit. 2018. "The Curious Case of Hungary: Why the Naturalisation Rate Does Not Always Show How Inclusive a Country Is." GLOBALCIT. Published on January 3, 2018. Retrieved from http://globalcit.eu/the-curious-case-of-hungary-why-the-naturalisation-rate-does-not-always-show-how-inclusive-a-country-is/.

Tsuda, Takeyuki. 2010. "Ethnic Return Migration and the Nation-state: Encouraging the Diaspora to Return 'Home.'." *Nations and Nationalism* 16, no. 4: 616–36.

Turudić, M. 2008. "Istorija naših pasoša" [History of our passports]. *Vreme*. Published on February 14, 2008. Retrieved from https://www.vreme.com/cms/view.php?id=584894.

UNIAN. 2018. "Klimkin Ready to Discuss Criminal Liability for "Concealed Russian Citizenship." Published on October 6, 2018. Retrieved from https://www.unian.info/politics/10288479-klimkin-ready-to-discuss-criminal-liability-for-concealed-russian-citizenship.html.

United Nations Development Programme (UNDP). 2013. "Under-five Mortality Rate (per 1,000 Live Births)." Retrieved from http://hdr.undp.org/en/content/under-five-mortality-rate-1000-live-births.

United Nations Office on Drugs and Crime (UNODC). 2014. "Intentional Homicide Count and Rate per 100,000 Population, by Country/Territory (2000–2012)." Retrieved from https://www.unodc.org/gsh/en/data.html.

United Nations Population Division, Department of Economic and Social Affairs. 2017. "Table 1: Total Migrant Stock at Mid-year by Origin and by Major Area, Region, Country, or Area of Destination, 1990–2017." Retrieved from http://www.un.org/en/development/desa/population/migration/data/estimates2/data/UN_MigrantStockByOriginAndDestination_2017.xlsx.

United States Census. 2012. "Table 52: Population by Selected Ancestry Group and Region: 2009." US Census Bureau, Statistical Abstract of the United States. Retrieved from www.census.gov.

University of Kent. 2015. "New Survey Shows US Citizenship Renunciation Intentions Not Linked to Income." Published on February 11, 2015. Retrieved from https://www.kent.ac.uk/brussels/news/?view=1973.

Univision. 2014. "El costo del cruce indocumentado a Estados Unidos varía entre $3 mil y $20 mil dólares." Published on December 22, 2014. Retrieved from http://www.univision.com/noticias/inmigracion/el-costo-del-cruce-indocumentado-a-estados-unidos-varia-entre-3-mil-y-20-mil-dolares.

Urry, John. 2012. *Sociology beyond Societies: Mobilities for the Twenty-First Century*. New York: Routledge.

Van Oers, Ricky, Betty de Hart, and Kees Groenendijk. 2013. "Country Report: The Netherlands." GLOBALCIT Country Reports. European University Institute, Robert Schuman Centre for Advanced Studies.

Vasiljević, Jelena. 2012. "Imagining and Managing the Nation: Tracing Citizenship Policies in Serbia." *Citizenship Studies* 16, nos. 3–4: 323–36.

Vasilijević, Jelena. 2014. "Citizenship as Lived Experience: Belonging and Documentality after the Breakup of Yugoslavia." CITSEE Working Paper 2014/36.

Velasco, Laura, and Marie Laure Coubès. 2013. "Reporte sobre Dimensión, Caracterización y Areas de Atención a Mexicanos Deportados desde Estados Unidos." El Colegio de la Frontera Norte. Tijuana, Mexico.

Verdery, Katherine. 1979. "Internal Colonialism in Austria-Hungary." *Ethnic and Racial Studies* 2, no. 3: 378–99.

Verdery, Katherine. 1998. "Transnationalism, Nationalism, Citizenship, and Property: Eastern Europe since 1989." *American Ethnologist* 25, no. 2:291–306.

Vink, Maarten P., A. Schakel, D. Reichel, Gerard Rene de Groot, and C. Luk. 2016. "The International Diffusion of Expatriate Dual Citizenship." Unpublished manuscript. Retrieved from https://macimide.maastrichtuniversity.nl/dual-cit-database/.

Vink, Maarten P., and de Groot, Gerard Rene. 2010. "Citizenship Attribution in Western Europe: International Framework and Domestic Trends." *Journal of Ethnic and Migration Studies* 36, no. 5: 713–34.

Vink, Maarten Peter, and Rainer Bauböck. 2013. "Citizenship Configurations: Analysing the Multiple Purposes of Citizenship Regimes in Europe." *Comparative European Politics* 11, no. 5: 621–48.

Vink, Maarten Peter, Tijana Prokić-Breuer, and Jaap Dronkers. 2013. "Immigrant Naturalization in the Context of Institutional Diversity: Policy Matters, But to Whom?" *International Migration* 51, no. 5: 1–20.

Volčič, Zala. 2007. "Yugo-Nostalgia: Cultural Memory and Media in the Former Yugoslavia." *Critical Studies in Media Communication* 24, no. 1: 21–38.

Vonk, Olivier. 2012. *Dual Nationality in the European Union*. Leiden: Martinus Nijhoff.
Vonk, Olivier. 2014. *Nationality Law in the Western Hemisphere: A Study on Grounds for Acquisition and Loss of Citizenship in the Americas and the Caribbean*. Leiden: Martinus Nijhoff.
Walla. 2005. "Eikh Lehasig Darkon Polani" [How to obtain a Polish passport]. Published on June 2005. Retrieved from www.walla.co.il.
Wallerstein, Immanuel. 1974. *The Modern World-System*. Cambridge, MA: Academic Press.
Wang, Horng-luen. 2004. "Regulating Transnational Flows of People: An Institutional Analysis of Passports and Visas as a Regime of Mobility." *Identities: Global Studies in Culture and Power* 11, no. 3: 351–76.
Warikoo, Natasha, and Irene Bloemraad. 2017. "Economic Americanness and Defensive Inclusion: Social Location and Young Citizens' Conceptions of National Identity." *Journal of Ethnic and Migration Studies* 44, no. 5: 736–53.
Washington Post. 1982. "How Japan Saved Jews From Hitler." Published on November 14, 1982. Retrieved from https://www.washingtonpost.com/archive/opinions/1982/11/14/how-japan-saved-jews-from-hitler/cbcd517b-4fcf-4812-85a8-9c687d6fc083/?utm_term=.911fe95d9677.
Waterbury, Myra. 2014. "Making Citizens Beyond the Borders: Nonresident Ethnic Citizenship in Post-Communist Europe." *Problems of Post-Communism* 61, no. 4: 36–49.
Waters, Mary C. 1990. *Ethnic Options: Choosing Identities in America*. Berkeley: University of California Press.
Weber, Max. 1961. *General Economic History*. New York: Collier.
Weber, Max. 2003 [1958]. *The Protestant Ethic and the Spirit of Capitalism*. Mineola, NY: Dover.
Weil, Patrick. 2001. "Access to Citizenship: A Comparison of Twenty-Five Nationality Laws." In *Citizenship Today*, edited by Alex Aleinikoff and Doug Klusmeyer, 17–35. Washington, DC: Carnegie Endowment for International Peace.
Weil, Patrick. 2005. "The Return of Jews in the Nationality or in the Territory of France." In *The Jews Are Coming Back: The Return of the Jews to Their Countries of Origin after WWII*, edited by David Bankier, 58–71. Jerusalem: Yad Vashem.
Weil, Patrick. 2011. "From Conditional to Secured and Sovereign: The New Strategic Link between the Citizen and the Nation-state in a Globalized World." *International Journal of Constitutional Law* 9, nos. 3–4: 615–35.
Weil, Patrick. 2012. *The Sovereign Citizen: Denaturalization and the Origins of the American Republic*. Philadelphia: University of Pennsylvania Press.
Weil, Patrick. 2017. "Can a Citizen Be Sovereign?" *Humanity: An International Journal of Human Rights, Humanitarianism, and Development*, 8, no. 1: 1–27.
Weiler, Joseph H. 1997. "To Be a European Citizen: Eros and Civilization." *Journal of European Public Policy* 4, no. 4: 495–519.
Weiman, Gabi. 2008. Orzei Ha-mizvadot Ha-hadashim [The new suitcase packers]. *Haaretz*. Published on April 10, 2008. Retrieved from https://www.haaretz.co.il.
Weinbaum, Laurence. 1999. "The Return of Jewish Property in Eastern Europe." *Bishvil Ha'zikaron* 31: 26–36. Jerusalem: Yad Vashem.
Wilkinson, Tracy, and Ken Ellingwood. 2011. "Mexico: Drug Lord's Wife has Twins in Los Angeles County Hospital." *Los Angeles Times*. Published on September 26, 2011. Retrieved from http://latimesblogs.latimes.com/world_now/2011/09/mexico-el-chapo-guzman-emma-coronel-twins-lancaster-antelope-valley.html.
Wimmer, Andreas. 2002. *Nationalist Exclusion and Ethnic Conflict: Shadows of Modernity*. Cambridge: Cambridge University Press.
Wimmer, Andreas. 2014. *Ethnic Boundary-Making: Institutions, Power, Networks*. Oxford: Oxford University Press.

Wimmer, Andreas, and Nina Glick-Schiller. 2002. "Methodological Nationalism and Beyond: Nation-state Building, Migration, and the Social Sciences.' *Global Networks* 2, no. 4: 301–34.

Wimmer, Andreas, and Yuval Feinstein. 2010. "The Rise of the Nation-State across the World, 1816 to 2001." *American Sociological Review* 75, no. 5: 764–90.

World Bank. 2016a. "Literacy Rate, Youth Female (% of Females Ages 15–24)." Statistics for 2010. Retrieved from http://data.worldbank.org/indicator/SE.ADT.1524.LT.FE.ZS?view =chart&year_high_desc=false.

World Bank. 2016b. "World Development Indicators: Gini Index." Retrieved from http://databank .worldbank.org/.

Yahil, Leni, 1983. "Raoul Wallenberg—His Mission and His Activities in Hungary." *Yad Vashem Studies* 15: 7–54.

Yan, Sophia. 2015. "How Far Chinese Moms Will Go to Have US Babies." CNN Money. Published on March 30, 2015. Retrieved from http://money.cnn.com/2015/03/30/news/china-moms -birth-tourism-fraud/.

Yang, Phillip Q. 1994. "Explaining Immigrant Naturalization." *International Migration Review* 28, no. 3: 449–47.

Yie. 2018. "Proposed Finnish Dual Citizen Law Stricter than in Neighbouring States." Published on February 8, 2018. Retrieved from https://yle.fi/uutiset/osasto/news/proposed_finnish_dual _citizen_law_stricter_than_in_neighbouring_states/10065407.

Yonhap. 2017. "Dual Citizenships among South Koreans Increasing." *Korea Herald*. Published on October 22, 2017. Retrieved from http://nwww.koreaherald.com/view.php?ud=20171022000180.

Young, Cristobal, Charles Varner, and Ithai Z. Lurie. 2015. "Millionaire Migration and Taxation of the Elite Evidence from Administrative Data." *American Sociological Review* 81, no. 3: 421–46.

Zelizer, Viviana. 2005. *The Purchase of Intimacy*. Princeton, NJ: Princeton University Press.

Žilović, Marko. 2012. "Citizenship, Ethnicity, and Territory: The Politics of Selecting by Origin in Post-Communist Southeast Europe." CITSEE Working Paper 2012/20.

INDEX

Alba, Richard, 69
Altan-Olcay, Özlem, 18, 167n80
American-Mexican dual nationality: births in the United States to nonresident mothers and, 76–77; categories of dual nationals, 68; categories of dual nationals in Mexico, 72–73; citizenship industry associated with, 82–83; demographics of Mexican birth strategizers, 68–69; family dynamics and, 84–86; legal and historical background, 69–72; motives for seeking, 78–79, 86–92; opportunities associated with, 86–88; pathways to, 158n32; process of acquiring, 79–83; security and risk-mitigation concerns associated with, 87–90; as social closure and status, 92–95; statistical data on, 72–77; strategic cross-border birth, as case study of, 12; travel freedom associated with, 90–92; trends reshaping the citizenship constellation of Mexico and the United States, 67–68; US-born persons in Mexico and, 73–75
ancestry-based citizenship acquisition, 11; demand for, evaluating variation in, 30–37; EU-Israeli dual citizenship as a case of (*see* EU-Israeli dual citizenship)
anchor babies, 164n9
Anderson, Benedict, 25–26, 133
Arendt, Hannah, 7, 117

Balta, Evren, 18, 167n80
Bancroft, George, 8
Bauböck, Rainer, 7
Bauman, Zygmunt, 132, 143
birthright citizenship (*jus soli*), 4, 6, 12, 68–70, 80, 164n10
birthright lottery, 7, 20, 126
birth tourism. *See* strategic cross-border birth
Black, Hugo, 137

Bourdieu, Pierre, 62, 87, 98, 112, 123, 170n36, 171n2
Brecht, Bertolt, v
Brubaker, Rogers, 3–4, 7, 45, 58, 139, 141

Calderon, Felipe, 88
Castles, Stephen, 132
CEE. *See* Central and East European countries
Central and East European (CEE) countries: demand for Hungarian dual citizenship in, 45–46; dual citizenship held by Israelis in, 98 (*see also* EU-Israeli dual citizenship); dual citizenship policies in, 39–40, 100; middle tier dominated by, 22–23; nationalization without nationalism in, 58; the West, movement towards, 57
citizenship: compensatory (*see* compensatory citizenship); dimensions of, 3–8; dual (*see* dual citizenship); exclusive, 1; flexible, 114, 135–36; global hierarchy of, 15–16, 19–22, 126; as global sorting mechanism (*see* sorting function of citizenship); identity and (*see* identity); instrumental attitudes toward, 6–7, 126–27; by investment, 128–29; *jus sanguinis* (right of blood), 4, 100, 107, 164n3; *jus soli* (right of soil), 4, 6, 12, 68–70, 80, 164n10; long-distance acquisition of, 30–37; opportunistic attitude towards, 129–31; post-exclusive and post-territorial shifts in, 8–9; quantifying, 21; resident, components of, 21; restitution and, 100–101; as rights (*see* rights); the "sovereign individual" as attitude towards, 2–3; as status, 3–4, 127–31; stratification by, 19–21; value of (*see* citizenship value)
citizenship hierarchy approach: Hungarian dual citizenship and, 45–47. *See also* global citizenship stratification
citizenship industries: American-Mexican dual nationality and, 82–83; citizenship

199

citizenship industries (*cont.*)
  by investment, global industry of,
    128–29; comparison across cases, 127–28;
    EU-Israeli dual citizenship and, 108–10;
    Hungarian-Serbian dual citizenship and,
    49–53; legitimation of dual citizenship
    and the growth of, 129
citizenship light, 6–7, 137
Citizenship Quality Index (CQI), 20–22
citizenship stripping, 70, 117, 140, 165n18
citizenship value: elements of, 21; global
  hierarchy of, 19–22; mapping tiers of,
  22–25; tiers of, dual citizenship and,
  25–26
class: American-Mexican dual nationality
  and, 86–88, 92–95; entry to the United
  States by land and, 91; EU-Israeli dual
  citizenship and, 120–22; strategic birth
  and, 68–69, 81; stratification by citizenship versus, 19–20
coethnic citizenship acquisition, 11–12;
  demand for, evaluating variation in,
  30–37; Hungarian dual citizenship in
  Serbia as case study of (*see* Hungarian-
  Serbian dual citizenship)
compensatory citizenship, 2; American-
  Mexican dual nationality as case study
  of, 69 (*see also* American-Mexican dual
  nationality); EU-Israeli dual citizenship
  as case study of, 97–98, 125 (*see also*
  EU-Israeli dual citizenship); Hungarian-
  Serbian dual citizenship as a case study
  of, 65 (*see also* Hungarian-Serbian dual
  citizenship); as an instrumental strategy
  of global upward mobility, 16, 127, 138;
  pathways to, 11–13 (*see also* ancestry-
  based citizenship acquisition; coethnic
  citizenship acquisition; strategic cross-
  border birth); populism and, 142; sentimental dual citizenship, distinction from,
  18–19
Cook-Martin, David, 17
cross-border mobility: of Serbs, 59–61.
  See also passports

Democracy Index, 21, 154n23
dual citizenship, 1–2; demand for, evaluating
  variation in, 30–37; to evade tax authorities or law enforcement, 156n4; the future
  of, 141–43; the global hierarchy of citizenship and, 16; global shift toward, 8–9;
  individual-level perspective on, 16–17;
  instrumental value of outside Western
  Europe and North America, 17–19;
  motives to obtain, 2; political rights and,
  133–34; populism and, 141–43; prevalence of, 27–30; reasons for the move
  toward, 10; sentimental value of in the
  West, 17; statistics on, 27–37; tiers of citizenship countries and, 25–26; traditional
  resistance of states to, 7

emigration: from Hungary, 58; from Israel,
  102–3; negative stereotypes regarding,
  58; from Serbia, 47, 56–59. *See also*
  immigration
ethnicity: coethnic dual citizenship as
  an agent of national homogenization,
  58–59; dual citizenship and, 92–94,
  120–24; EU membership and, 66;
  national and citizenship, 4, 101; "nationality" in Central and Eastern Europe as
  synonymous with, 159n7; paradox of
  politicization in Central and Eastern
  Europe, 65; preference based on, 42–43.
  See also coethnic citizenship acquisition
EU. *See* European Union
EU-Israeli dual citizenship: citizenship specialists facilitating acquisition of, 108–10;
  commodity/restitution perspective on,
  110–11; compensatory citizenship, as case
  study of, 97–98; emigration and, 104; EU
  expansion and, 103–4; family dynamics
  and, 111–14; legal and historical background, 99–101; motives for seeking, 98,
  105–7, 113–20; opportunities associated
  with, 114–16; process of acquiring, 107–11;
  the security situation in Israel and, 103,
  116–18; as social closure, reclaiming Ashkenazi privilege and, 120–24; statistical
  data on, 101–4; travel freedom associated
  with, 118–20
European Union (EU): benefits of citizenship in a member country, 114–15; citizenship in as "citizenship light," 6–7; citizenship reacquisition programs in, 39; ethnic
  nationalism and, 39, 42–43; expansion
  of, opportunities created by, 97, 103–4;
  long-distance citizenship acquisition in,
  31–37; middle-tier citizenship countries
  and, 25–26

family dynamics: American-Mexican dual
  nationality and, 84–86; EU-Israeli dual
  citizenship and, 111–14; Hungarian-
  Serbian dual citizenship and, 53–55
FitzGerald, David, 16, 93
flexible citizenship, 114, 135–36

Germany: acquisition of citizenship and emigration to, 102–3; dual nationals among immigrants to, percentage of, 156n6; German citizenship for Israelis, 103–4; Israeli immigration to Berlin, 115; liberalization of citizenship laws after 1999, 4; restitution of citizenship for German Jews, 101
global citizenship stratification: dual citizenship and, 30–37, 138–40; mapping tiers of, 22–25; prevalence of dual citizenship and, 27–30; tiers of citizenship countries and, 25–26; travel freedom and, 59–61, 132–33 (*see also* travel freedom). *See also* citizenship hierarchy approach
global inequality: the birthright lottery and, 7, 20; the hierarchy of citizenship and, 15–16, 19–22
Guzman, Joaquin "El Chapo," 94

Henley & Partners, 22–23, 129
Herder, J. G., 161n28
Hindess, Barry, 18
Howard, Marc, 4
Hoyo, Henio, 71
Human Development Index (HDI), 21
Hungarian-Serbian dual citizenship: as case study of compensatory citizenship/coethnic citizenship acquisition, 2, 12–14, 40; citizenship industry developed around, 49–53; as citizenship reacquisition program, 39–40; collective status hierarchies and, 63–65; demand for, 33–35, 45–47; effects of, 65–66; family dynamics and, 53–55; legal and historical background, 41–43, 45; motives for seeking, 40, 48–49, 54–61; nonresident voting and, 134, 161nn25–27; opportunities associated with, 56–59; social closure for individuals from, 61–63; strategic (non-Hungarian) applicants for, 47–48, 50–53, 55, 61–62, 66
Hungary: birth rate and population of, 43; coethnic citizenships approved, 2011–2016, 31–32; criticism of citizenship policy, 42–43; emigration from, 58; openness to dual citizenship held by nonethnic Hungarians, 50–51; rejection of dual citizenship in 2005, 160n16; territorial designs on Vojvodina, concerns regarding, 63

identity: citizenship as, 5–7; of immigrants, 5–6; from national to individual, dual citizenship and, 134–38; as sovereign individual, 2–3, 137–38
immigration: dual citizenship and, 16–17; of East Europeans, Hungary's citizenship policy and concerns regarding, 42–43; liberalization of citizenship laws and, 4; between Mexico and the United States, 67–68, 72, 89, 96; "migration hump," 72, 165n27; national identity and, 5–6; naturalization rate of immigrants, 165n23. *See also* emigration
Immigration Reform and Control Act of 1986, 70
Israel: as case study of ancestry-based citizenship acquisition, 11, 14; as case study of compensatory citizenship, 2; citizenship policy in, 99–100, 168n13, 169n28; class and ethnic stratification in, 121; the discourse of the sovereign individual in, 136; emigration rate from, 155n67; EU-Israeli dual citizenship (*see* EU-Israeli dual citizenship); exports, distribution of, 155n67; GDP per capita, 155n67; generational structure of the Ashkenazi family in, 111; Law of Return, 6, 100; motivation to acquire dual citizenship for citizens of, 2
Italy: ancestry-based citizenships approved, 1998–2010, 31; demand for dual citizenship from, 35–36

Jansen, Stef, 59
Joppke, Christian, 3, 6, 137, 141
jus sanguinis citizenship (right of blood), 4, 100, 107, 164n3
jus soli citizenship (right of soil), 4, 6, 12, 67–70, 80, 164n10

Kälin, Chris, 129
Kennedy, John F., 6
Kim, Jaeeun, 127
Knott, Eleanor, 18
Kochenov, Dimitry, 154n25, 157n19, 157n23, 159n1, 171n17
Kovács, Mária, 43
Kranz, Dani, 115

Lake, David, 154n42

Macklin, Audrey, 7, 20
malinchismo, 91–92, 94
Malkki, Liisa, 7
Marshall, Thomas H., 5, 131
Martin, Phillip L., 165n27

Marx, Karl, 19
Massey, Douglas, 70
Mateos, Pablo, 17, 68, 74, 93, 140
Mau, Steffen, 8
methodology: for the Citizenship Quality Index, 157n22; data, sources of, 147–49; interviewer effect, 172n30, 172n32; interviews, 149–52; US nationals, estimating the number of, 165n32
Mexico: as case study of compensatory citizenship, 2; as case study of strategic cross-border birth, 12, 14; citizenship policy in, 70–72; class position of birth-strategizing parents, 68–69, 86–88, 92–94; the discourse of the sovereign individual in, 135–36; emigration rate from, 155n67; exports to the United States, percentage of, 155n67; GDP per capita, 155n67; map of, 71; motivation to acquire dual citizenship for citizens of, 2–3; nationals/nationality and citizens/citizenship, distinction between, 153n5, 164n2; racial bias in, 92–93; violence in, 88–89. *See also* American-Mexican dual nationality
migration hump, 72, 165n27
Milanovic, Branko, 19
Milošević, Slobodan, 57, 62
Molnár, Judit, 163n67

nationalism: ethnicity and (*see* ethnicity); long-distance, 26, 133; nationalization without, 58; post-territorial, 45
naturalization, 5
Nietzsche, Friedrich, v

Ong, Aihwa, 18, 113–14, 135
opportunism, 129–31
opportunity: American-Mexican dual nationality and, 86–88; as a component of resident citizenship, 21; EU-Israeli dual citizenship and, 114–16; Hungarian-Serbian dual citizenship and, 56–59
Orbán, Viktor, 42–43, 51–52, 57, 134, 161n24

passports: focus on for Israeli dual citizens, 98; as a gift within the family, 112–13; ranking of, 20–23, 34, 36, 157n23; as status symbol, 120–24; travel freedom and, 47, 59–61, 90–92, 118–20, 132–33
Paz, Octavio, 92
Pocock, John, 131

Pogonyi, Szabolcs, 17, 42, 45
Portes, Alejandro, 17
post-territorial nationalism, 45

rights: citizenship as, 5; civil and social, 133; as a component of resident citizenship, 21; political, 133–34; territorial, 131–33

Salvini, Matteo, 141
Sasson-Levy, Orna, 121
Scheppele, Kim, 43
security: as a component of resident citizenship, 21; as a factor in American-Mexican dual nationality, 88–90; Israeli dual citizenship acquisition and, 103, 116–18; territorial rights and, 131–32
Serbia: coethnic dual citizenship policy of, 43, 45; emigration from, desire for, 47, 56–59; emigration rate from, 155n67; exports to the EU, percentage of, 155n67; GDP per capita, 155n67; Hungarian-Serbian dual citizenship (*see* Hungarian-Serbian dual citizenship); identity and citizenship in, 136–37; map of, 44; political history of, 160n9; travel freedom as an issue in, 59–61; Western Europe and, gap between, 56–57
Shachar, Ayelet, 7, 20
Shamir, Ronen, 132
Skeldon, Ronald, 72
social capital, 87
sorting function of citizenship: as dimension of citizenship, 7–8; as hierarchical, 7–8, 126, 138–40
sovereign individual: as attitude towards citizenship, 2–3; rise of, 134–38
Spiro, Peter J., 173n53
State Fragility Index (SFI), 21
statelessness, 7
status: citizenship as, 3–4; citizenship industries and the commodification of citizenship, 127–31; passports as a symbol of, 120–24
strategic cross-border birth, 12, 96, 164n10. *See also* American-Mexican dual nationality

Telles, Edward, 92
Tintori, Guido, 17
Torpey, John, 154n20
travel freedom, 47, 59–61, 90–92, 118–20, 132–33

Trianon, Treaty of, 41–42
Trump, Donald, 95, 141, 172n23

United States: citizenship policy in, 68–70; citizens living abroad, 96; dual nationals among immigrants to, percentage of, 156n6; Fourteenth Amendment, 6, 69; strategic cross-border births to secure dual citizenship in (*see* American-Mexican dual nationality)

Vučić, Aleksandar, 62

Wallerstein, Immanuel, 22
Weber, Max, 88
Weil, Patrick, 4, 69–70, 99, 135, 137–38

Yugo-nostalgia, 57

Zelizer, Viviana, 84, 112, 170n36

A NOTE ON THE TYPE

This book has been composed in Adobe Text and Gotham. Adobe Text, designed by Robert Slimbach for Adobe, bridges the gap between fifteenth- and sixteenth-century calligraphic and eighteenth-century Modern styles. Gotham, inspired by New York street signs, was designed by Tobias Frere-Jones for Hoefler & Co.